THE OFFICERS OF THE COMMONS
1363–1965

PHILIP MARSDEN

The Officers of the Commons 1363–1965

BARRIE AND ROCKLIFF
LONDON

377,520

CONTENTS

ACKNOWLEDGEMENTS

Without the help of my colleagues, of all ranks, in the service of the House of Commons, this book could never have been completed. Personal reminiscence, expert interpretation and informed comment have been showered upon me ungrudgingly, when asked for, by men whose days are already full; but their patience has been monumental, and their aid invaluable, and I am happy to record it and to thank them all for their generosity.

Special thanks are due to Sir Barnett Cocks, KCB, CBE, Clerk of the House, for the many precious hours he afforded me; and to Richard Barlas, OBE, Second Clerk Assistant, who read my script on behalf of the Clerk. To Lt. Col. P. F. Thorne CBE, the Deputy Serjeant at Arms, and to Sir Francis Reid, CBE, the Speaker's Secretary, who read it on behalf of the Serjeant at Arms and the Speaker I am also especially grateful; and to Strathearn Gordon, OBE, the Librarian, and his expert staff, without whose assistance I would not have known even where to begin.

I only hope they all may feel that *my* effort is worth *their* trouble.

Horsham   PHILIP MARSDEN
1965

Preface

The House of Commons consists of elected representatives of the people, and its colourful history is that of the growth and development over seven hundred years of what is now a fully fledged democracy.

But Parliament itself, like government as a whole, could not exist for a day on the mere work of elected representatives. The House of Commons, like the town council or county council, like any Government department, consists of a body which deliberates and makes decisions, and a parallel body which not only records and implements decisions, but also provides the whole apparatus of administration which makes it possible for the Commons even to meet at all, to deliberate in an informed way, and which protects them in carrying out their duties.

As Parliamentary democracy grew over the centuries from very humble beginnings, so did the team of Servants of the House, without which the Commons could not function.

The recording of what Parliament *does*—in Acts of Parliament and in day to day decisions of the Commons recorded in the *Journal*—has a long and eventful history.

The building up of what might be called the case-law of the House—the collecting and collating of precedents and the shaping of Standing Orders—is another story of steadily expanding labour over the centuries.

The protection of the House, which began with the King appointing one of his Serjeants to keep an eye on the safety of the members, has also grown into a complex department.

For centuries after the House first met, its debates were secret, and the last thing the Commons wished anybody to know was who said what. But now every word spoken in the House is accurately recorded and most of it is in print and in the hands of members before they begin the next day's work.

Today then, the Palace of Westminster houses not only the elected members, but an able and industrious professional team who render a thousand and one invaluable services, led by Officers of high calibre and rigorously selected and trained.

The House is proud of the character and quality of its Servants. One Speaker expressed the views of all members when he paid tribute to "the Clerk and other Officers and Servants of the House, whose services we can command, but whose loyalty and devotion are so generously and lavishly given to every honourable member of this House".

Philip Marsden, himself one of the officers of Mr. Speaker and a faithful servant of the House, has devoted much thought and labour—a labour of love—to tracing the growth of the various departments from their crude beginnings.

Here we may read of men like Seymour, who perhaps began the *Journal*; of Jodrell, who began its collation and printed publication; of Rushworth, who preserved for history one of the great moments of Parliament; of Hatsell, whose noble work on procedure was the *fons et origo* of the even greater work of Erskine May and a succession of great Clerks.

Mr. Marsden pays a tribute long overdue to those who serve the House so magnificently, and traces the history of their offices—a history as chequered as that of the Mother of Parliaments.

This history, together with Mr. Marsden's detailed picture of the present complex organisation of the House, will be of value to all who love Parliament and its ways.

HORACE MAYBRAY KING
Speaker

Introduction

Introduction

Much has been written about Parliament—Parliament as a place
of legislature, as court of law, as defender of the liberties of the
people (and their oppressor at times)—and even more has been
said about those who have achieved fame or obloquy as Members
of one House or the other. But the great machinery of Parliament, as distinct from the machinery of government, is not kept
running by politicians, nor does it run itself; it is kept in motion,
cared for and continually brought up to date by men who are
carefully chosen and meticulously trained to carry out this
peculiarly subtle task.

Seen against the background of contemporary politics, the
internal organisation of Parliament, and especially the House of
Commons with which this book is concerned, may appear complicated—to some, even chaotic—but the endless efficiency of
the machine itself is undeniable. And this efficiency, which has
been maintained through every crisis thrust upon it by Parliament and the nation's affairs, is simply the product of the efforts
of all those men who are part of this specialised little world.

Like Parliament itself and its Members, its servants are hedged
about, inspired and often frustrated by the unbreakable precedents of tradition which have not only shaped their duties but
have defined the form in which they must be carried out, and
unless these formative influences are understood it is difficult
to appreciate exactly what does go on behind the public performance of Parliamentary government. History, therefore, must be
at least touched upon in the following pages, but it is upon the
servants themselves that attention will principally be focused—
holders of such ancient titles as Clerk of the House, Serjeant at

Arms, Doorkeeper, Trainbearer, Deliverer of the Vote and many more, whose functions must appear as enigmas to the uninitiated.

Seven hundred years have passed since the Model Parliament of Simon de Montfort was summoned for its first sitting in 1265; seven momentous centuries during which a new and significant form of democratic government struggled into being. Slow and painful at first, shrinking at times before the massive power of the Crown and the Baronage, and threatened often by violent assaults of ambitious commoners, the idea of government by the people for the people continued to inspire the minds of men in England until it developed into an instrument that was to become the envy of the world.

All over Europe, during those seven eroding centuries, kingdoms and principalities disappeared from the map. Crowns toppled, kings died, whole dynasties were submerged under seas of blood, but in England the role of Parliament remained, unbroken—indeed, uninterrupted—in the face of every threat to its existence. Though its form changed, and changed often, it was only changed by the will of Parliament itself. More and more power was wrested from the Crown; greater authority was ceded by the people; wider privileges were won over both king and commoners; stage by stage the will of Parliament asserted itself until it became predominant. And within Parliament itself, the Commons at length assumed the real control.

The story of Parliament is an open book. The history of England itself is virtually the history of Parliament, since practically every event that remains memorable either occurred in Parliament, or was planned there, or had some sort of connection with one House or the other. The pages of England's long pedigree are liberally studded with names that made *Parliament* illustrious. From de Montfort himself, through Cromwell, Gladstone and Disraeli, to mention only a few, down to Churchill in our own times, the nation's heroes have been mostly men of Parliament's breeding, and their names and deeds are known to every schoolboy. This honourable and illustrious line, unbroken down the centuries, continues even today, the raw material for tomorrow's historians.

But behind it, unsung by the bards and almost unheard of by

the man in the street, that other line of men has quietly scored its tale upon the flank of history, throwing up from time to time its own heroes and villains and creating almost from nothing its own tradition of discreet, specialised service which is excelled nowhere in the world. Without them the function of government as we know it in Britain could not be carried on; without them, the Parliamentary system of which we are justly so proud would never have become the pattern it is for almost every democratic government in the world.

These men are not Civil Servants. By an odd quirk of history the people's representatives in Parliament are served, guided and sustained by the staff of one of the palaces of the Crown. Some members of the staff, indeed, are still appointed directly by the monarch, in spite of the seemingly decisive intervention of Cromwell in the control of Parliament during the authoritarian government of the Commonwealth.

The beautiful Barry building which is known the world over as "The Houses of Parliament" is in *fact* the Royal Palace of Westminster, staffed by its own servants and used as a meeting-place for Parliament only by the courtesy of earlier kings of England, the costs of its upkeep being met by a special Vote from the Treasury. It is almost by chance that Parliament now meets there; had things been different, and another place had been chosen, the ancient buildings beside the river might well have crumbled away unnoticed after Henry VIII moved out to occupy his proud new palace at St. James's. But by then the die had been cast; Parliament and Westminster had become synonymous.

In its earlier days, when the power of Parliament was much more circumscribed than it is today, the king summoned "his advisers" (usually only when he wanted money) to attend upon him wherever he might be in residence. Thus, Parliaments have met as far afield as St. Alban's and Oxford, to mention only two of the provincial towns so "honoured", as well as at Hampton Court and in many other temporary homes in London itself. The Public Departments, however, like the Treasury (in 1307) and the Law Offices later, became centralised in London—or, more particularly, in and around the Great Hall of William Rufus, the Westminster Hall of history.

There were two main reasons for this. First, the fact that the Old Palace at Westminster had been the life-long residence of Edward the Confessor, who was both King and Saint, had lent to the place an atmosphere of magic and mysticism that made it sacred to the minds of all Englishmen; and not only to Englishmen, for the Norman dynasty that claimed its succession from the Confessor chose to set up its Court on the ground that its predecessor had hallowed. The Conquerer himself insisted upon being crowned in Westminster Abbey, whether from a feeling of genuine respect or for reasons of simple propaganda is open to question, but the fact remains—the Norman kings did make Westminster their centre of government, and the kings that followed them continued to show a predeliction for the Old Palace of the Saxons.

The second reason was purely physical. Not only did the vast size of Rufus's new Hall make it the ideal meeting-place for large numbers of people, but it was surrounded by the lesser halls of the Old Palace which were themselves commodious enough and conveniently enough placed to house those Public Departments through which the will of the Government was expressed. Most of these, of course, though much too big now to occupy their former quarters, are still centred around the Parliament building —principally in Whitehall—and although the modern emphasis is increasingly on decentralisation it is certain that the main executive Ministries will remain there within easy reach of their political heads.

The distinction between the staffs of these Departments and the staff of the Palace itself has always been very strongly maintained, and the historical reasons for this are easy to follow. When Parliament was summoned to the Palace, or to one of the other royal residences, their needs were served by a staff already in existence (i.e. the king's own servants) and it was never necssary for them to set up any kind of organisation of their own. Indeed, it would scarcely have been possible to do so, since it was never known when—or where—the next meeting would be held; and if the king's advisers were to retain their required mobility they could not encumber themselves with secretariats. Clearly, to use the *king's* servants and domestic offices on these occasions was the ideal arrangement. It had the added virtue, too, of economy, since the Crown must foot the bill.

When the Departments were brought within the Palace, however, they brought with them their own specialised staffs, men whose allegiance (in the professional sense) was not to the king but to the Head of their own Department, and it was from staffs like these that the great Civil Service was to develop. In modern times the Civil Servant is still responsible to his department's professional head, who is in turn responsible to the *political* head, or Minister, in overall authority. Thus, the Civil Servant —theoretically in the main, but sometimes in actual fact—is at the mercy of the Executive, and may be acted against not only for lack of efficiency but upon political grounds, too. This has happened in our own time.

The staff which serve the Commons within the Palace of Westminster, on the other hand, are not answerable in any way to the Government of the day. Nor are they appointed by politicians or political organisations; if they were, their usefulness would disappear overnight. They are the servants only of the House, and it is this long-preserved independence from political control that has endowed them with their own special value to the smooth running of the machinery of government. Within the Palace precincts they are rigidly, almost religiously, nonpolitical. Whatever the complexion of the Government in office the House can be certain of receiving that completely impartial and professionally expert service for which its Officers enjoy a reputation second to none, and upon which all Members can, and do, rely unhesitatingly, regardles of party affiliations, religious distinctions or personal differences of temperament.

Because these officials *are* servants of the House, and have not to rely on political patronage either for their appointments or for their continuation in office, they are able to devote the whole of their lives to their task and to develop their individual capacities to a very high standard of professionalism. None of them seek appointments in the House for mercenary reasons—even today, the pay is by no means extravagant—and unless they possess special aptitudes of character and temperament they will soon find the work unbearable.

For one thing, the hours of duty can seem almost unbelievable in this era of Trades Union representation and thirty-five-hour weeks. During the great nationalisation debates of 1945–1948, when all-night sittings were more the rule than the exception, it was a commonplace experience for many of the staff to put in well over eighty hours a week, month after month—and in most cases without overtime pay, since "night-duty" is normally covered by a modest flat-rate allowance which takes no account of the numbers of hours worked. Some officers, in fact, draw no extra-duty pay at all.

Though such conditions may seem a hardship they have their value—no one would put up with them unless he loved his work. And since an absolute devotion to his duty is one of the indispensable qualities of a good servant of the House, this sort of consideration soon separates the sheep from the goats. Men who remain in the service, one can be sure, do so from the highest of motives—the desire to serve, and the will to serve usefully.

Service in the House is a way of life. Unlike other professions, it cannot be taught—it is only by living and working in the very special atmosphere that exists uniquely within the walls of Westminster that one begins, after a few years' experience, to absorb that intangible "something" that makes the place what it is, and then to act and react in the way it demands. For make no mistake about it; even in this dynamic, progressive twentieth century the Palace of Westminster is full of magic still, a magic strong enough to grasp the imagination of everyone who works within its walls and to mould into his personality that undefinable characteristic that marks him out as a House of Commons man.

If the House accepts them, these men are in a unique position and they must become unique people to survive there. They must know not only their own particular duty, but also why it is performed in a particular way, for in Parliament precedent is everything. Though divorced from party politics, they must yet be so saturated in political awareness that they are sensitive to every slightest political nuance both in the House and in the country outside, for otherwise it would be impossible for them to interpret the functions of their ancient offices flexibly enough to meet the needs of the modern moment.

In addition to a thorough knowledge of his duties and the possession of a sure instinct to discharge them properly, an

Officer of the House must be blessed with a special sense that will recognise the *shape* of Parliamentary problems even before they arise. He is constantly consulted by Members—busy men, all of them, with no time to waste—and if the work of the House is not to be delayed his answers to their queries must be immediate and generally without reference to the "authorities". Though his replies must be given quickly they must, above all else, be accurate. Mistaken information passed to a Member could easily result in a catastrophe on the Floor of the House—and that would be unthinkable. The Officers of the House enjoy a reputation for discretion that is unparalleled, and were they unworthy of it their fault would be a serious one. The corridors of the House, as well as its committee-rooms, dining-rooms, bars and lobbies, are constantly alive with rumour, gossip and speculation, much of it political dynamite if spread abroad, and since an Officer enjoys virtually the same privileges as a Member and moves about the building at will he inevitably becomes the involuntary recipient of a great deal of information that is highly confidential. An ability to hold one's tongue in company is essential.

The overall organisation of the staff of the Commons is fairly easy to follow, since it is divided into three main Departments; but the sub-divisions of the Departments themselves are more difficult to understand.

Under the controlling authority of the Commissioners for Regulating the Offices of the House of Commons (comprising the Speaker, the Chancellor of the Exchequer and the Principal Ministers of State) the three Departments are administered by the Speaker, the Clerk of the House and the Serjeant at Arms respectively, and between them these three chief Officers control every aspect of life and work in the Commons while the House is sitting. Prior to the setting up of the Select Committee on the Palace of Westminster in 1965 (see below) the Serjeant only operated while the Commons were in session; when they went into recess, or were prorogued, he relinquished his command of the domestic side and the House reverted to its Palace status under the Lord Great Chamberlain on behalf of the Crown.

This duality of control was often irritating to Members of the Commons, who felt, understandable enough, that they should be able to exercise complete authority over their own facilities and resources.

They asked, for example, why the Lord Great Chamberlain should still have the power to pre-empt large areas of accommodation on behalf of the Crown while the Commons were practically bursting at the seams for lack of space. They were irritated to find that if they wanted to take photographs or park their cars on the premises at weekends, when the Commons were not sitting, they had to go to the Lord Great Chamberlain for permission—in writing. The Commons, they rightly felt, should no longer occupy their quarters by courtesy of the Crown; the time was long overdue when they should have a place of their own where *their* will was paramount, not only on sitting-days but during weekends and recesses too.

Two ways of achieving this had been canvassed over the years. When the rebuilding of the Commons Chamber was debated after its destruction by bombing in 1941 some Members were in favour of moving the Commons out of Westminster altogether, to start afresh on some completely new site in a modern Chamber specially designed to facilitate the increasingly intricate work of government. The vacated accommodation, they suggested, might perhaps be used to house some form of Parliamentary museum. This rather drastic idea was rejected overwhelmingly at the time, in spite of the fact that the old Chamber—and its projected replacement—was furnished with only enough seats for about three-quarters of the 630 Members, and it has never been seriously raised again. The Commons are unwilling to break away from the continuity of their long traditions.

The second idea, more recent than the first, was that the Crown should relinquish control of the premises, withdraw the Lord Great Chamberlain and hand over the building (deconsecrated, so to speak) completely to the Commons for their own undisputed use; but if this were to mean the disappearance of the Lords from the Palace a new complication would appear. Parliament does not consist, constitutionally, of either the Lords *or* the Commons *or* the Crown. It is only when these three estates are met *together* that Parliament is deemed to "sit"; individual action by any one of them would be unconstitutional—and therefore illegal.

It was on this point that Charles I challenged the authority of the Commons to bring him to trial in 1649. The Commons alone, he claimed, meeting in the absence of both the Lords and the Crown, were constitutionally incapable of passing an Act of Parliament; and since laws can only be enforced in England as the consequence of such Acts, the whole procedure under which Charles was arraigned was itself unlawful in the true sense of the word. The action of the Commons on that occasion was more the action of a Revolutionary Tribunal—which the French adopted with such glee 140 years later, and applied very much more widely than their predecessors had done. Argument still continues about the propriety of Cromwell's act; but whatever it was, it certainly was *not* an Act of Parliament.

Thus, to divorce the Commons from the Lords, even physically, could do nothing to facilitate the work of Parliament; it must inevitably slow it down and produce a system even more cumberous than the traditional one. The two Houses *must* remain, somehow, under one roof while the present constitution remains. (The problem of the Monarch's presence has long been solved. In modern times the Queen normally attends in person only for the State Opening of Parliament each autumn; at other times she is represented in the Lords by one of the high Officers of State, usually—though not necessarily—by the Lord Chancellor as Speaker of the House of Lords.)

So it was between these two extremes of control by the Crown or complete autonomy for the Commons that a *modus operandi* had eventually to be found. Clearly, the will of the Commons must be sovereign; and if the present constitution is to be maintained—with all its strength—it is equally clear that the desires of the Commons to be beholden no longer to the hospitality of the Crown must be met. This being so, the historic statement made by the Prime Minister on 23rd March 1965 seems to present the ideal compromise:

"... Her Majesty the Queen has graciously agreed that the control use and occupation of the Palace of Westminster and its precincts shall be permanently enjoyed by the Houses of Parliament. Her Majesty's Government have decided that the control of the accommodation and services in that part of the Palace and its precincts now occupied by or on behalf of the House of

Commons shall be vested in you, Sir [i.e. the Speaker] on behalf of this House. The House will wish to know that the control of the accommodation and services in that part of the precincts now occupied by or on behalf of the House of Lords will be vested in the Lord Chancellor as Speaker of the House of Lords on behalf of that House. The control of Westminster Hall and the Crypt Chapel will be vested jointly in the Lord Great Chamberlain as representing Her Majesty the Queen and in the two Speakers on behalf of the two Houses."

So, in the year of their 700th anniversary, the Commons have at last become master in their own House and the Speaker's authority has become paramount. The Select Committee on the Palace of Westminster, set up immediately after the Prime Minister's statement, is now considering how best to make the Commons' new powers effective, and though organisational changes—some of them considerable—can be expected in the years ahead, they clearly cannot be included within the scope of this book—which appears, appropriately enough, at the precise end of a definite era in the Commons' history. During the period it covers (1363–1965) the powers of the Crown in the Commons, at first quite absolute, have gradually but progressively declined, until, in 1965, they disappeared altogether and freed the Lower House from any kind of outside interference. It is worthy of note, however, that this freedom was not wrested from an un-willing ruler by some newly powerful Commons (as has hap-pened more than once in days gone by) but was granted un-grudgingly by a Monarch who cared more for the wishes of her people's representatives than for the sometimes anachronistic dictates of precedent and protocol—a Royal gift indeed, and one that underlines yet again the strength and texture of our own form of Parliamentary government. *noble*

The following pages are divided into three distinct sections. The first describes the conditions under which the several Depart-ments of the House came into being, and pays particular atten-tion to the three Departmental Heads—the Speaker, the Clerk and the Serjeant at Arms—around whom the Commons' offices were evolved. Part Two deals with the findings and recommenda-tions of the "1833 Committee", whose deliberations provide a natural dividing-line between ancient and modern practice. The final chapters give an outline, as brief as possible, of the shape and function of the contemporary Commons' machinery up to the year 1965; future changes which may be made as the result of the "1965 Committee's" work (even those that can be foreseen now) have not been touched on. They will provide an interesting subject for future students of the Commons scene.

The gap which I have intentionally left from about 1850 to the present day will appear a pity to some, since the Victorian Clerks were a colourful lot, but the omission of recent history (which is, anyway, available elsewhere) excuses the discussion of personalities either still living or only lately dead, and this must surely be preferred. This much, however, should be said; during the period of the "gap" the service rendered to the House by its officers has been continuously refined and improved, and it is better today than at any time in its history.

This book has not been easy to assemble and put on paper, since the area to be covered is enormous. Every Office of the House has enough of a story behind it to fill a volume of its own, while most of the Speakers, Clerks and Serjeants could each provide enough material for a large biography. So from a mass of detail I have attempted to select the thread of continuity and to express it in uncomplicated terms so that *some* picture may emerge of the domestic interior of the Commons, of those who began it and built it up and of those who inherited its greatness. If these researches should contribute even a fraction towards the public understanding of the machinery of the Commons and its officers the labour will have been as well-spent as it was willingly undertaken.

Part One

The Officers of the House
1363–1833

CHAPTER I

The Clerk of the House 1363–1833

On the 28th July 1964 the Commons met to move a vote of thanks to Winston Churchill, who had announced his intention of retiring from the service of the House with the ending of that current Session. As he had been a Member, with only insignificant interruptions, since the year 1900, and since he had already accumulated in his lifetime more honour and greater distinction than any other figure in our recorded history, his departure from the stage of Westminster was no ordinary event. It was unique; and unique means had been sought to make it memorable.

The decision of the House, apparently so commonplace, to move a motion "to thank the right honourable Gentleman for these outstanding services to the House and to the nation" was in fact far from ordinary. Certainly, in days gone by, Parliamentary motions of thanks and congratulations were not uncommonly accorded on the occasion of famous victories—the most recent of these being that to the Duke of Wellington almost exactly 150 years before—but for the House to take such action in respect of one of its own sitting members was rare enough to be almost unheard-of. Not since the year 1700, in fact, had a Member of the Commons been so signally honoured by his colleagues.

On the present occasion, the Motion was moved by the Prime Minister, supported by the Leaders of the opposition parties and by the three elder statesmen present, and carried by the House —to use the Speaker's words—*nemine contradicente*; that is to say, "with none speaking against". The Motion, having been thus carried was entered in the Journal, there to mark the moment for all time in the history of Parliament and the country.

A small committee was appointed to carry the feeling of the House to its illustrious pensioner, and for the purposes of greater accuracy the Resolution recorded in the Journal was embodied in a letter to be handed over at the same time as a tangible and lasting token of the occasion.

The interesting thing about this document was the signature it carried. It was not subscribed, as might reasonably be expected, by the Speaker, or even by the Prime Minister; this historic message was sent over the name of the Clerk of the House of Commons—a fact which may serve to underline the celebrity and significance of this most distinguished officer of the House.

The long, unbroken lineage of the Clerks of the House is more ancient even than that of the Speaker, reaching back as it does to the year 1363. But centuries before that date, long before representatives of the *communes* (or commons) were summoned into the councils of the King, before even the Upper House was a recognised entity, there were men whose job it was to record the decisions of the King and his advisers. In the earliest days, this work was done by the King's own scrivener who normally knelt at his master's side with a cushion on one knee for a table, to jot down such orders as might be given him. When the "advisers" were required for counsel, it was the Scrivener who sent off the necessary summonses.

But as the conception of "parliament", or talking-place, began to develop, and the King's council began to meet with some sort or regularity, it became clear that *some* more or less permanent officials would be required if the work of the advisers was to be carried out in a useful and expeditious manner. (It should be remembered that the earlier parliaments contained no "commons" element.)

The King normally called his Council into "consultation" only for two reasons—and neither of them was that he really wanted advice. First, he was fairly constantly in need of troops, either to defend his throne at home or to pursue campaigns abroad, and for the supply of these he was completely dependent upon his Tenants-in-Chief—as the nobles were called in pre-Norman times. Under the feudal system then existing, it was the Tenants-in-Chief, and their sub-tenants under them, who recruited and maintained armed forces at their own expense for the protection of their own domains, and since the King had no large forces at his own disposal he was obliged to call upon those of his tenants' when the need arose. Since, however, no tenant was *compelled* to lend his soldiers, it was necessary for the King to make out a good case for borrowing them, and it was this fact that gave reality to the "advisory" capacity of the Barons. It was their one power over the Crown.

The King's second need was for money—no new problem this. Although he was supposed to maintain his own estate from private sources, and generally did so, he was in no position to finance a war—or even a major domestic campaign—and for funds under these circumstances he had to rely on contributions from the principal landowners, in those days the Church. So two bodies of subjects, very different from each other in both outlook and interest, had some form of control over the King and could to some extent (even in early times) influence both his domestic and foreign policies—though it should not be forgotten that if individual Barons were *too* argumentative the axe was a powerful advocate of the King's point of view!

Be that as it may, however, even the Saxon Kings were subject to a certain control and had around them the nucleus of a parliament made up of the Lords Spiritual (the Church leaders with their money) and the Lords Temporal (the Barons with their trained bands), but the trouble was they were only summoned when the King *wanted* something from them. That being so, attendance in Council was not a popular duty and was avoided whenever possible.

In very early times indeed, therefore, the King realised that the appointment of a special officer was necessary to ensure both that summonses were delivered to all members of the Council and that the members answered to them in person; and for that, some sort of register—or roll—must be kept and Acts recorded. So we find, in 1315, the first creation of the official post of the Clerk of the Parliament by Edward II. William Ayremin, a direct appointee of the King, was charged with the duty of keeping the Rolls of Parliament and informing his master of absentees, and since his work virtually was to censor the comings and goings of the chief dignitaries of both the Church and the State, one can imagine that it was no sinecure. However, at this stage there were no Commons to cope with; that was to come later.

It was earlier, in 1265, when Henry II summoned "burgesses" to meet with the parliament, that common folk were first called into consultation by the Crown—though they were not accepted *into* the parliament, but were made to meet separately. Nor were they permitted to speak in the presence of their august and powerful superiors; their collective views were to be made known in the council-chamber only through the mouth of one whom they would elect as "parlour" to speak for them.

Simon de Montfort, who was the architect of this plan to widen the representation in parliament, has gained great retrospective acclaim as the founder of our modern democratic system of government, though his motives at the time were probably much less high-minded than history has liked to admit. Granted that he was the champion of the Barons against the autocratic power of the Crown, he was never ever suspected of being champion of the common people against the waxing power of the Barons. It is much more likely that his intentions were purely practical and expedient, not to say mercenary, for by that time the ancient milch-cow of Kings and Council—the Church— was showing signs of exhaustion, and fresh treasuries were required to sunstain the power of the mighty. Whose better, then, than those of the newly arisen merchant classes, who for too long —in the opinion of hungry government—had enjoyed their gains in peace?

So the knights and burgesses were co-opted, and though they were permitted to meet together to *discuss* the demands made upon their purses by the King and his advisers, little notice was taken of any objections they might raise and the influence of their opinions on actual policy was for a long time precisely nil. Neither were they provided with any kind of meeting-place. The conception of a "house" for the commons was a long way in the future, and the unfortunate citizens who were summoned into council had not only to produce the (often enormous) sums of money required of them by the King, but had to pay their own expenses into the bargain. Naturally enough, summonses to the parliament became as unpopular with the commoners as it had been with their more distinguished predecessors; and naturally enough, too, it soon became necessary to keep tabs on *them* in the way that had proved successful with the Barons.

It fell to the Lord Chancellor to provide the earliest clerical assistance to the Commons, though the precise date of this innovation is not known—principally because we do not know exactly *when* the Commons were first recognised as a "House" with rights of its own as well as duties to the Crown. At all events, it was probably early in the fourteenth century that the Chancellor was ordered to provide "a clerk" for the service of the Lower House and it is almost certain that one or other of his own Clerks in Chancery was seconded to the (comparatively unimportant) task. A "clerk", in the language of the times, was simply one who could read and write; a Clerk in Chancery possessed, in addition, legal training and qualifications.

It is interesting to note that the original appointment (made by the Chancellor but on behalf of the Crown) was not made directly to the Commons; the new officer was designated as Under-Clerk of the Parliament—i.e. he was no more than the assistant of the Clerk already established in the Upper House, lent to the Commons by the Crown (who paid his salary) to help them with their business. The necessity for his presence there is obvious—most of the Members could neither read nor write! The principal function of the Lower House at this period, apart from finding money, was the presentation of petitions on behalf of local interests (what we would recognise now as Private Bills) and since they needed to understand what these petitions were all about before discussing them, *someone* clearly was required to read them out aloud to the House.

This was an important part of the Clerk's function in the Lower House and an interesting relic of it remains in our procedure today. When the Speaker calls a Bill for discussion, the Clerk will rise in his place and read out the Title of the Bill in a loud voice for all to head; since Bills are printed nowadays, and all Members have copies, it is no longer necessary to read the document in full, the Title is enough, but the ancient precedent is observed and tradition is continued.

The first Clerk to be officially appointed as the Clerk of the Commons, though still described as the "Under-Clerk to the Parliament" (i.e. assistant to the officer in the Lords) was Robert de Melton in the year 1363. Like his part-time predecessors and his contemporary superior in the Lords, he was a Chancery clerk, and one might wonder what attraction such a man could see in a post whose emolument was a mere 100 shillings a year for life. But as will be seen later, there were other inducements. (The Clerk received a 100 per cent pay rise in 1592, but even then the salary itself was still insignificant.)

It can be gathered from this that the earlier Clerks were far from being the professional experts their successors were to become—Hasely, Bayen and Seymour, in fact were actually Members of the House before assuming the duties of clerkship—and it is not surprising that two of them have left little impression on the rolls of history. William Underhill (1510), perhaps, is worth a mention, since he was the first to be officially described as Clerk of the Parliament of "our *Lower House*"—the Commons, it seems, were beginning to "arrive".

Under the Tudors, Parliament continued to increase in stature and the voice of the Commons, though still subdued, was heard more than formerly. Henry VIII's strong support of the Commons in their "privilege" complaint against the City of London (see p. 80) was indicative of the growing recognition accorded at that time of the rights which the Lower House were at last beginning to establish; and as the Commons learned to treat their own House with respect and dignity, so too did their servants. The Clerk, still a servant of the King by appointment, began to identify himself more directly with his immediate employers; to use initiative where his duties were concerned, to *think* about his job and to *care* for it; to lay down, in short, the first foundations of that tradition of highly professional expertise that is the hall-mark of modern Clerks.

The first of this new generation, John Seymour, had served as Member of Parliament for West Bedwin in the last parliament of Henry VIII and he brought with him to the Clerk's chair a considerable personal experience of what the House needed to carry out its work efficiently. He was no fly-by-night, simply accepting a royal appointment as a stepping-stone to better things, but was to occupy his post for twenty years and to make it memorable by a very significant innovation.

Although Seymour's patent (i.e. his letter of appointment

under the Great Seal) was dated 26th May 1548, his actual assumption of office coincided with the first parliament of Edward VI in 1547, and his tenure of the Clerkship covered completely the reigns of three sovereigns and overlapped by nine years into the reign of a fourth (Edward VI, the tragic fourteen days of Jane Gray who was beheaded at the age of seventeen, Mary I and Elizabeth I). Certainly, by the end of that long service, Seymour was a very experienced and knowledgeable Clerk, but the innovation that was to give him a special place in the clerkly hierarchy dates from his earliest days in office. Being obviously of an orderly mind, he began—quite unofficially (it was no part of his accepted duties)—to keep a rough record of the day's proceedings in the House, a mere scribble which was at first simply a note of the presentation and progress of petitions.

But Seymour was blessed with imagination, too, and he soon saw what a useful document his simple "diary" could become. As time went by he widened the basis of his entries to include, not only the histories of individual motions, but such items as records of attendance by Members, instructions of the House on matters affecting its privilege, etc.; and in 1553 he included for the first time detailed figures of all divisions taken in the House. This daily record, which occupied a mere three pages in Seymour's first Session, had grown into eleven pages per Session by the time he retired, and it was to develop with time, into the Commons' most indispensable document—the Journal (see p. 49).

Seymour was succeeded in 1567 by Fulke Onslow, whose brother Richard Onslow had been elected Speaker the previous year, and the new Clerk continued the self-imposed task of his predecessor. In some ways he improved upon it. One considerable improvement, for example, was the legibility of Onslow's script; Seymour had simply jotted down his notes in the Chamber and filed away his jottings, but Onslow—more painstaking, perhaps—made it a point to copy out his rough notes later in proper journal form, leaving a clearly readable record for posterity.

Another of Onslow's "improvements", however, was to cause trouble—he attempted to cram into his journal the gist of the actual speeches made in the House. This might have been a good idea, but it established bad precedents. For one thing, the Clerk

could scarcely be expected to carry out his statutory functions
and listen to all the speeches—and not only listen to them, but
summarise their arguments, too—and Onslow's attempt to do so
was really derogatory to the very dignity he wished to see
invested in his own position. Secondly, the mere practice of
recording speeches in the Journal was itself a dangerous move,
though the House was not to awaken to this fact until sixty years
later when Charles I demanded to see the Journal to check on
the utterances of a particular Member.

Although this was one of the earlier of the many pinpricks
Charles was to inflict on the House in the course of his long
—and eventually fatal—contention with its members, it was
nevertheless met effectively and dealt with promptly. The House
resolved that "the entry of the clerk of particular men's speeches
was without warrant at all times"—and, one might add, in *all
places*. Reporting of individual speeches was completely prohibited (though of course the ban was frequently evaded, unofficially) and it was not until 1909 that the House felt on firm
enough ground to broadcast *all* its proceedings to the public.
Even then, properly enough, the task was not given to the Clerk
but to a completely new staff specially recruited and equipped
to do it as it should be done (see p. 191).

The Journals of Seymour and Onslow, which are still known
by the names of their authors, did not at once become official
documents of the House; they were regarded as no more than
what, in fact, they were—private notes of the Clerk. But in 1581,
when the Speakership fell vacant and the House was at a loss for
what precedent to follow, the Journals really came into their
own. Onslow was ordered to read to the House from "the original
book of notes"—i.e. Seymour's journal, where an invaluable
account of a previous Speaker's Election had been faithfully
recorded—and the House was reminded of the Speaker's traditional three requests to the Crown for privilege: free speech in
the House, freedom from arrest for Members and their servants,
access to the Crown.

Forty-two years later, in 1623, the Clerks' journal became the
Journal of the House when a committee was appointed "to
survey the clerk's Book of Entries every Saturday in the afternoon". Seymour's jottings had become respectable; his brain-

child had achieved maturity. It was to become more cherished than any other possession of the Commons, and its maintenance one of the Clerk's most important duties.

Apart from their founding of the Journal, however, the Elizabethan Clerks added little of distinction to their appointments, and neither did Ralph Ewens and John Wright who followed them. The Commons under Henry VIII were a very docile lot—no one can blame them for *that*, remembering Henry's ferocious Welsh temper and his use of the block and axe in place of argument—and under Elizabeth they were little better. Still servile, never "demanding" but always "requesting", their long service under that redoubtable Queen nevertheless began to foster in the House a certain corporate backbone and aggressiveness that was to show its final development unmistakably in that cataclysmic clash with the Crown under Charles; and when that occurred, it was found that their Clerk had developed a backbone, too.

Henry Elsyng, who was appointed Clerk in 1640, fifteen years after the accession of Charles I, was the son of a former Clerk of the Parliament. In 1637 he had petitioned the King for the reversion of his late father's appointment, but when his petition was rejected he doubtless considered the post of under-clerk to be the next best thing, and with the recommendation of Archbishop Laud (so it was said) behind him he secured the appointment.

He came into the service of the House at a time that was intensely interesting, both historically and in the Parliamentary sense, for the Commons were at last becoming really alive. This was the period of the Long Parliament (1640–1653). Protracted debates, bitter and stormy to a degree never known in earlier days, made the introduction of some sort of strong framework of procedure and order absolutely vital if the Commons were to continue as a House, and it was from this urgent need that the Clerks first drew their eventual importance in the organisation.

Elsyng was exactly the man for the moment. Being the son of his father, he had spent the whole of his earlier life against a background of Parliamentary affairs, and though his father's experience had been confined to the Upper House one can be sure that both father and son were no strangers to either the practice of the Lower House or to its problems. The fact that

Elsyng went so far as to petition the King direct for his father's old post must indicate that he considered himself amply equipped to fill it—and as events were to show, he was.

Elsyng's own stature was greatly enlarged by the fact that the Speaker, William Lenthal (see p. 96)—who owes his great name in Parliamentary history simply to the great events with which he was to be associated—was a personal nonentity. The following extract from Wood's *Athenae Oxonienses*, quoted by Hatsell (a later distinguished Clerk), paints a reasonable picture of both men :

"This (place) crowned his former labours and by it he had opportunity to manifest his rare abilities; which in short time became so conspicuous, especially in taking and expressing the sense of the House, that none, as it was believed, that ever sat there exceeded him. . . . His discretion also and prudence was such that though faction kept that fatal, commonly called Long, Parliament in continual storm and disorder, yet his fair and temperate carriage made him commended and esteemed by all parties. And therefore it was that, for these his abilities and prudence, more reverence was paid to his stool than to the Speaker's chair; who being obnoxious, timorous, and interested, was often much confused in collecting the sense of the House and drawing the debates to a fair question."

The friendly bias of this testimony cannot detract from its importance; Elsyng was a rare Clerk in trying and dangerous times. Having asserted his personality in the House, he added significance and lustre to the Clerk's position; from a mere keeper of records and reader of bills, the Clerk became principal adviser to the House and the Speaker on everything to do with procedure —and so remains to this day.

Elsyng, however, was called upon to distinguish himself even more signally—and at terrible cost—when Parliament seized the King for trial and began to hurry through an enabling Act in 1648. Elsyng, as Clerk, would have none of it. To lay hands on the King, in his opinion, was bad enough; but to attempt to carry through an Act in an improperly constituted Parliament (the absence of the Crown made it so, under the Constitution) was something he would not endure. He resigned his post in protest, and died six years later—a sad and forlorn figure, in such circumstances of poverty that friends had to pay for his funeral. (After the Restoration, in 1660, the new House voted £500 to his children, who were even then still destitute as the result of their father's brave defiance against something which he believed wrong.)

On Elsyng's abrupt departure at the end of December 1648, the Clerk's chair was briefly filled by his recently appointed assistant, John Phelpes, but when Elsyng's patent was called in on the 5th January 1649 it was Henry Scobell who was appointed to the vacancy, with Darnall as his Clerk Assistant. Phelpes was to be one of the two Clerks to the court that tried the King, and was attainted later as a regicide—though he escaped trial and fled to Switzerland.

Scobell, in his day, was the centre of one or two very interesting experiences in his dealings with his militant masters of the interregnum Parliament. When he took his seat at the opening of the Session of 1654 the House, it seems, suddenly remembered that he had been appointed by letter patent; they had no liking for patents, they told him (a relic of Royal prerogative!) and ordered him to leave his place and withdraw from the Chamber. One can imagine with what astonishment he did so, having already served the House faithfully for five years!

However, he had no sooner withdrawn than he was called back again and informed that he had now been *chosen* as Clerk; he was to resume his place and carry on as before—purged, one assumes, of all taint of the monarchy. The House of Lords having been abolished under the Commonwealth, the Commons decided to regularise Scobell's position by passing a special Act appointing him Clerk of the Parliament (singular), and this was done in proper and regular form; the Common's Clerk was now Clerk of the Parliament.

But when the House of Lords was revived (as the "Other House") in 1658, Scobell, under his new title, automatically became *its* Clerk—a promotion he was not slow to seize, taking with him, under the authority of his special Act, all the records of the Commons, which he refused to surrender. How true was the Speaker's comment in the *impasse* : "The Clerk is gone, and ye could not carry on your business without one"! The *impasse* was resolved, however, when on the 25th January 1658, the

Commons passed a specific order and the Journal and other documents were at length returned safely to the custody of the House.

During the following two years the Clerk's chair was occupied by three transient incumbents—John Smythe, Thomas St. Nicholas and William Jessop—none of whom offer any claim to distinction and may be passed over without loss. It was only in 1661, after the Restoration, that the next "real" figure emerged. William Goldsborough's appointment on the 13th April that year swept away for all time the expediences of the Commonwealth Parliament, which "had no liking for Patents" and simply "chose" its Clerks; he was appointed formally in the old style by letters patent under the Great Seal of the new King. Also, he was designated by the old title of Under-Clerk of Parliament; the wheel had come full circle.

The appointment of Goldsborough as Clerk revived another interesting tradition which had fallen in abeyance under Cromwell—the ancient connection between Clerks of the House and the clerks of Chancery. Goldsborough had been a deputy register of the Court of Chancery since 1650, and though his political sympathies had undoubtedly been towards the cause of the Royalists he must have kept them fairly well hidden for in 1658 he had even taken on the duties of full (acting) Register—no mean position to hold under the Commonwealth.

When Goldsborough died in office in 1678 he was succeeded by his son, William Goldsborough junior, who had been granted the reversion of his father's office five years before he left it, and who was a member of Lincoln's Inn. Both father and son did well, financially, from the many sidelines (see p. 118) then available to officers in the Commons, but the bulk of documentary evidence they have left to mark their tenure of office seems to be concerned with their never-ending struggle to secure payment of their official salaries (then £10 per year) from the Crown. Charles II, of course, was notoriously always short of funds—one remembers the story that he was supposed to have bribed Captain Blood to steal the Crown Jewels (and certainly Blood was never punished for it!)—and the Goldsboroughs seem to have had little success with their applications for proper payment.

The salary of Goldsborough senior was ten years in arrears

when he died, and the son seems never to have received any salary at all since when *he* died, in 1683, the whole of his five years' salary (£50) was paid over to his executors. Still, salary or no salary, they must have found their appointments both profitable and enjoyable; if they had not, there would have been ample scope for their qualifications and abilities *outside* the House in the Courts.

Paul Jodrell, who became Clerk in 1683 and held his appointment for forty-three years, was a man of significance in several ways. He was, for one thing, the only practising *solicitor* ever to occupy the Clerk's chair; and though this was during a period of increasing business in the House and increasing complexity in procedure and detail, he not only added to the distinction of his Parliamentary office but managed to keep his private practice flourishing throughout his career. This was no mean feat, since neither of his interests suffered in the least by the division of his attention, and it bespeaks a man of tremendous energy, capability and application.

Jodrell possessed all these qualities to a high degree, but he possessed another that was to be particularly important both to the House in which he actually served and to those that were to follow. His legal training followed by the disciplined exercise of his solicitor's practice, had produced, in a mind naturally acute and incisive, a passion for system and order that coloured everything he did, and it was fortunate indeed for the House that he brought this characteristic into its service just when he did. The records and papers of the Commons, he found, were in a state of indescribable confusion—to him, unbearable—and he made it his first and most urgent task to bring them back into some sort of recognisable order. But first, they had to be *found*. Since the invaluable Journal had always been regarded as more or less the chattel of the Clerk in office its custody had become very casual indeed and it was by no means unusual for sections of it to be "lent out" to individuals whose interests may have been affected by decisions of the House, and who, perhaps, may have wished to study the relevant ruling at first-hand. The return of the borrowed manuscript was not always as prompt as it might have been, and when Jodrell assumed the guardianship of the Journal he found that many of its pages were missing.

Some of them, which were traced to "William Henchman and Thomas Fox, booksellers of Westminster, and others" (who apparently proposed printing and publishing them) were only recovered after Jodrell obtained an Order in Council for their return. The pages recording the proceedings from the 18th March to the 27th May (1678) were found to be in the possession of Samuel Pepys—who, it will be recalled, had found himself in trouble with the Commons over Navy matters in that year—and who had borrowed the relevant pages in order to check the references.

The rounding-up of the complete Journal must have cost Jodrell a great deal of trouble and effort, and he clearly took steps to see that the performance would never need repeating. The Journal manuscript has never since been lent to anyone for any reason, and it is not likely to be.

Jodrell's passion for proper organisation prompted him into another step which, though doomed not to mature in his own lifetime, was to benefit his successors greatly. In 1685 he petitioned the King with a new idea. The petitioner, he said, had lately come in to the office of Clerk of the Commons and ". . . had endeavoured to his utmost for the preservation of the books and other things belonging thereto, for future service, he finding the same in a very disordered manner; that he apprehend such disorders have happened by reason there hath not been for many years any place of habitation appointed for the Clerk of the Commons (as the Clerk of the House of Lords has had, which is annexed to his office) for the more convenient execution of the said office".

There was a litle plot of land, he said, at the west end of Westminster Hall, and on it a ruined old house to which the King had title; he would be glad to rebuild this place at his own expense, if permission were forthcoming, and use it both as a residence for the Clerk and for the safe storage of essential records and documents. His petition, however, failed, and he continued to live at his old address in Chancery Lane. But his solicitude for his beloved Journals was in no way lessened by this set-back to his plans. Not long afterwards he appointed a new clerk to be specially in charge of the House's records, lodging him in his own house and paying him a salary of £40 out of his own pocket—and in so doing laid the foundations for what was to become the very important Journal Office (see below). Jodrell's long tenure of office extended over the reign of James II, William III, Queen Anne, and into the quieter days that came into the Commons with Walpole, and he retired in 1726 a rich man. Perhaps the best memorial remaining (among many) to this distinguished Clerk—certainly the one which would have pleased *him* best—was the statement of Speaker Spencer Compton (in a letter to the Treasury) that "his keeping of the Journals (was) in a better manner than had ever been done by any of his predecessors". Because of the new sense of order and organisation that Jodrell brought into his department, it is fair to say that he was the first of the modern generation of Clerks—though with the important difference (only to be altered much later) that he, like some of his predecessors, still drew payments direct from the Lords of the Treasury in return for specific work done on their behalf, and he was—to that extent—far from independent of the executive. Today's Clerks, as will appear, are completely so.

Edward Stables, who occupied the Chair for five years after Jodrell's death, was quite unremarkable; undoubtedly good at his job (he, too, was a member of Lincoln's Inn), he quietly and efficiently carried out the duties required of him in a House that ran easily and well under the strong leadership of Walpole. It is, perhaps, typical of his whole life that the monument he had arranged to have put up to mark his tomb in Wandsworth church was never erected; only his name remains.

His successor in 1732, Nicholas Hardinge, was a very different kind of man, celebrated in many spheres. A brilliant classic scholar, from Eton, he became a Fellow of King's and a member of the Middle Temple, and by the time he reached the age of thirty-two (when he was appointed Clerk) he was already recognised as a master of the composition of Latin verse and an authority on his own branch of the law. Though he was without any form of Parliamentary experience prior to his appointment he was chosen by Walpole on sheer merit, and the choice was amply justified.

Hardinge brought a new air of social distinction into the Clerk's position in the House—a position occupied hitherto by men whose merits were, at best, the dry, prosaic merits of lawyers coming to grips with a strange environment—and the Clerks who have followed him have much to thank him for. Hardinge was an *elegant* man, acceptable everywhere in Society, and with his advent the appointment was given a new—and lasting—gloss. The story of Walpole's wager with William Poultenay is a fair example of the Clerk's new dignity among the great ones of the land.

On the 11th February 1741 (according to Cox's *Life of Walpole*) Walpole made use of a quotation from Horace to reinforce a point during his speech from the Treasury Bench and Poultenay (later the Earl of Bath) challenged his accuracy. Walpole, stung by the criticism, thereupon bet Poultenay a guinea that the words he had used were correct, suggesting that the learned Clerk should be called upon to arbitrate. Hardinge at once ruled the Prime Minister in error, and such was his authority that there was no more argument—Walpole tossed his guinea to his triumphant opponent, who remarked as he caught it, "It is the only money I have received from the Treasury in many years, and it shall be the last!"

But it was not only elegance and erudition that Hardinge added to the Clerk's office; he brought in practical improvements, too. It was under his administration that the practice of *printing* the Journal was first introduced, and he was imaginative enough to persuade the House to have the earlier Journal printed as well as the current ones—he arranged, in fact, for all the Journal right back to the *Seymour* to be put into print by the well-known printer and novelist Samuel Richardson. This was a signal service to Parliament and one for which he deserves to be remembered. He will be remembered, too, as the first Clerk to draw a salary from the Civil list in addition to the £10 a year that came with his letters patent.

Like most of us, however, Hardinge had his blind spot—and in his case it was money. He extracted enormous sums from the Treasury in respect of the printing of the Journals; in addition to the £15,000 which he drew during his own lifetime towards this expense, a further £3,778 16s. 5d. was voted to his widow after his death—the odd seven hundred pounds being "in full satisfaction of the balance of an account for printing the Journals up to the end of the 8th Parliament of Great Britain", and the main sum "as recompense for the pains and services of Nicholas Hardinge in preparing copies of the Journal for the press and in directing the printing".

Certainly, his task had been a notable one; but then, so was the reward! But in spite of the generosity of the payment, and the promptness with which it was made, Hardinge showed himself by no means anxious to meet the just accounts of Samuel Richardson the printer who had done the actual work. Time and again Richardson applied to the Clerk for settlement, and just as often Hardinge put him off with promises to pay—promises which were never kept until Speaker Onslow himself intervened and insisted upon the bills being met.

The elegant Hardinge resigned his post in 1747 to enter politics—and did well out of both transactions. On leaving the Clerk's chair, he "sold" the reversion of the appointment to his successor for £6,000 (to be fair, it should be said that this practice was common among his predecessors, both in respect of the reversion of their own appointments and the appointment of subordinates). Hardinge's action, then, was in no way dishonourable—but his "golden handshake" was a good one. He became Member of Parliament for Eye, in Suffolk, the following year, and joint Secretary to the Treasury four years later, a post which he held until his death in 1758.

The man who paid £6,000 for Hardinge's appointment was very different from his polished, man-of-the-world predecessor. Jeremiah Dyson, young (he was a mere twenty-six when appointed), well-to-do, highly literate and of pronounced radical views, had joined Hardinge's staff in a subordinate capacity some years before and had already decided on a political career. It seems clear that he bought Hardinge's reversion simply to gain at first-hand what he considered an essential grounding in Parliamentary procedure and practice, and although he was prepared to pay such a handsome price for it he obviously disapproved of the market he had dealt in, for he never himself sold a place in the House and on his retirement the appointment passed on without fee to his successor. In this, he set a good precedent—one that has been followed since.

Dyson is remembered for one or two procedural innovations—

for example, it was under his supervision that a system for cal-
culating the fees chargeable on Private Bills was finally worked
out—but perhaps his most important achievement lay in the
fact that he was the first to obtain an official residence for the
Clerk. In 1760, at a cost of £3,159 4s. od., a house was put up
for him on the site of Sir Robert Cotton's former house (where
Charles I was held before his appearance in Westminster Hall),
and though its design was poor and its foundations rotten it
served to shelter successive Clerks until it disappeared, merci-
fully perhaps, in the great fire of 1834, when a replacement was
provided. Dyson established a precedent for which many who
followed him have had cause to be grateful.

When he resigned in 1762 to pursue his political ambitions he
was followed by Thomas Tyrwhitt, who—though a great and
noted scholar, was undistinguished as a Clerk and left nothing
behind to commemorate his six years of office. This could certainly not be said of the man who succeeded him in 1768.

Henry Hatsell had been appointed Clerk Assistant by Dyson
in 1760 and had been expected to fill the vacancy left by Dyson's
retirement. He was a brilliant man, a member of the Middle
Temple (of which he was to become successively a Master of
the Bench and Treasurer), well connected socially and with a
zest for living that was never to desert him. Also, he knew what
he wanted in life and always had a pretty good idea how to get
it. He was the first Clerk ever to discharge his functions through
a deputy—John Ley was appointed in this capacity in 1797—
and even though he abandoned his seat at the Table at that
juncture, he still retained all the (considerable) fees and payments
of his office, which he shared, at his own pleasure, with his
assistant.

Hatsell studied the Journals as other men might study the
Bible. The Journal *was* his Bible, and from its references he drew
a prodigious store of the precedents, which, added to his own
considerable personal understanding of the parliamentary machine, made him the world's principal authority on parliamentary
procedure. Between the years 1776 and 1796 he produced his
celebrated *Precedents of Proceedings in the House of Commons*,
a formidable work in four volumes dealing respectively with—
Privilege; Procedure, the Speaker and the Clerk; relations be-

tween the two Houses; Impeachments. This work, more vast in
its authority than even in its size, became *the* handbook of Parliaments—not only in England, but in the newly emerged Congress
of the United States—and has only been exceeded, in much
later days, by the monumental volume of Erskine May, which
is the acknowledged standard work of modern times.

Just as Hatsell was outstanding as a man, so was his tenure
of his office. From his appointment in 1768 until he quitted the
Chair in 1797—a period of over thirty years—he ruled the
offices of the House with a rod of iron and impressed upon their
functions a pattern that was to be long remembered and respected. When he withdrew his physical presence from the
Chamber in 1797, already sixty-four years of age, and handed
over day-to-day authority to the man who had been his Clerk
Assistant for thirty years, John Ley, it might have been supposed
that his intention was to devote the declining years of his life to
quieter and less demanding pursuits. But not at all; from 1797
until he died in 1820 this remarkable man retained his iron grip
on the affairs of the Commons. He not only continued to control
almost every action of every clerk in his department, but continued—though absent—to collect the very considerable fees
which had by now become the perquisite of the Clerk; he continued, too, to occupy the Clerk's House in Cotton's Gardens,
and it is small wonder that he died a very wealthy man indeed.

The John Ley who was appointed to the vacancy caused by
Hatsell's death in 1820 was not the same John Ley who had
been Hatsell's Assistant from 1768–1797 and Deputy thereafter.
That John Ley had pre-deceased his master by six years, dying
in office in 1814, and Jeremiah Dyson (son of the earlier Clerk)
had succeeded him as Deputy. The new Clerk, who had been
Dyson's Assistant, was the nephew of the elder Ley and was
distantly related to Hatsell himself by marriage; he was the pro-
genitor of a minor dynasty of Leys whose service was to extend
up into times within living memory.

This is an excellent point at which to break off this retrospect
of the Clerk's succession, since it was during the tenure of John
Ley that decisive changes were made in the office of the
House. Once these changes had been completed, service in the
Commons took on a completely new look—a change certainly for

CHAPTER 2

The Clerk's Officers, 1363–1833

THE CLERK ASSISTANT

While it is obvious that no Clerk could discharge single-handed the multifarious duties of his office, there is very little reliable information about what assistance he had during the earlier days of the Commons. Even in Seymour's time (1548–1567) the Clerk's status was a humble one, and there is no record that his subordinates enjoyed any official recognition at all. Indeed, as Hooker was to say in his *The Order of Kepinge of a Parliament*, the Table of the House was at that juncture no more than "a little board before him (i.e. the Clerk) to write and lay his books upon".

What little can be gleaned from contemporary records and observations, however, suggests that the earlier Clerks normally made use of their own servants to assist with the work of the House—not "servants" in the domestic sense, but in the sense that they were men whose obedience was to the Clerk personally and not to either the House or the government. Bearing in mind the Chancery background of most of these Clerks it is reasonable to assume that they brought in as assistants men who had already established themselves in the clerical posts of the legal offices; certainly, they could read and write, for without that facility they could not have attempted the work they had to do and would have been useless to the Clerk. And the fact that they were literate must have placed them, culturally, a long way above most of the Members who used their services.

Whoever these early assistants were, however, they remain anonymous, and it was not until the year 1640 (when the

Clerk's appointment was already nearly 300 years old) that a Clerk *Assistant* was first officially appointed into the service of the House. This new departure was made at the specific request of Henry Elsyng when he took up his own appointment in that year, and it is interesting to note that while Elsyng himself was enough of a Royalist to resign over the trial of the King, the man he chose as Assistant, John Rushworth, was flexible enough to hold high offices under both King and Commonwealth and to survive the Restoration.

In 1661, long after he had quitted his service at the Table, Rushworth became Member of Parliament for Berwick and Secretary to the Council of State, but his brilliant career was ruined by drink (brandy, so it was said). He died, graceless and sodden, in 1690 in the King's Bench prison, where he had been committed for debt and drunkenness—a pitiable figure who could not even remember his days of power and greatness.

He left his mark, however, in the annals of Parliament. On that famous occasion on the 4th January 1642 when Charles burst into the House to arrest the five Members—an act against privilege for which the Commons have not forgiven the Crown to this day—it was Rushworth who took down the King's actual words in "shorthand", to embed them for ever in history.

Rushworth's Account

"Gentlemen," said the King in halting sentences, "I am sorry of this occasion of coming unto you. Yesterday I sent a Serjeant at Arms upon a very important occasion to apprehend some that by my command were accused of high treason; whereunto I did expect obedience and not a message. And I must declare unto you here, that albeit no King that ever was in England shall be more careful of your privileges to maintain them to the uttermost of this power than I shall be; yet you must know that in cases of treason, no person hath a privilege. And, therefore, I am come to know if any of these persons that were accused were here."

Then casting his eyes upon all the Members in the House, he said : "I do not see any of them : I think I should know them. For I must tell you, gentlemen, that so long as these persons that are accused (for no slight crime, but for treason) are here, I cannot expect that the House will be in the right way that I do heartily wish it. Therefore I am come to tell you, that I must have them, wheresoever I find them!"

Then his Majesty said: "Is Mr. Pym here?" to which nobody gave answer. "Well, since I see all my birds are flown, I do expect from you that you shall send them unto me as soon as they return hither. But I assure you, on the word of a King, that I never did intend any force, but shall proceed against them in a legal and fair way, for I never meant any other. And now, since I see I cannot do what I came for, I think this is no unfit occasion to repeat what I have said formerly, that whatsoever I have done in favour and to the good of my subjects, I do mean to maintain it."

(It is interesting to note that Charles was aware that Rushworth was "taking him down"; he subsequently sent for the report, and returned it later—with corrections.)

Of John Phelpes, and his fate after the Restoration, we have already heard; and of his successor, Ralph Darnall, it is only necessary to say that he was Clerk Assistant to every session but one of Cromwell's interregnum parliaments. It is true to say that, as Clerks Assistant, the majority of those who held this appointment seldom achieved distinction in it—though some Assistants did become distinguished as Clerks and made their mark in the top appointment. Of these, the most notable were undoubtedly Goldsborough, Jodrell, Hatsell, and J. H. Ley, and it may well be the case that they owed their eventual fame as Clerks as much to their sound apprenticeships at the Table as to their own native talents.

In 1801 the increasing business of the House made such demands upon the attention of both Clerk and Assistant that it became clear a third clerk would have to be brought in to the Table, and the post of Second Clerk Assistant was created. First to occupy it, in that first year, was John Henry Ley, nephew of Hatsell's deputy (John Ley)—who was to become Assistant in 1814 and Clerk of the House in 1820.

On J. H. Ley's succession to the Assistant post in 1814 he was succeeded as Second by a very interesting character indeed, a man who was—in one respect at least—unique. John Rickman, son of the vicar of Newburn in Northumberland, had enjoyed a fine classical education, and with his friend Robert Southey had interested himself in the problems which complicated and bedevilled the structure of the every-day society in which he lived. The lower-class strata, he found, were very little understood by those who framed the laws to govern them; it was not even known, for example, how *many* of them there were or where they were concentrated.

John Rickman "invented" the National Census to discover the answer to these basic questions, for he believed that it was only when they had been properly answered that a start could be made on the great social reforms that were becoming glaringly more necessary in the new environment of industrialisation. Rickman's idea of a counting of heads was taken up with enthusiasm by Charles Abbot, M.P. for Helston, and after its passage through Parliament as the Population Act of 1800, it was not surprising that its originator should be invited to supervise the actual work it entailed. Rickman, in fact, personally organised the first censuses ever taken in this country— those of 1811, 1821 and 1831— and was drafting the Act for the 1841 count when he died.

When Charles Abbot (see p. 108) became Speaker in 1802, Rickman was appointed Speaker's Secretary and served in that capacity for twelve years—efficiently enough, by all accounts, but with no great enthusiasm since the duties were by no means taxing. The offer of a clerkship by Hatsell (at Abbot's instigation) in 1814 came as a godsend and Rickman seized it with alacrity and gratitude, and though he admittedly found *that* work tedious and boring, too, when he got into it, be became an excellent Second Assistant and served with notable efficiency until his death in 1840. He was the only Speaker's Secretary ever to become a Clerk at the Table.

In concluding this very brief retrospect of the Clerks Assistants' appointments it is as well to mention that up till that time (i.e. the mid-nineteenth century) the Clerk's power of appointment, discipline and dismissal was absolute over the whole of his staff. The changes which came into practice *after* the "1833 Committee"—they included taking away from the Clerk the power of appointing his Assistants at the Table and vesting it henceforth in the Crown—will be discussed in their place at a later stage.

THE JOURNAL OFFICE

As Orwell said, ". . . all animals are equal . . ." etc. So, too must be the Offices which together make up the Clerk's Department; since each has an absolutely vital place in the machinery of the House it would be idle to designate any one as "more equal" than the rest. But if any one of the Clerk's Offices must be singled out for prior treatment it must be the Journal Office—if only because it carries the responsibility of custody of the Commons' most valued possession. (Its functions, however, by no means end with that particular duty (see p. 200).)

The House first accorded official notice to "the Clerk's Book of Entries" early in the seventeenth century, and once it received recognition it ceased to be merely a private chattel : its custody became, overnight, one of the Clerk's most important and onerous responsibilities. We have seen how seriously Jodrell (1683–1726) regarded this duty, and we have seen to what lengths he went, not only to reassemble the scattered records into a composite whole, but to provide for its safeguarding in the future. His attempts to secure specific accommodation for its care proving unsuccessful, he had paid a clerk £40 a year (plus board) specially to look after it and in so doing laid the foundations for what was to become—in time—the Journal Office.

The title did not accompany the birth of the idea. At first—around 1740—a certain Samuel Littlemore was appointed as the Clerk of the Papers (almost certainly by Nicholas Hardinge) and this appointment was made, whether by design or chance is not certain, just when the House had decided to have the whole of the Journals put into print (see p. 40), starting with the very first manuscripts and gradually bringing the whole set up to date. This was an enormous undertaking and called for some reorganisation by the Clerk, who was in overall command of the operation; a reorganisation apparently still in progress when Dyson succeeded Hardinge in 1748, for it was in that year that Littlemore's appointment (as Clerk of the Papers) was described for the first time as the Clerk of the Journals and Papers—which has remained the correct title of the principal Clerk of the Journal Office ever since.

But though the clerk's title was changed at this time, the title

of the office was not; his office continued to be known by its
adoptive title—of ancient origin—of the Court of Wards. I say
"adoptive" because there was no relationship whatever between
"Journals and papers" and "The Court of Wards", the old name
of the latter being transferred to the former more or less by
chance. The original court, properly called the Court of Wards
and Liveries, had been abolished in 1660, leaving vacant its
premises at the south end of Westminster Hall, and in 1674 the
inner room of the building had been given over to the Commons for the storage of records—among which, of course, were
the Journals. When the old building was pulled down in 1678
to provide access from the Old Palace Yard into St. Stephen's
new storage area—still called by the name of the office it replaced
—was provided in another part of the building, so that the place
where the Journals were kept continued to be called the Court of
Wards long after the Court itself had disappeared into oblivion.

It was not until Hatsell's occupancy of the Clerk's chair
(1768–1797) that the old form of title fell in disuse and was
replaced by the now-familiar "Journal Office" and it was under
this title that the duties of the office were reported on by Arthur
Benson (then Principal) to the Select Committee on the State of
the Public Records set up by Speaker Abbot in the year 1800. His
responsibilities, he told the Committee, included not only the safe
custody of all the manuscript Journals since 1547, the Clerk's
books of Minutes since 1685 and the minutes of the Committees
of the whole House since 1688, but also the filing and maintenance of all petitions, bills, accounts and reports. In addition to
these documents, which were referenced and indexed in schedule
books, there was a further mass of earlier papers (all manuscript,
of course) stored in a "lumber room" above the House; and it
is interesting to note that included among the latter were some
sealed bags of documents referring to "plots, secret communica-
tions and Irish affairs" around the time of the Revolution. Interesting reading!

It might be noted here that it was only after the Act of
Union with Ireland, in 1800, that it became the practice for the
Commons to have *all* its papers printed; some of them—Bills,
for example—had been printed since 1733, but there still re-

mained a mass of documentation in manuscript form and looking after it was not easy.

The way in which the official Journals were maintained changed several times over the year. It will be remembered that the Journal consisted originally of merely the actual notes written by Seymour as he sat behind his "little board", filed away subsequently, unaltered, for the record. When Seymour was succeeded by Onslow, however, the Clerk's rough manuscript was copied up at the end of the day in a good fair hand and the respectable version was the one which was preserved. During later years some Clerks followed the example of Seymour and some that of Onslow; some of them cherished the Journal and guarded it as their own lives, while some were so casual in their regard to its safety that parts of it were actually lost—indeed, the entire set of volumes from 1584–1601 were mislaid and have never been recovered.

Once the Journals were got into print, however, their custody and maintenance became a simpler matter since there were now several copies available for filing. The decision of the House in 1742 to print all the Journals "from the earliest times" had not been put into effect overnight; it was not until about the time of Hatsell's appointment (1768), in fact, that the work was finally brought up to date and the printer was able to direct his efforts towards the current issues of the Clerk's notes—which should have made the production of the Journal (as distinct from its custody) a very much more leisurely affair for all concerned. This happy result was not forthcoming, however. In order to provide continuing payment of "copy money" for the clerks the Clerk decided that the carefully written-up manuscript copy of the Journal should still be produced in addition to the printed version, and it was not until 1833 that this practice was finally abolished by the Select Committee.

One good thing about producing the Journal, however, from the clerks' point of view, was the fact that it was a document *for the record*; it was not something that had to be produced overnight for use by the House next day—and this being so, both the manuscript and printed versions could be prepared and produced as time allowed during the sitting-days of the House and the (inevitable) back-log in the work could be made up at leisure during the long recesses. This consideration, unfortunately, did not apply to another document which was one of the major responsibilities of the Journal Office—the Vote.

Even today, the Vote is often referred to as the "Members Bible", and it has always been the most important single document in the day-to-day functioning of the House. The Vote might be described as a condensed version of the Journal, compiled overnight and delivered to the House next day so that Members can know what business has been got through and what has been left over for another time. Although it has been printed, for easier circulation, since 1681, its preparation entailed a considerable amount of painstaking and accurate hand-copying from the Clerk's manuscript, and several clerks were kept fully occupied far into the night to have it ready for the next sitting. Both Clerks Assistant were required to remain for one hour after the rising of the House to make sure that everything was properly in hand.

As the years passed and the business of the House increased the Vote grew both in importance and size. More and more new items were included in its pages to bedevil the work of its compilers; large numbers of accounts presented for the inspection of the House had to be examined, summarised and entered; petitions (sometimes as many as 300 in a single night) required similar treatment; the business for the morrow, notice of motions and advanced notification of remoter business; all these, as parts of the Vote and its appendix, were to be sorted and arranged, written out in legible longhand and sent off to the printer in time for him to have the printed version off the presses before breakfast time! There was a heavy demand for his wares, not only from Members and departments of the government but from the general public, who bought large numbers of the Vote almost like a newspaper.

By the early nineteenth century the document had become almost unmanageable. In fact, when Abbot became Speaker in 1802 the Vote, almost indispensable to the sittings of the House, was at times up to a week in arrears and delays of two or three days were regarded as normal, while the Journal itself was actually two years behind. The precincts of the House were jammed every morning with Members' servants, sent to discover—by whatever means they could—the state of current business and details of the Order Paper for that afternoon's sitting, and it became clear to Abbot that if some remedial action were not put quickly in hand the House would risk grinding to a standstill. Abbot put a great deal of work into examining a host of suggested solutions to the problem, but it was solved eventually by a memorandum from the 2nd Clerk Assistant—John Rickman—who, it will be remembered, had been formerly the Speaker's Secretary, and had moved to the Table on Abbot's recommendation.

Rickman's scheme, which was adopted by Abbot, completely reformed the preparation and presentation of the Vote. The actual items from the Journal were included in a new, drastically streamlined form, and were numbered consecutively, while petitions were cut out completely and were presented to the House as a separate document to be issued once or twice a week. Forthcoming business, the Order Paper, Notices of Motion and Public and Private Bills for second Reading were also relegated to separate sheets—which were, however, to be issued daily *with* the Vote. Rickman's intelligent proposals, upon which the Vote has been modelled ever since, were accepted with enthusiasm by the House and when finally put into practice in 1817 were instantly successful. Though the work of compilation remained just as arduous and entailed the burning of just as much midnight oil, the Vote never again got into arrears and from that day to this Members have never had to enter upon a day's sitting without the proper documents—no matter *how* late the House may have sat on the previous night.

Mention should be made here of another duty laid upon the Clerk of the Journals up to the early part of the nineteenth century. He was responsible for the custody of a collection of records, pamphlets and assorted books—a small collection by modern standards, but extremely valuable—which was kept in his warehouse at No. 1 Abingdon Street and were available for consultation by Members. When the Library was established in 1818 (see p. 177), this collection was taken over and transferred into the precincts of the House to form the nucleus for the new service, but, sad to relate, they perished in their entirety in the fire of 1834 and their loss was irreplaceable.

THE COMMITTEE OFFICE

It might be said that Committees of the House represent the House itself in miniature. The rules of procedure and debate are identical; the state of the parties in the House is reflected faithfully in the composition of its committees; the Speaker in the House is paralleled by the Committee Chairman, who represents the Speaker's overall authority outside the Chamber—or "without doors", to use the ancient term. And in the same way, the Clerk ("and ye could not do your business without one!") is represented in all Committees by one of his subordinates. In a "Committee of the Whole House"—i.e. a Committee sitting in the Chamber itself—the Clerk, is always represented by the Clerk Assistant; in Committees "without doors" the duty is done by Clerks of the Committee Office, experts and specialists all of them. Their office is by far the most venerable of all the Clerk's departments.

For something like 300 years successive Clerks had been obliged to rely on what might be described as amateur assistance; amateur, certainly, in the sense that none of their subordinates received anything in the way of salary from Treasury sources. Neither did they receive official recognition—from the Treasury or anywhere else; they were the "Clerk's servants", completely without status as far as the House was concerned and virtually anonymous to history. But that they did a job, and did it well, is apparent, for the House got through its business and the Clerk carried out all the functions allotted to him; without the assistance of a skilful and experienced staff neither the House nor the Clerk could have continued to operate as their work became increasingly sophisticated. So while the early Clerks' subordinates may have been "amateur" in the professional sense, they were certainly not wanting in the skills and experience which their duties demanded.

A few years prior to 1696 (the precise date is unknown) the then Clerk, Jodrell—whose far-seeing innovations were to benefit the House so greatly—decided that the time had come when he should have more *official* assistance than was presently allowed him in the person of the Clerk Assistant. His principal worry was the increasing number of the Committees to which the

House was referring more and more legislation of a specialist nature—in the discussion of which only expert opinion was really relevant and for which appropriate Members were empanelled —or lesgislation so relatively unimportant that to have taken it on the Floor would have been to waste the time of the House at a stage when there seemed less and less time available, so full was the Order Paper.

It will be remembered that during the later 1680's Jodrell had appointed a Clerk (see p. 38) (Zachary Hamlyn) to take over the custody of the Journal and had paid his salary out of his own pocket, but the problem of providing clerks for the Committees was too big to be resolved so simply. Philanthropy, to be sure, can only go so far. To Jodrell, it seemed obvious that some proper, officially recognised organisation should be established—under his control but paid for by the Treasury—and that the Clerk should have the professional assistance that was undeniably necessary *as a right* and not simply if he could afford to pay for it. Jodrell, of course, was a man who knew his job thoroughly, and it is not surprising that he got his own way in this. He was authorised to establish four new clerical posts under himself and the Clerk Assistant, posts described by the Treasury as for "four under-clerks without doors attending the House of Commons", and the names of the men he appointed are still on the record—John Hookes, George Cole, James Courthope and Hicks Burrough. They were the first full-time subordinate Clerks of the House—the nucleus of the present professional staff.

For some strange reason, the Treasury Warrant authorising the payment of their salaries describes their work as "writing, copying and ingrossing several bills, writings and other papers for His Majesty's Service"—which, of course, it was anything but. That sort of work was being done quite satisfactorily by the "common clerks" and scriveners (who were paid at piece-time rates), and the four new appointees were "gentlemen" in the old sense of the word. It may be that the Treasury had no idea what work it was, precisely, that was involved in the new appointments and simply applied an old and accepted formula to justify the new payments—or perhaps the wording in the warrant reflects the outcome of some deep manoeuvring on Jodrell's part to get the posts accepted in the first place with a firm footing

on known territory (i.e. "writing, copying", etc.), breaking the
Treasury in gently to the idea of *new* appointments after they
had become established. We shall never know.

There is no actual documentary evidence still in existance
to prove by chapter and verse that Jodrell did indeed initiate
these appointments, but evidence supporting the fact from other
sources is conclusive. Their salaries, as "under-clerks", appeared
in Treasury records for the first time in 1696, by which time
Jodrell had been Clerk for thirteen years, and since all Clerical
appointments were at that time completely in the hands of the
Clerk himself it is obvious that Jodrell was responsible for the
innovation of "under-clerks without doors".

Their duties were of two kinds. First, they were required to
attend all Committees sitting on Public Bills and to give them a
similar service to that given by the Clerk to the House itself—
i.e. to keep the register, organise meetings and witnesses (if any),
advise on procedure and keep the minutes—and for this they
were paid the ridiculously small salary of £50 a year by the Treasury. Their second duty was to similarly attend the *Private* Bill
Committees, receiving fees from both the proposers of the Bills
and their opponents. It was this aspect of the appointments which
made them attractive and sought-after and which brought in the
real money to the appointees.

It would be unreasonable to expect that the numerous, and
increasing, Committees sitting in those times should be coped
with satisfactorily by only four clerks, yet there is nothing in the
records to suggest that they had any assistance—how did they
manage? From what we can glean from the fragmentary records
extant, it would appear that there existed a body of casual clerks
who, offering their service wherever employment might be found
(not only in Parliament), were engaged to attend particular
Committees as they were empanelled and were paid a specific
fee for the job. It seems likely that these clerks were selected and
supervised by the four Clerks without doors, but that their fees
were met out of a lump-sum paid by the Treasury and shared
out by the Chairman of each Committee—an arrangement that
was to lead later to a very unsatisfactory situation in the Clerk's
Department.

Around 1760 (again the exact date is unknown) official

Deputies were appointed to assist the four principal Committees clerks—still called clerks without doors—and we know that by 1772 these deputies had completely taken over all the public duties of their seniors! The posts of the clerks without doors had become sinecures. By the time that assistants to the *deputies* were appointed in 1812, and a Committee Office in more or less modern form was beginning to take shape, the four principals were all completely detached from the "public" duties of the office and were living in various degrees of retirement on the fat fees from private bills which they continued to draw until their deaths. The top posts in the Committee office became, therefore, simply well-paid "paper" appointments involving no actual work and providing a form of pension for the deputies when they wished to retire from active service. Unlike the normally accepted principle of "pension", however, these sinecure posts carried considerable emoluments, and the strange situation arose in which a clerk might work for a lifetime—and work hard—for a comparative pittance, and only begin to make real money after his services were withdrawn.

A system of 'closed shop" promotion inevitably developed around this system—aided, of course, by the Clerk's inalienable right to make and control all appointments in his own Department. On the death of one of the four principals the vacancy was logically filled by the senior of the four Deputies, and what began as logic soon became regarded as absolute right. The senior Assistant could expect to become a Deputy when a vacancy appeared at the top end, and the senior of the junior (unestablished) clerks or scriveners could expect to be placed on the establishment. And their fortunes depended on one thing—if they lived long enough, they would do well in the autumn of their days; if they died young, or even middle-aged, they died poor. Life in the service of the House for any but the Crown's appointees remained a chancy business.

By the year 1812, when some reorganisation was made in the office of the Committee Clerks under Speaker Abbot, the Deputies seem to have been well on the way to becoming sinecurists like their four seniors. There were other employments within the House, more lucrative, to which they could turn their hands, and they apparently did so—leaving more and more of the actual Committee to their assistants. Abbot mentions in his diary that Mr. Ley (the Acting Clerk—under Hatsell) and Mr. J. H. Ley (the Clerk Assistant) had put forward a reorganisation scheme under which the four Deputies would "be made more efficient"—by which they no doubt meant more "effective"—and additional junior clerks appointed to bring the office up to a really effective strength.

Abbot accepted Mr. Ley's proposals, and with the approval of the House they were carried into effect towards the end of that year (1812), enlarging the staff of the Committee office considerably, and defining its functions much more closely. Nothing could be done at once, of course, about the four sinecurists—*their* positions having become virtually hallowed by time—but notice was clearly given that the abuse was to be brought to an end on the retirement of the then incumbents. Future Clerks without doors, it was understood, were to be full-time practitioners. For the present, the four Deputies would be required to concentrate their labours much more exclusively upon the work of the Committees, their four Assistants were to establish a duty-rota so that each should be called in turn for Committee attendance, and five extra clerks were to be added to the recognised establishment to be called upon as required when their superiors were fully committed. This made an operational total of thirteen clerks (excluding the sinecurists) and the office began, at last, to resemble its modern self, though much refining was to be done by the 1833 Committee before its final form and function was to be defined.

A further enormously important step in the direction of efficiency was made under Abbot's direction in the following year (1813) when W. B. Gurney, a free-lance shorthand writer, was appointed "shorthand writer to the House" and he and his staff thenceforward took down all the evidence given before the Committees. This move not only speeded up the work of the Committees and produced fuller and more accurate accounts of their proceedings, but served also to relieve the Committee Clerk of the onerous duty of note-taking and allowed him to devote more time and attention to the other aspects of his work and to develop it to the point of high professionalism that is its hallmark today.

Speaker Abbot retired in 1817, and the House thereby lost the services of a keen and informed innovator. Hatsell, the Clerk, died in 1820, and was succeeded at the table by J. H. Ley (i.e. the younger of the two) who, like both the retired Speaker and his own late uncle, was an intelligent and determined reformer. But the further re-organisation and improvements which might have been expected to carry on the excellent beginnings of Abbot and Ley (senior) did not immediately materialise. As will be seen when we come to study the findings of the 1833 Committee, too many vested interests were still in the way—vested interests which were by no means dishonourable, but simply anachronistic, and their dissolution without injustice or hardship to *someone* would clearly be very difficult to arrange. Suggestions were put forward from time to time, impracticable in the main and generally half-hearted, by both the House and the officers themselves, but none of them went to the length of proposing an all-out frontal attack on the main problem and they remained no more than suggestions. The 1833 Committee, however, determined as it was to settle all these matters in a grand "final solution", went to work with an axe on the tangle of tradition and unplanned development and last-ditch stands by some of those whose interests were threatened and cut its way through a Gordian knot that had existed for centuries. As will be seen, the Committee was merciless.

THE PUBLIC BILL OFFICE

Although the *title* of this office is of comparatively recent origin (it was, in fact, first adopted by the 1833 Committee at the suggestion of J. H. Ley), the office itself is impressively venerable under its original designation of "the office of the Clerk of the Fees"—changed later to simply the Fees Office. And strangely enough, when the Clerk of the Fees Office ceased officially to exist and his ancient functions began to be discharged by his newly created self as Clerk of the Public Bill Office, the old title did not disappear. It was simply handed on to another officer—in the Speaker's Department—who uses it to this day, though the duties for which he is responsible are very different from those of the original Clerk of the Fees.

By "public bills" we mean, broadly speaking, legislation initiated by the Government—as opposed to "private" bills, whose initiators are private concerns outside Parliament (e.g. local authorities, business interests, private individuals, etc.). In modern times most of the Government Departments (Ministries) are responsible for the preparation and presentation of measures which their Minister wishes to lay before the House, and working —as they do—in co-operation with the Parliamentary draftsmen and the officers of the Public Bill Office, they find this part of their work reasonably straightforward. But it was not always so. There was a time—not so long ago, historically speaking— when the bulk of the public legislation laid before Parliament was initiated by the Treasury, prepared and drafted by Treasury draftsmen and presented to the House in the name of the First Lord of the Treasury—which is, of course, the legal title of the Prime Minister. (It was not until Walpole asserted himself so forcibly in the Commons in the years following 1721 that any *one* of the King's ministers assumed an importance greater than that of his colleagues. Walpole was the first "prime" minister, but it was during the long years of the Regency that the title Prime Minister was really adopted and came into general usage. It still, however, has no existence in law.)

The correct drafting of legislation is not one of those simple, straightforward processes that could be done by just anyone with a thorough grounding in the Queen's English and a flair for the *mot juste*. The work is fraught with difficulties unimaginable to a layman. For one thing, the finished product—the Bill—must be a definite and unambiguous statement of intention and its terms must be capable of withstanding the most minute scrutiny by the whole machinery of the Law. There will always be someone looking for loopholes in legislation—fortunes have been made for some who have found them!—and a piece of legislation that is either indefinite or ambiguous can cause untold trouble if it gets on to the Statute Book as an Act of Parliament. Fortunately, this seldom happens (*political* viewpoints apart!) since before a Bill can become an Act it must pass the severe, and sometimes protracted, examination of both the Commons and the Lords, and one can be sure that it fairly represents the majority view of the elected Parliament before it passes into Law.

This procedure, which has long served to protect the interests of the people against the power of both the Crown and a potentially dictatorial Executive, brings added difficulties into the life of a Parliamentary draftsman; not only must his Bill be *legally* watertight and specific, it must be correct also according to the forms and traditions of Parliamentary procedure and not likely to run into trouble in the House because, say, one of its clauses is "out of order". It is surprising what nonsense a determined opposition can sometimes make out of an apparently simple and serious statement of intention in a Government Bill.

Clearly, then, no Treasury draftsman could be expected, on his own, to produce a perfect Bill—and in practice he was never asked to. In earlier days a senior member of Parliament with a specialist knowledge of the particular subject was usually brought into the work of preparation to assist with the definition of intention (in the case of revenue Bills, this was always one of the Law Officers—the Attorney General or the Solicitor General), and the Clerk of the Commons was consulted on the Parliamentary aspects. Certainly, by the latter half of the seventeenth century William Goldsborough was being paid by the Treasury for the work he did on their behalf in connection with "public" Bills, and so was his successor, Paul Jodrell—payments which had nothing at all to do with their official appointments as officers of the Commons. They were, in effect, agents for the Treasury inside the House, doing the Treasury work in their "spare time" for extra pay.

Some time around the turn of the century, however, this service by the Clerks seems to have been discontinued—perhaps because their official duties made greater calls on their time—and the Treasury appears to have fallen back on its own resources to check the Parliamentary angles of its bill-drafting; at all events, from about 1700 to 1733 the Treasury paid one of its own clerks for this work. But in 1733 a significant innovation was brought into the picture; the appropriate Treasury clerk of the day, Christopher Lowe, was sent into the House itself to do his work and was paid his salary as an officer of the Commons. Since this was during the administration of the ever-efficient Walpole it is reasonable to assume that he considered the Treasury's resources not up to the standards of accuracy then

more than ever required in Parliamentary drafting (he faced
a particularly active Whig opposition!) and that his was the hand
behind the move.

The change once made, stayed. Lowe was succeeded in 1756
by William Plaxton, another Treasury clerk, but it is interesting
to note that from 1750 onwards both of them, in turn, enjoyed
the assistance of Robert Yeates, one of the four Clerks without
doors—an officer of the House, who drew an additional sessional
payment from the Treasury for this extra work. Plaxton, the
Treasury Clerk, disappeared altogether from the service of the
House only a year after his appointment and his place was taken
over by an officer of the Commons—Hardinge Stracey, nephew
of Nicholas Hardinge the former Clerk. The wheel had turned
full circle; supervision of Parliamentary drafting had come
back from the Treasury into the House itself and into the Clerk's
department. Stracey's appointment lasted for only a year or so,
however, for when Uncle Hardinge died in 1758 and was translated to a place where his patronage could do *nobody* any good,
Stracey was replaced by the experienced old Yeates, who continued to see Treasury business safely through the House for the
next ten years. (Hardinge Stracey, it might be said, was a hard
man to beat; only five years later, in 1763, we find him
appointed as Clerk without doors—a post he occupied for eleven
years before handing it on to his son Edward in 1774. It will be
apparent that much work was building up for the 1833 Committee's attention around this time!) However, back to the
Treasury business in the Commons. After Yeates' death in 1769
the Treasury continued to appoint a Commons officer to look
after its interests—though still as a Treasury agent, separately
paid. A Treasury minute of 20th November 1769 shows:

My Lds. are pleased to appoint Danby Pickering, Esq., to do
the Parliamentary business of this office performed by the late
Mr. Yeates with a salary of £600 a year to be paid by Mr.
Davis at the end of each session of Parliament.

My Lds. Likewise appoint John Rosier, Esq., to assist Mr.
Pickering in the execution of the said business at a salary of
£100 to be paid in the same manner.

At the time of this appointment Rosier was Clerk of the

Journals and Papers, and he continued in that post until 1744 when he took charge of the newly created FEES OFFICE—still, of course, carrying out the work required of him by the Treasury. There had always been *some* officer responsible for collecting various fees that were chargeable on legislation passing through the House—generally the senior of the four clerks without doors—but when the new office was established for that specific work, it carried with it the appointment of a new Principal Clerk —the Clerk of the Fees. The strange thing about this appointment, to modern eyes, was the fact that no salary was attached to it. Moreover, though the Clerk of the Fees was required to maintain a competent clerical staff of his own to do the work of the office, he received absolutely nothing towards his costs from the Clerk of the House, who was himself at that time enjoying enormous fees from various quarters.

Obviously, then, the Clerk of the Fees was in everything but name a Treasury official within the Commons, and convenient though this arrangement must have been at the time it would appear quite shocking today. On paper, Rosier was a fully established Officer of the House; in practice, he owed sole allegiance to an outside body—the Treasury—who defined his duties and paid his salary. The salary, as we have seen, was by no means negligible, amounting as it did to £600 per annum in 1769 when the post was created, and by the time the 1833 Committee came to look at the appointment it was found that the then Clerk, John E. Dorington (whose father had succeeded Rosier) was drawing £1,100 a year from the Treasury, plus 10s. for every Private Bill that came before the House. He enjoyed in addition a steadily mounting expense account which in some years topped £1,300. Not bad pickings, even by modern standards!

The post itself was no sinecure, as Dorington's evidence before the 1833 Committee was to show. After giving an account of his work in connection with Private Bills (in respect of which, of course, he drew separate fees from their promoters, since they were unconnected with his official duties) he was questioned about the work he undertook on behalf of the Treasury. The following extract comes from the minutes of the 1833 Committee (H.C. 648 (1833) Questions 395–411).

Q 395 : With regard to the charge of £1,100 paid to you by the Treasury, have the goodness to explain to the Committee the duties performed for that sum?

A : The Committee are perhaps aware of the sort of duties which are performed by a Parliamentary agent for Private Bills. The duties of the Parliamentary agent to the Treasury are to conduct the Treasury business in Parliament much as a Parliamentary Agent conducts a Private Bill. I am in perpetual communication with the Treasury, Board of Trade, and with the Solicitors of the Boards of Stamps, Excise, Asssessed Taxes, etc., both on the business relating to their departments before Parliament, as well as any Bills which may affect them; for example, in the alterations just proposed as to Assessed Taxes, Stamps, etc., the Solicitors of the Boards have been with me for a considerable time, drawing up the proper form of resolution to be submitted to the House, according to the plan of the Government. I prepare the resolutions of Supply and Ways and Means and all those other resolutions and proceedings which on the perusal of a Bill I deem necessary, preparatory to its introduction. In the course of this I must occasionally (especially when any new measure of taxation is about to be brought forward) be entrusted confidentially with a knowledge of the intentions of the Government; my duty is, that in all proceedings in public business the forms of the House are attended to, and the greatest facility given to the progress of the business. I take care that all the amendments sent from proper authority are introduced into the Bill at the proper stage, and that ultimately the Bill is ingrossed correctly and sent to the Lords as agreed to by the Commons; and I also draw most of the Finance Bills, and various clauses for different Bills in progress. With regard to the manner in which the duties of my office are executed, and also the necessity for it, I feel I can confidently appeal to any gentleman who has held the Office of Secretary to the Treasury, and to the Solicitors of the Public Boards.

Q 396 : Do you go on with the Bill in the House of Lords?
A : If there is anything particular in it; but Public Bills are scarcely ever altered there.

Q 397 : Does the charge include the actual work on the Bill?
A : No; the work actually done is charged for by the gentlemen in my office, in the same manner as law stationers; the

sum charged is that which I pay to the persons who do the work.

Q 398 : The £1,100 is for personal superintendence?

A : It is.

Q 399 : Is all the work done in regard to those Bills done in your office?

A : Yes.

Q 400 : And charged by you as a private agent?

A : No, they are paid as clerks, so much for copying; their rate of pay amounts to about 3s. an hour, if they are able to go on the whole day.

Q 401 : Are the sums charged there regulated in the same way as those of Parliamentary Agents?

A : No; a Parliamentary Agent for Private Bills charges a profit on the labour of his clerks.

Q 402 : But you charge the Treasury only the sum you actually pay?

A : No more; and my contingent account is audited at the Treasury by the production of the receipts of the persons who receive the money for the work done, having no profit myself upon what I pay.

Q 403 : There is a charge of £42 for passing the Militia and Mutiny Acts, paid by the War Office, and £26 5s. od. for passing the Marine Mutiny Act, paid by the Admiralty; what is the nature of these charges?

A : The Mutiny Act was formerly conducted by another gentleman in the House of Commons; about fifteen years ago, the War Office did not like his charges, he having charged, as a Parliamentary Agent, a profit on the copying, and so on; and they proposed to my father to do it for a certain sum; with regard to the Marine Mutiny Act, that has been, as long as I can recollect, in the office in the same way.

Q 404 : Take, for instance, the Marine Mutiny Act which is charged at twenty-five guineas; that is for superintendence?

A : Yes.

Q 405 : Supposing that were put to the other charges in the office, would that amount to as much as the charges by the Parliamentary Agent formerly?

A : No, not to anything like it.

Q 406 : In point of fact, you are a kind of counsel, in the first instance, to the Treasury, in respect of those Bills?

A : Yes; and to take care that all the proceedings during the whole time are correct.

Q 407 : For general supervision you receive that sum?

A : Yes, and for carrying on correspondence with the Public Boards, and drawing the attention of the Treasury to the different Bills in the House which I think they ought to see.

Q 408 : In your opinion, such an officer is necessary to the public business?

A : I do not think they could get on without somebody to do it.

Q 409 : What is the time it occupies?

A : It comes in jumps and starts; sometimes every moment of time we have is occupied in it; the Clerks of the office come, as I used to do when I was junior, before breakfast; they are always here from ten o'clock in the morning till ten at night; it varies a good deal with regard to the necessity; it is always necessary they should be in attendance, but they are not certainly filled up during the whole Session with it.

Q 410 : You said you gave vouchers to the Treasury for the work you performed, signed by the parties who did the work?

A : Receipts for the payment for that work.

Q 411 : Is there not a sum charged also for things done for private Members of the House?

A : Yes; that is charged to the Treasury, just in the same way.

As I have said, the situation revealed by Dorington's testimony would have been intolerable under modern procedural arrangements and it is clear that the 1833 Committee were the first to realise it, for—as will be seen—they were to extinguish for all time the Treasury's intervention in the machinery of the House, and to make an "honest man" of the Clerk of the Fees.

THE PRIVATE BILL OFFICE

Unlike most of the other offices in the Department of the Clerk —which, like Mopsy, "just growed"—the Private Bill Office was created specially to fill a special need; it came into being at the instigation of a Select Committee of the House; it was provided from the very beginning with a properly established staff; and, above all, its functions were clearly prescribed in a set of regulations which were laid down as the Standing Orders for Private

Business. A latecomer on the Parliamentary scene, its debut was immaculate—and welcome.

As will be remembered, "legislation" in the modern sense had sprung from the earlier conception of petitioning the Crown, through Parliament, either for the redress of grievance or for the granting of rights or favours. Petitions, as such, had gradually developed a recognisable shape, suitable for presentation to Parliament, and as order and form began to assert themselves in the day-to-day proceedings of the Commons, and convention and rules became more and more accepted, the bulk of the petitions presented were introduced in the regularised pattern of Private Bills.

The new sense of orderliness in the Commons, however, brought new problems to those outside who needed to bring in private legislation. For one thing, the standardisation of the requirements for presentation meant that the *form* of the Bill must conform exactly to a pattern previously laid down by the House; many of the pitfalls which might trap an unwary (or inexperienced) draftsman in this respect could well render his Bill out of order even before proceedings were begun on it—and one can be sure that when there was opposition to a private measure the Bill's opponents would go through it with a toothcomb in search of exploitable flaws. Secondly, the more sophisticated proceedings in the House itself made it necessary for the Bill's sponsors to keep a constant vigil over its progress through the machinery of Parliament. Amendments, when made, had to be made properly and at the appropriate "stage" of the Bill; they had to be correctly entered on the "House copy" of the Bill and then "ingrossed" in proper form in order to produce the new Bill which resulted from the accepted amendments. (Ingrossing, for which there was a special branch in the Clerk's department until 1849, was an ancient art. It was a particular way of recording any material which had to be *kept*—e.g. the new form of an amended clause, as opposed to the original form which could now be scrapped—and it was done by writing with a thick quill on parchment, in such a way that both the up-strokes and the down-strokes were of equal thickness, a type of script which was easily recognisable.)

The House ruled in 1640 that no ingrossed Bill, public or

private, should be brought to the Table for its third reading
until the Chairman of the Committee which had amended it
had checked the ingrossed copy against the paper original and
certified it as correct, and had this procedure been carried out
all would have been well. But alas for the best-laid schemes.
Chairmen soon grew tired of what was an irksome and finicky
task, and the duty of checking was soon shuffled off on to other
shoulders—in the case of Public Bills, upon the clerks'; and in
the case of Private Bills on to those of the responsible agent.

This procedure rendered the passage of legislation much less
easy than before, and while that was no doubt all to the good,
it did complicate the lives of those whose interests depended on
the successful passage of Private Bills through Parliament.
Where, for instance, were they to find as Agents someone so
thoroughly familiar with Parliamentary procedure that, whatever
else their Bill might fail for, they could be certain it would not
be for lack of competent handling? No provincial lawyer—and
not many London ones either—could be expected to have the
Parliamentary Rules of Order at his fingertips, and the few who
were competent were constantly overwhelmed with work. So it
is not surprising to find, under these circumstances, that the clerks
who worked actually in Parliament itself were in great demand
to act as agents for Private Bills. Most of them did it, and to
many of them the fees they received for these duties—extraneous
to their official work—made up the bulk of their income.

By the beginning of the nineteenth century the state of private
legislation had become chaotic. Everyone who fancied himself
as a likely pilot among the eddies and cross-currents of the still
almost-uncharted depths of Parliamentary procedure found it
easy to set himself up as a Parliamentary Agent; officers of the
House vied with each other to tout for the lucrative trade that
continually poured in from private sources; whole staffs appeared
in the wake of each "agent" and crammed themselves into the
already bursting confines of the Parliament building. By modern
standards the amount of private business was fantastic. During
the period from 1809 to 1814, for instance, the average number
of Private Bills passed *per year* was nearly 300—how many were
projected and not passed, of course, we do not know. But it is
clear that with business going through at such a dizzy rate *some-*

thing had to suffer (unless the House were to sit through twenty-four hours a day—which it did not) and in this case it was quality and accuracy that became the casualties. No matter with what celerity Bills were rushed through their required stages; no matter with what errors of amendment or ingrossment they were brought forward for their third, and final, reading, there still remained at the end of each Session a backlog of private business that *had* to be completed before the close. And needless to say, those thus left were inevitably pushed through with scant regard for the proprieties, and the standard of legislation suffered accordingly. Half-baked and half-digested Bills, many of them completely unchecked, passed into law as Acts of Parliament, and the chaos that reigned increasingly inside the House bid fair to spread out into the Courts.

It was not surprising that the Speaker, the indefatigable Abbot, should have met little opposition to his proposal that a Select Committee be appointed to look into the whole field of private business. The House welcomed his initiative with enthusiasm and the Committee that met in 1810 were given simple, but comprehensive, terms of reference—". . . to consider of providing more effectually for the accuracy and regularity of proceedings on private bills".

The tangible outcome of their deliberations was the Private Bill Office, which—as I have said—emerged fully fledged. Its organisation was placed under the control of a new Principal Clerk, Henry Gunnell by name (who had been a Deputy Committee Clerk since 1776), and its functions were all-embracing in respect of private business. Gunnell was required to institute a register of all Private Bills in a standardised form, together with information as to the Bill's Agent in Parliament and its progress through the various stages of debate in the House. His office was to be accessible both to Commons Clerks and to outside Agents and was intended to become a kind of clearing-house where information relevant to private business could be passed in both directions; thus, Agents could give the House early notice of likely future proceedings, and the House could keep Agents informed about which Committees were sitting, or were proposing to sit, on which Bills—this being promulgated by means of a daily list to be exhibited in the Private Bill Office.

Here also, both sides were able to check on current legislation, comparing amended and ingrossed Bills against their originals —in fact, the belated establishment of this new office admirably filled the need it was created to fill, and the conduct of private business was placed for the first time on a sound and regular basis.

One further provision in the regulations governing its functions, however, was to be even more significant. All clerks employed in the Private Bill Office were expressly prohibited from taking any active part themselves in the promotion of private business; they could advise—indeed, they were *required* to advise —but their days of partisanship were over. The loss to them, in prospective fees, was considerable—and the prohibition was to be extended eventually to disbar *all* officers from personal practice—but the reform itself was the prelude to two further improvements which were to prove of inestimable value to both the House itself and to its officers. First, it led—eventually—to the establishment of all the clerks of the Commons on a *salary* basis, an arrangement infinitely preferable to the former undignified grab for fees and appointments; and second, it freed them from both financial and political dependence on either Government or outside sources and laid the first real foundations for that independent and reliable impartiality for which the entire service was soon to become renowned. So, in more ways than one, the emergence of the Private Bill Office was an event of real significance in the domestic history of the Commons.

OTHER OFFICES—NOW EXTINCT

Before concluding this all-too-brief retrospect into the pre-1833 history of the Clerk's Department, mention should perhaps be made of one of two offices which—though ancient in themselves and important enough in their day—are no longer in existence. Some of them, victims simply of reorganisation, bequeathed their functions—in more appropriately modern form—to latter-day successors; others, established originally to discharge procedures which themselves were swept away by progress, disappeared altogether. Yet all of them left their mark on the machinery of the modern House; even those that sank without apparent trace had their share in establishing the tradition of the service, a tradition which today provides a background and framework without which the personal qualities of the House's officers—no matter *how* sparkling—would appear mundane.

THE CLERK OF ELECTIONS

Controverted elections are rare occurrences in modern times. In earlier days, elections were by no means as orderly as now and each was followed invariably by a flood of petitions seeking to invalidate particular results. Ever since 1672, when Parliament had finally asserted its right to determine contested elections domestically, Committees had been appointed in the Commons for this purpose and a clerk made available to attend their sittings. Sometimes a particularly difficult petition would be heard at the Bar of the House, in which case the Clerk Assistant would officiate; when the proceedings took place in committee outside the Chambers a Committee Clerk would do the work.

Whichever officer did the job, however, his earnings were handsome, since in addition to a basic salary of £100 from the Treasury he was able to charge an additional fee for every petition. (The Clerk of Elections' fees in 1835, for example, amounted to £2,089 9s. 0d.!) During the "season"—which was always the first session following a General Election—the Clerk and his men had work enough to keep them all at their desks until far into the night, but once the rush was over they were likely to find themselves almost completely without work. What they *did* have, however, was an office inside the House, a qualified Principal Clerk, and a staff of men expert in the handling of petitions—a combination that put them right at the top of the list of would-be Agents for private business. It is not surprising, then, to find that some of the most flourishing and prosperous firms in the history of Parliamentary Agencies were founded and run by Clerks of Elections.

During the late eighteenth century, proceedings on election petitions became farcical. Objections were brought more and more on simply party lines, whether irregularities had been committed or not, and the ensuing trial of the petition in the House degenerated into no more than a sterile parade of party strength

—or guile. The judicial function of the Election Committee became buried under a mountain of manoeuvre—or of plain brute
force—and the Committee itself began to fall into disrepute. It
was abolished, after 1835, on the recommendation of the 1833
Committee, and thirty years later the power to determine election
misdemeanours was taken out of the hands of the protagonists
altogether; since 1868 all controverted elections have been decided in the High Court of Justice.

THE CLERK OF RECOGNISANCES

The need of an "Office of Recognisances" first began to be felt
during that period, mentioned above, when it became the practice among the political parties to challenge election returns
merely to gain some advantage over their opponents, and not
because some real election offence had been committed (though
it must be admitted that in those days many election offences
were committed, not least the bribery and corruption of
electors!). Irresponsible and frivolous petitions were increasingly
brought forward and their hearings ate disastrously into the time
of Parliament, this at a time when "legitimate" legislation was
itself demanding more time than it had ever done before so that
the machinery of the House was becoming strained to the limit.
After the election of 1784, for example, there were no fewer than
fifty-two election petitions and only nine of these managed to
gain a hearing, the remaining forty-three being "put off to another occasion"—which, of course, never came.

Needless to say, the House itself was not unaware of the bad
odour that was beginning to surround the whole question of
controverted elections and the resulting petitions, and in 1788
they passed a measure to try to deal with it. This became known
as Wynn's Act, after its proposer, and it laid down that no
election petition was to be proceeded with unless properly identified with the petitioner, by signature; further, the petitioner
would be required to deposit a security, or recognisance, of £200
with the Speaker and to provide two additional sureties of £100
each, that he would appear, when the time came, and pursue his
petition. If, in the opinion of the Election Committee when it saw
the petition, it was frivolous and irresponsible, both the petitioner

and his guarantors would be liable for costs—to be deducted from their deposits. (Two elections later, in 1796, the number of petitions had dropped by half—to twenty-three—so it would seem that Wynn's Act did filter out a lot of the time-wasters.)

However, to operate the new system staff was required and the office of the Clerk of Recognisance was created under W. G. Rose who was, at that time, the senior of the Committee Clerks (Rose was to hold this appointment during the whole of its existence—surely a unique distinction for any officer of the House!). The Clerk Assistant (after 1801 it was the Second Clerk Assistant) and one of the Masters in Chancery were made responsible for reporting to the Speaker on the correct payment of recognisances and on the taxing of such costs as were to be raised when petitions were condemned by the Committee. They were empowered in all cases to charge an agreed fee for their services in respect of both the examining and taxing of petitions.

Even this process, however, soon became impracticable. The appointed Master in Chancery fell into the custom of setting four o'clock in the afternoon (after the Courts had risen) as the meeting-time for the examiners and this meant that the Clerk Assistant had perforce to absent himself from the Table—often protractedly—when the House was likely to be at its busiest. It was for this reason, more than any other, that the office of Recognisance was abolished (by "Peel's Act") in 1839 and J. B. Booth, then appointed as first Counsel to the Speaker, was made also the permanent examiner of recognisances. The Clerks at the Table were thus relieved finally of an onerous and irksome duty which had always been more nuisance than it was worth.

THE INGROSSING OFFICE

Reference has already been made to the way Bills, both Public and Private, were *ingrossed* to record and preserve any change in meaning between an original and an amended draft, and there had been an ingrossing clerk in the Clerk's Department from the very earliest time—though not, perhaps, with official title. The first *official* Clerk of Ingrossments was probably appointed by the indefatigable Jodrell at or about the time he created his four "clerks without doors". Certainly, at the time the appoint-

CHAPTER 3

The Serjeant at Arms and his Officers, 1415–1833

Of all the Departments and sub-departments of the House of Commons, that of the Serjeant at Arms is markedly the least documented. Clerks and Speakers, and even lesser Officers, who have occupied positions in Parliament—many of them quite without distinction—have invariably left *some* published record of their tenures for the inspection of posterity; since the earliest times the names of Members have been recorded and preserved in the Rolls of Parliament; even obscure people like printers and clerks in Government departments whose duties brought them within the ambit of the House can still be identified from the records of the day. But of the Serjeant at Arms, high Officer though he was—and still is—printed history says almost nothing.

The blank wall that faces any researcher into the colourful past of the Commons' Serjeant is at the same time both irritating and intriguing, and is made more so by the fact that reference is made to him on practically every page of Parliamentary history. Distinguished prisoners appeared at the Bar "in charge of the Serjeant at Arms"; by Order of the House "the Member for X was arrested by the Serjeant"; in times of unrest and disorder "the Serjeant was bidden to clear the galleries and lobbies of the House". As the executive Officer of the Commons the Serjeant was never out of the news, but he seldom reached the headlines. Speakers and Clerks became personally famous and left behind them reputations and names splendid as those of any statesman or soldier of their times—but the Serjeant at Arms remains simply "the Serjeant", a seemingly anonymous figure who, down the centuries, has done no more than carry out the orders of the House. There are several possible explanations for this (very sad) state of affairs for which history is undoubtedly the poorer. First, the Serjeant at Arms was never in fact the Commons' Serjeant at all; he was the King's Serjeant lent to the Commons only for the duration of the House's sittings. Secondly, since the Serjeant's duties were executive in nature rather than clerical he was hardly likely to employ clerks (i.e. writers) among his staff as the two other Departments did perforce, so that the keeping of records would not have come easily. Also, in spite of the several unique powers possessed by the Serjeant, he was very much more the servant of the House than either the Speaker (whose voice was the voice of Parliament itself) or the Clerk (who was the chief keeper of the records and accounts and was the undisputed overlord of all the clerical services of the Commons). His life must often have been a very trying one, caught as he always was between the Crown, the Speaker, the Clerk and the Members themselves.

Though published information about the Serjeant at Arms in the Commons is so scanty as to be practically non-existent, the evolution and the development of the office of Serjeants in general is easier to study and is not without interest. According to some accounts Serjeants were first created in Rome under Romulus, who himself had twelve carefully chosen patricians to act as his personal bodyguard; Consuls, likewise, each had twelve of these early "serjeants" (or Lictors, to use their proper title), while inferior officers of state had six. In the pursuance of their duties—and this is the continuing feature which links them with their more modern counterparts—these men possessed virtually unlimited powers of arrest, and were not dependent upon the warrant of any legal authority. They were a sort of super elite corps, answerable only to their own master and taking precedence according to his rank.

The actual title of Serjeant *at Arms*, however, is not met with until the days of the Crusades when Philip the August, King of France, instituted a special corps to guard his person in the Holy Iand in 1192. *Men*-at-arms, of course, were common enough in all armies of the time, but Philip's escort—being Cavaliers, or gentlemen—were styled *sergents* d'Armes to distinguish them from the lower orders, and whenever they appeared in public they did so encased from head to foot in armour. Also, partly as a weapon and partly as a badge of their particular office, they carried a decorated battle-mace—a useful weapon for close-fighting on horseback, and one which probably owed much of its popularity to the fact that it was used with devastating effect by the redoubtable Saracen cavalry.

It is almost certain that the "Serjeant" conception came over to England with the Normans, although the tenure was not at once established in any functional sense. In its earliest form (in England) it was an alternative form of land-tenure to the knight-age, though with the important difference that whereas a knight was required to give *military* service in return for the lands he held from the King, the return demanded from a Serjeant was not confined to the bearing of arms. It could be much more, or much less, according to the amount of the debt, and in consequence not all Serjeants were Serjeants "at Arms" and not all duties were concerned with the safety of the King's person. Thus, there were Serjeants with special responsibility for such odd things as royal game preserves, crewing of ships, collecting taxes and keeping an eye (on behalf of the King, of course) on local administration and the processes of justice.

During the thirteenth century, however, the principal Serjeants—i.e. those with the biggest land-grants—*were* Serjeants at Arms, and in 1278 a corps of twenty were recruited as a mounted close escort for the Sovereign, Edward I—the first glimmer of the conception of a standing army in England. Like their remote Roman prototypes, they wielded almost royal authority over their fellow-citizens; wherever treason was even suspected against the Crown the Serjeant at Arms's power of arrest and imprisonment was unquestioned, and no Court in the land could wrest a victim from his grasp once the arrest had taken place. If the victim really *was* a traitor, of course, this may have been well enough—though very much contrary to the established principles of *observable* justice—but when the arrested person was no more than merely a political undesirable, or a commercial competitor, a situation could, and often did, arise when ordinary folk began to protest.

And not only "ordinary folk". During the twelve years 1386–1397 Parliament itself protested no less than four times to Richard II about the arbitrary behaviour of his Serjeants at Arms, accusing them of making arrests, causing extortions and "other evil deeds *outside their franchise without warrant*", and praying the King to assert at least some control over their activities. The grave rebellion in Kent in 1381, for example (the Peasants' Revolt) had almost certainly been sparked off by the ruthless actions of John Legg, the Serjeant at Arms attached to the Commission of Inquiry in Kent whose lust for extortion—he was officially there as a tax-collector—was only halted when the blood began to flow.

The Royal Serjeants, however, were not the whole of the trouble. During the fourteenth century the "serjeant" idea proliferated to such an extent that almost every city and borough in the Kingdom, adopting the example of their royal overlord, appointed their own City Serjeants and Serjeants-at-Mace to take over the administrative and police duties formerly carried out by the bailiffs and reeves, and these lesser officials were not slow to imitate the behaviour of their Royal counterparts. Quite soon, City and Borough Serjeants, it seemed, were running loose all over the country, arresting, imprisoning and extorting at will and without any regard to the statutory boundaries of the authority which had appointed them. No man, in fact, was safe from either the King or the local authorities and Parliament appeared to be pushed out of the picture almost completely. This, too, was subject of complaint by Parliament to the Crown.

Why then, one might well wonder, should the Commons accept one of these malign creatures right into its own Chamber in 1415, still smarting though they undoubtedly were from the grim experiences of the preceding century? The theory that the assignment of a Serjeant at Arms "to attend upon the Speaker" was some deep scheme by the King to extend his power over Parliament will not hold water. For one thing, the House of Commons was not yet enough of a power to warrant such a move—the Speakership itself was a mere thirty years old and the Commons was very much a "Lower House" in every sense of the word. Also, as inspection of the Close Rolls for 1415 will show, the Serjeant at Arms was introduced at the request of the Commons themselves:

"... At the special petition of the Commons in the Parliament at Leycester by letters patent of 20th May last the King granted

that the said N [i.e. Nicholas Maudit] should during his life
attend upon all his Parliaments and the Parliaments of his heirs
so long as they should last as Serjeant at Arms for the Commons
coming thereto; and should take for this service and attendance
£10 a year of the issues of the City of London."

So the Commons *wanted* a Royal Serjeant, and for a very
good reason—the enforcement of Parliamentary privilege. In
modern times privilege is fairly well defined, having been contested in the Courts on many occasions during the centuries by
those who have sought to challenge it, and the Commons today
are their own arbiters when complaints of breach are made. But
it was not so in the fifteenth century. Members of Parliament, it
seemed, were subject to interference from every Tom, Dick and
Harry who carried a mace or baton of office, and on the basis
of the dictum "if you can't fight 'em, join 'em" it must have
appeared as obvious good sense to the Commons to have a
Serjeant of their own—and the bigger the better. Hence a *Royal*
Serjeant, and hence his *attachment* to "wait upon the Speaker"
and not his outright appointment to the staff of the House. He
was still the King's officer of state, and by virtue of the King's
insignia on his mace he was empowered to exercise royal
authority over ordinary citizens—*but on the instructions of the
Speaker*. When Parliament was not sitting he was withdrawn, he
and his mace returned to duty in the Royal Household and his
powers were temporarily suspended in the Commons. But when
Parliament *was* in session they were now armed with complete
powers of arrest, trial (if desirable) and imprisonment, and were
ready to embark upon the centuries-long battle to establish those
well-recognised rights and "privileges" under which they work
today—and without which they could not hope to work successfully.

The first recorded real clash between the Commons and the
growing powers around it came in 1542, and the event makes
interesting reading for several reasons. For one thing, it occurred
at a time when the authority of the Crown was at its height—the
despotic Henry VIII was in the thirty-fourth year of his reign—
and when the Commons themselves had little to offer in the
way of either strength or dignity, and it is surprising that the
House should have taken the determined stand it did. Even more

surprising, however, is the fact that the fire-eating Henry should have come out, as he did, unequivocally on the side of Parliament, when expediency might well have counselled his support of the City of London—which even then was one of the treasure-houses of the world.

Since the earliest days of Parliament it had been accepted by all civil authorities that no Member could be arrested for debt; proceedings, certainly might be taken against him for recovery, but to lock him up while enquiries pended would be to prevent his attendance in Parliament and this was something which clearly could not be permitted. But in 1542 a Member, Ferrers by name, was seized for debt by order of the City of London and was committed to the Counter Prison to await trial. The House, normally so timorous a body and with little to say for itself, on this occasion took a serious view of such interference with one of its Members and commanded the Speaker to send the Serjeant at Arms into the City to demand the prisoner's release.

The Serjeant, John Sent John, accompanied by two or three of his servants and carrying the mace as symbol of his authority had no sooner presented himself at the City gates and announced his errand, however, than he was set upon by a band of the Sheriff's men and badly beaten up. Worse still, the mace was broken in the fracas, after which both he and it, and his servants, were unceremoniously thrown out of the City gate to make their sorry way back to Westminster to report to the Speaker. The House had been angry enough at the City's original action but this latest insult drove them wild. The City Sheriffs and the Clerk of the Counter Prison were seized at once and committed to the dreaded Little Ease in the Tower and the Chancellor and the Speaker, representing the Lords and the Commons, sought audience with the King to seek his support.

Surprisingly, Henry commended the action they had taken. "For," he said "I understand that you, not only for yourselves, but also for your necessary servants, even to your cooks and housekeepers, enjoy the privilege insomuch as my Lord Chancellor hath informed us that he being Speaker of the Parliament, the cook of the Temple was arrested in London, and as he served the Speaker in office during the Parliament, was taken out of execution by the privilege of Parliament."

So there was no support for the City from Henry, and after a few days in the rigour of the Little Ease the Sheriffs and the Clerk came docilely to the Bar of the House to make their submission to Parliament and to crave its pardon. Interference with the liberty of Members did occur again from time to time in later years and it was always punished, and the sovereign authority of the Serjeant at Arms and his mace at length became universally acknowledged throughout the country.

The principle referred to by Henry that Parliamentary privilege was wide enough to protect even a Member's "cook and housekeeper" remained in force until as late as the eighteenth century, causing many scandals and abuses in its day. There was a great buying and selling of "places" in M.P.s' households —which soon became staffed by rogues and thieves seeking immunity from the just punishment of their crimes—and even Members themselves were not above offering "domestic posts" to rich friends or relations in trouble with the law (for a consideration, of course).

Clearly, such abuse had to be brought to a stop; and when it was, the whole extent of Parliamentary privilege was defined more clearly. Henceforth, its mantle was to cover Members of Parliament in the execution of their duty and the servants of *Parliament*, and so it remains to this day.

A century or so after John Sent John's public discomfiture in the City of London another Serjeant at Arms found himself in even greater peril—this time, at the hand of his own masters. In 1675, following a finding by the High Court in respect of a civil action in which a Member of Parliament had come off victorious, an appeal was made by the loser to the Lords—a procedure which, under normal circumstances, is commonplace enough. But in this particular case, the Commons decided that the prosecution in the Lords of any suit involving a Member of the Lower House must in itself constitute a breach of the privileges of that House, and they issued an order forbidding the counsel for the appellant to plead his client's case before the Lords under penalty of both fine and imprisonment.

The Lords, however, refused to accept this interference with what was, after all, no more than a normal lawful process, and they issued an order of their own, armed with even greater penalties, commanding counsel to appear before them in West-minster Hall on the appropriate day. Accordingly, when the case was called, Sir John Churchill rose to plead his client's cause, and was promptly arrested by the Serjeant at Arms (Sir James Northfolke) who had been sent into the Hall by the Commons for just this purpose. Churchill was committed to the Serjeant's prison room to await the House's pleasure.

To the Lords, of course, the Commons' action was not entirely unexpected, and as soon as they heard what had happened they sent Black Rod to have words with the Serjeant. Exactly what words he used were never revealed, but they were certainly effective. Without even consulting the Speaker, Northfolke released his prisoner and Churchill returned to Westminster Hall. The Commons, furious over the loss of face they felt they had suffered in this stupid little quarrel with the Lords, turned all their anger on the unfortunate Northfolke, dismissing him peremptorily from his post for "betraying his trust in not executing his office according to the orders and directions of this House", and sending him to the Tower. And this after fifteen years' unblemished service, for Northfolke had served the House with distinction ever since the Restoration!

Nevertheless, the dismissal was effective—in spite of poor Northfolke's letters patent from the King—and Sir William Bishop was appointed to replace him. The House *has* this power of dismissal over the Crown's appointee in cases of "misconduct", even today, but Northfolke's was the only case in which it was ever invoked.

The Serjeant soon developed into an essential figure in the ceremonial of Parliament, and since he was the sole executor of the orders of the House, as expressed by the Speaker, it followed naturally that he should appear in practically every scene of the grand drama of Westminster as it unrolled down the centuries. Strange tasks fell his way. Under Protestant monarchs, Catholic books condemned by Parliament were burned personally by him in the Old Palace Yard, and vice versa; impeached "criminals" were carried away in his custody to torture or death; illustrious prisoners, under the displeasure of the House, were confined under lock and key in his quarters—and made to pay him 6s. 8d. a day for the privilege. On every great occasion of State at which the presence of the Commons or their Speaker was required, the Serjeant at Arms with his gilt mace was an essential figure, "attending upon the Speaker" by order of the King—and yet, down the long generations of the Commons Serjeantcy, its occupant has remained, in the main, virtually anonymous. How many names in the list of Serjeants are household words today, even in esoteric circles?

Strangely enough, probably one of the best-known Serjeants of them all—renowned not for his qualities, which were sadly deficient, but for the drama in which he played so conspicuous a part—does not even appear in the official records of the holders of the office. According to them, the period from January 1646 to April 1660, was covered by the unbroken Serjeantcy of one Edward Birkhead, who was appointed in the normal way by letters patent from the King. But by the end of January 1649 that King was dead and his letters patent discredited, and Serjeant Birkhead, like his master—though less finally—had disappeared from the scene. Perhaps, like General Fairfax, "he had too much sense to be there!" During the whole of Charles's trial, in fact, the Serjeantcy was occupied by William Dendy, a man of questionable background who, as the tool of Cromwell and Bradshawe, served his new lords well by adding what miseries he could to Charles's last wretched days in Westminster Hall. And for this, officially non-existent though he may be since his appointment was not from the Crown, he is remembered—the prime example of Shakespeare's remark that "the evil that men do lives after them". Much good, however, was interred with the bones of others.

The outward show of Parliament, important part though it was in the duties of the Serjeant, was by no means their total. Quite early in his history he became the Commons' Usher, Keeper of the Doors, and Housekeeper. Unlike the Lords, who had Black Rod to carry messages to the Commons, the Commons had no analogous officer, and as the importance of the Lower House developed to a point where an official messenger was often required to convey resolutions, protests, petitions, etc., to the Lords, they decided to add this task to their Serjeant's duties. Then, too, as the public became aware of the regular sittings of their representatives in Parliament and began more and more to crowd around—and often into—the Chamber, it became necessary to find someone to keep order, and once again it was the Serjeant who filled the bill. After all, the man was *there*, and had to be kept busy one way or another!

And finally, the housekeeping—an aspect of the Serjeant's work that has increased steadily down the centuries until it far exceeded (in rigour, if not in importance) the ceremonial side of his duties. The "Houses of Parliament", of course, are still a Royal Palace (the Palace of Westminster) and the people who work there professionally are its staff—which is why they are not Civil Servants. In earlier days, the place was a Palace in fact as well as in name and successive Kings of England lived in it from the time of Edward the Confessor, through the Norman period and into the Tudor; its domestic upkeep and maintenance were the responsibility of the King's own servants and it was furnished in splendour or in squalor according to the inclinations of its current occupant. But when Henry VIII tried to bring up his red-headed daughter within its walls, he soon found that the old home was not big enough to hold two such Tudors at the same time. And Henry built himself a new Palace on some land at St. James's which he "acquired" from Cardinal Wolsey, while the stormy and imperious Elizabeth was sent to fret herself half to death in distant Greenwich. It was the end of Westminster Palace as the home of the English Kings.

When it became the home of the English Parliament, however, and became more packed with people than it ever had been before in the whole of its long history, new problems of staffing and servicing called for urgent attention, and once more the poor Serjeant found himself in demand. He became responsible for the housekeeping of the Palace of Westminster and a Housekeeper was appointed under his supervision.

The trouble was, however, from his point of view, that no funds were made available to him to pay for the services he was expected to provide—and these were fairly extensive. As we have seen, the Serjeant's own salary was negligible. Under the Terms of his original appointment in 1415 a mere "£10 a year from the issues of the City of London", it had later been revised to the rate of one shilling and twopence per sitting day, and it is of course obvious that he could not have been expected to provide

services out of *either* sum. Money had to be found from somewhere, however, both to hire staff and to pay for supplies, and to
this end various fees were introduced and allocated to the
Serjeant in the same way as fees had been made use of to pay
for the services of the Clerk's department. Exactly how they
started and what they amounted to we have no way of knowing,
but it is clear that they must have been introduced quite early in
the Serjeants' history for they were certainly an established
feature even before Tudor times.

(During the days of the Interregnum (1649–1660) the
Commons, anticipating history by almost two centuries, abolished the system of payment by fees and put its principal officers
on a regular salary, but after the Restoration the old system was
revived—doubtless much to the gratification of the collectors, if
not of those who had to pay.)

By mid-eighteenth century the pattern of changes was clearly
regulated and almost hallowed by long usage, and the 1731
Table of Fees gives a good idea of the varied sums which the
long-suffering Members—and those of the public using the
Commons' legislative services—were required to pay the Serjeant
and his men. (These fees were, of course, additional to those paid
to the Clerk and *his* assistants.)

TABLE OF FEES DATED 1731

The Serjeant	£	s	d
For every Private Bill or enacting clause	1	5	0
(Double fees for "double" Bills)			
For taking a knight into custody	5	0	0
For taking a gentleman into custody	3	6	8
For every day in custody	1	0	0
For every knight of the shire when sworn into the House		10	0
For every burgess when sworn into the House		5	0
For every person sworn at the Table ordered to be naturalised		12	6
For every Counsel pleading at the Bar or before a Committee		10	0
For bringing a criminal to the Bar		6	8
Riding charges per mile			6

The Housekeeper	£	s	d
For every Private Bill or enacting clause		5	o
(Double fees for "double" Bills)			
For every Private Committee		5	o
For every hearing at the Bar		10	o
For every prisoner discharged by the House		5	o

The Two Doorkeepers			
For every Private Bill or enacting clause		5	o
(Double fees for "double" Bills)			
For attending the House in private matters		7	6
For delivering papers at the door		5	o
For discharge of prisoners, each		2	6
For every Member sworn		5	o

The Four Messengers			
For serving any summons of the House in private matters		6	8
For serving the orders of Committees in private matters		2	6
For attending a prisoner, *per diem*		6	8
For keeping the door at a Private Committee		2	6

It is apparent from this extract from the 1731 Table of Fees that under the system of charges then in force the Serjeant and his staff did very well for themselves, particularly when one remembers that the bulk of the legislation passing through the House in early times was *private* legislation. The gross fees raised were enormous. In addition, considerable gratuities were collected by the Serjeant's staff from everyone using the House's facilities, gratuities which—as will be seen from the evidence given before the 1833 Committee—became themselves so established with time as to form virtually a second tier of fees superimposed over the official ones.

The final element in the total of the incomes of the Serjeant and his officers was that proportion that derived from the selling of appointments—a quite respectable and accepted procedure throughout the Commons, as we have seen. Little evidence exists, of course, of these financial transactions, but it can be taken for granted that they were not inconsiderable. They probably took the form of a cash payment at the time of appointment and a continuing "cut" of fees and gratuities for as long as the appointment lasted. From the evidence given before the 1833 Committee we know that each of the four Messengers paid the Serjeant no less than £500 for his appointment, and that the Deliverer of the Vote made a regular contribution to the Serjeant's income *in addition* to whatever lump sum he paid.

THE DELIVERER OF THE VOTE

The appointments which came within the gift of the Serjeant were by no means negligible and the total income of his staff was considerable—though not from official salaries. Like their more illustrious colleagues in the Clerks' department, the Serjeant's Officers made a good thing out of House fees on private business (in addition to those fees which were specially paid for Serjeantcy duties), but they made even more from gratuities and other "private enterprise" ventures that were not available to the Clerks.

By the seventeenth century the Serjeant's department was fairly well established, and consisted of the Vote Office, the Deputy Housekeeper, two Doorkeepers, four Messengers and various watchmen and firelighters. It is impossible, now, to fix the date upon which these offices were first created but one can make a reasonable guess at one of them—the Vote Office. Since the original duties of this office were concerned primarily with the distribution of the document known as "the Vote", and since the Vote was first produced in *printed* form in 1681 (it had appeared only in manuscript previously), the Deliverer of the Vote must have been appointed either in 1682 or very shortly after. The Vote, which was basically a copy of the Clerk's minute-book (the Journal), was—and is—so essential to the conduct of business in Parliament that it has been delivered daily to all Members ever since it was first printed, and even today it is one of the few types of Parliamentary paper that qualify for the "full delivery" treatment. Its importance in its earliest days lay in the fact that its reiteration of the Clerk's minutes of the previous day's proceedings informed Members of exactly what business had been reached and dealt with, and what still remained for "today's sitting". But as time went by the Vote became more sophisticated by the inclusion of a great deal of additional information, so that while it retained its original importance to Members it also attracted a great deal of interest outside the House. During the very long period when the reporting of Parliamentary proceedings was prohibited the Vote was the only authoritative account the public could refer to, and outside demands for it were heavy. Not unnaturally, then, it came to have a cash value which the Deliverer of the Vote was able, quite legitimately, to turn into a profit to himself.

His duties were fairly complex. In addition to delivering the Vote to London-based Members by hand—he employed up to ten early-morning porters, or Walkmen, for the purpose—he was responsible for ordering and maintaining a stock of all papers "ordered to be printed" by the House and for keeping the necessary accounts. Once a paper had been orderd by the House, it was up to the Deliverer to estimate the number likely to be required, order them from the printer and make them available to Members and to other users of the Commons machinery. If he ordered more than could be used it would cause him a loss in his accounts; if he ordered too few, on the other, hand, and found himself unable to satisfy a Member's legitimate request for a copy, he would be in serious trouble from the House. The estimating part of the work has always been tricky—and remains so today, though the *financial* responsibility no longer rests on the shoulders of the Deliverer.

Until 1833 his Treasury salary was a mere £14 12s. 6d. a year —a sum hardly likely to support the payment of printing costs and the salaries of his Deputy, three clerks and ten Walkmen! It really *was* an iniquitous system that forced its officers to scratch about as best they could to find funds enough to keep the Parliamentary machine in movement; and if their search for money took them into some odd places and gave rise to some strange expedients it is hardly to be wondered at.

The Deliverer, however, clearly scratched about with some success. He was empowered to charge every Member a fee of £2 12s. 6d. a year for the delivery of his Vote, though the Vote was not delivered unless the Member specifically claimed it at the beginning of each Session. Many Members simply did not bother themselves with their Vote or printed papers, and those that were not claimed remained as perquisites of the Vote Office —at nearly £9 a set, the income from this source was considerable. Thus, for *not* delivering the Vote to Members the Deliverer collected £2 12s. 6d. per head, whereas when he did deliver it he not only received the standard delivery fee but a handsome tip into the bargain. This gratuity, which varied over the years between 10s. 6d. and a guinea, became in fact so established that it was really a recognised (though unofficial) charge for delivery. A further "gratuity" of half a guinea was payable by Members for the delivery of every Public Act, and the Vote Office itself was entitled to no less than fifty-one sets of papers to sell for its own profit. Also, in addition to Votes and papers unclaimed by individual Members, a considerable number remained in the Deliverer's hands because the Government offices and Ministries to which they had originally been allocated had disappeared over the years, either because of amalgamations or through simple abolition, and the instructions regarding the supply of their papers had never been cancelled. Other officers of the House, too, who were allowed sets of papers as part of their emoluments, left these in the Vote Office for the Deliverer to dispose of to the best advantage, and there is no doubt but that he would show *some* profit on these transactions as he did on all the others.

As will be seen from the findings of the 1833 Committee, the income enjoyed by the Deliverer was substantial but it should be pointed out, in fairness, that his office was completely self-supporting and that he paid out very nearly one half of his income in running expenses. What he kept, he certainly earned, for his office was open from 7.30 a.m. until the rising of the House each day and either he or his Deputy were in constant attendance—not only for the delivery of the Vote and other papers, but to inform Members regarding the availability of current papers and to advise them concerning older papers having relevance to current debates in the House. His duty was an onerous one and there was a long history of illness and breakdown among successive holders of the office. As the Serjeant was to say before the 1833 Committee, "I do not think it could be done by one [person]: it is so excessively laborious that one in-

dividual could hardly get through it; Mr. Paskin [the Deputy
—the Deliverer had been away ill for nearly a year] appears to
have suffered in his health from it; it is very laborious indeed."

An interesting tradition developed around the Walkmen who
delivered the Vote around London. As can be imagined, it was
not always easy to find reliable men able to report for duty
between 7 and 7.30 a.m. and to work hard until 9.30 or 10—
if they were worth employing they would already have full-time
jobs which would certainly require their presence long before
9.30 in the morning, and if they were *not* of sufficient quality
to hold down full-time employment they would be useless to the
Vote Office. The problem was solved eventually by arranging
to employ gas-lighters from the nearby Gas Company. According
to the time of year, they were able to light or extinguish their
lamps either before reporting for duty at the House or after
they had delivered their Votes; or, by arranging their "walks"
to coincide more or less with their "beats" they could even do
the two jobs simultaneously.

This unofficial arrangement lasted into my own time (1945
onward), and very satisfactory it was, though as the gas-lamps of
the City of Westminster gradually gave way to more modern
lighting our long-standing supply of gas-lighters began to dry
up, and by the mid-50s it was no more. The old problem,
"solved" for well over a century, was with us again and had to
be solved anew.

THE DEPUTY HOUSEKEEPER

Although the duties of housekeeping officially devolved upon
the Serjeant it was obvious that he could not be expected to
carry them out personally, and until 1812 he was authorised to
appoint a Deputy. The duties were both multifarious and onerous, and when one thinks of the problems involved in keeping
such an enormous "house" clean, heated and fed, the wonder is
that it was done at all by so small a staff as the Deputy had—
and almost without Treasury support. The Deputy's salary was
a mere £15 6s. 6d. a year, but he was expected to employ enough
staff to clean the whole House daily (as well as certain accommodation belonging to the Speaker), to supply and equip with

stationery all the rooms required for Committees, to light and maintain all fires throughout the building and to provide candles as necessary and to buy in, cook and serve such food and drink as Members might demand.

Naturally, the Deputy Housekeepers had to find the money from somewhere, and though he did eventually receive certain allowances from Treasury sources he nevertheless had to work like a Trojan and at the same time rely heavily on gratuities from Members, Private Bill Agents, Counsel and others who used his services. As will be seen, the Deputy Housekeeper in 1833, Bellamy, drew his income from an astonishingly wide variety of sources, and as well as doing very nicely for himself in this respect he was in the happy position of running a private business on the side *and* employing his own son as Assistant on a Treasury salary. Exactly how much he paid the Serjeant for his appointment, however, was not stated—the sum was probably enormous.

THE DOORKEEPERS AND MESSENGERS

These officials (2 Doorkeepers and 4 Messengers) were of fairly equal status, drawing a Treasury salary of £12 13s. 6d. (The First Doorkeeper received, in addition, a special payment of £37 10s. 0d. a year from the same source.) But apart from this, their main income came from fees and gratuities—once again, the machine was kept going from the pockets of Members and the public. All six received fees on Private Business passing through the House—as did the Housekeeper. The Doorkeepers had fees for collecting, registering and distributing Private Bills; they had a gratuity of about two guineas a head from Members and a share in the fees charged for the admission of strangers into the Gallery. The First Doorkeeper was also entitled to certain fees from agents in addition to fifty copies of Private Acts which he made up into sets to sell at a guinea a time. All in all, they made a handsome living from their jobs—as did the humbler Messengers.

The four Messengers, in addition to their salaries of £12 13s. 6d. and their fees on Private Business, were paid by the Treasury to deliver the Orders of the House—2s. 6d. per Order plus 6d. a mile plus coach hire. They received a share of the strangers' admission fees, a two-guinea gratuity from each Member and three guineas for every Newspaper for each reporter it had in the Gallery (after the prohibition on reporting was lifted.) They also had fifty-four sets each of Public Acts to deliver at half a guinea a time—a not inconsiderable addition to their incomes. A "lower doorkeeper" appointed in 1826 had an official salary of £4 a year from the Treasury, but collected in 1832 no less than £360 in tips (according to his evidence before the Committee—and one can be sure he quoted an absolutely minimum figure to *them*!). It was estimated, in fact, that every Member paid out over £9 a year in tips, and these were *recognised* gratuities which custom had hallowed into virtual fees paid over and above the official ones.

An interesting feature about the "mileage and coach hire" fee charged by the messengers for delivering the Orders of the House outside Parliament was that it was only paid when the delivery address was "off the stones". This was a survival from the early days when only a few main streets in central London were actually paved and the "made-up" area defined the limits of delivery; but as time went by the criterion of "on" or "off" the "stones" became ridiculous. Whitechapel, for instance— several miles away—was "on", and delivered to free of charge, while Westminster Bridge was "off" and was charged for. This anomalous situation was still in existence in 1833.

WATCHMEN, PORTERS, FIRELIGHTERS, ETC.

These minor officials, who were often employed on a somewhat casual basis and in some cases combined their humble Parliamentary duties with other jobs outside, were paid a small salary by the Treasury which, by 1833, varied between £30 and £50 a year. They were not, however, in sufficient contact with Members or the public to make anything from gratuities.

CHAPTER 4

The Speaker, 1377–1833

To describe the Speaker of the House of Commons as "an important person" is to reiterate the obvious, yet his real importance is by no means as widely understood outside Parliament as it might be. He is exceeded in precedence among commoners, for example only by the Prime Minister and the Lord President of the Council; he takes precedence over all Peers except for the Archbishops of Canterbury and York, and his presence at all major State functions is taken for granted. Within the Commons, his voice is the law; his rulings and actions can only be challenged by a substantive Motion *after* the event, a Motion which is necessarily debated by the whole House—and which is rarely carried.

The office of the modern Speaker is an ambiguous and enigmatic combination of functions which makes it no easy subject for examination vis-à-vis the domestic machinery of the Commons. For one thing, the Speaker is simultaneously the master of the House and its absolute servant; his rulings are dictated by precedent—it is a legal axiom that without precedent there is no law—and his power is the power of the Commons themselves expressed through him. It is not simple to interpret a modern dilemma in the light of a three-hundred-year-old tradition, to do it often "off the cuff", and to produce a ruling which, at one and the same time, will redress a wrong with obvious justice, conform with the precedents and express the will of a modern House. Nor is it easy to sit hour after hour in the Chair, mentally alert during interminable debate—much of it tedious stuff enough—to safeguard the rules of order and the rights of minorities; harder still, one might think, to divorce his sympathies completely from participation in the all-important political clashes of opinion, to empty his mind of bias—perhaps after a lifetime of protagonism—and to rule the bitterly engaged parties with judicial firmness and impartiality.

Domestically, the Speaker's office is complicated again by the dual role of its occupant. He is the First Officer of the House, with a Department to administer and a service to provide and maintain, but he is also an elected Member of Parliament with a Parliamentary duty to discharge—were he not to discharge it, the people who elected him would be virtually disfranchised. It is small wonder, then, that any modern Speaker is a man of great distinction and incredible capacity, a man who not only enjoys the respect and confidence of the highest authorities in the land, but *merits* it. But it was not always so, and to contemporary eyes a quick backward glance might prove surprising as well as interesting. . . .

Like most things relating to Parliamentary history the earliest antecedents of the Speakership are lost in time, made more difficult to trace with certainty because of its humble beginnings. It is not generally appreciated that the great and dignified position which is the office of the Speaker today is one of the *results* rather than one of the *causes* of the constitutional development of democratic parliamentary government. As we have already noted, in the chapter on the Clerk, the earliest Commons were summoned into Parliament mainly in order to provide new funds; they were neither addressed directly by the King nor were they allowed to address him, and it can reasonably be assumed that even as early as Norman times some individual was appointed to carry the necessary messages backward and forward between the King-in-Council and the Commons (such as they then were).

But it was not until the year 1377, towards the end of Edward III's reign that the continuing line of identifiable Speakers was first founded with the appointment of Sir Thomas Hungerford as *parlour*, or "mouth", of the House. Unlike today, these early Speakers were appointed for one year only and many of them—as a glance at the list of Speakers will show—did not last out even the twelve months. Two Speakers in one year was a commonplace occurrence; in 1449 there were even three—possibly the indignity of the job was more than any real man could stomach for more than a few months at a stretch. For those earlier Commons were obsequious to a degree unimaginable today, constantly on their knees in the presence of royalty, insisting on their utter inferiority and choosing as their "mouth" a man who could express better than his fellows the kind of grovelling sycophancy that kept bloodthirsty kings quiet and reasonably happy. During the reigns of the Tudors, particularly, the attitude of the Commons reached what must have been the all-time low of their long history. We find Speaker Inglefield, for example, early in the reign of Henry VIII, referring to that murderous monarch's "promising valour, wonderful temperance, divine moderation in justice and avowed desire of clemency". And a quarter of a century later, when the same Henry's insatiable lust for wine, women and blood had made his name a by-word throughout Europe, Speaker Rich could still "compare the King for justice and prudence to Solomon, for strength and fortitude to Samson and for beauty and comeliness to Absolam". Was language ever more violently perverted!

The imperious Elizabeth, who could happily absorb as much flattery in a day as most normal people hear in a lifetime, was served up so much of it by her "faithful Commons" that even she was frequently disgusted with them. Small wonder that she treated them invariably like idiot children—they almost begged for contempt.

Yet, inevitably, there were exceptions, men whose lives and actions showed clearly enough that somewhere beneath that time-saving place-seeking jelly-like mass that the Commons had become, a backbone was developing. Among these, perhaps, Sir Thomas More—Speaker in 1523—may be accorded pride of place. In office, he stood up against both Henry VIII and his all-powerful Cardinal, Wolsey, insisting on the Commons' right to a voice in State affairs; later, out of office, in disgrace and imprisonment in the Tower, he preferred to die rather than to agree that "the Parliament could make the King supreme head of the Church". Sadly, such men were few and far between and it cannot be said that the Elizabethan Speakers did much that added lustre to their office—one good reason, perhaps, why the

Clerks began to develop the stature of *their* office during that period.

Strangely enough, it was with the ascent of Charles I to the throne of England that both the Commons and their Speaker first began to show and express the beginnings of that independence and authority that were to become their hallmark in later years. Since, as early as 1626 when Sir Heneage Finch was elected Speaker of Charles's first Parliament, Charles had not yet "offended" the Commons, it is obvious that the sturdy spirit that was developing in the Lower House was *not* the result of the King's intransigence (as later Parliamentarians were to claim), and that no matter how much Charles's attitude may have exacerbated the situation that did arise between the Crown and Commons it can be seen, in retrospect, that he had an entirely new element to contend with. It would almost seem as though Fate had brought a particular King face to face with a particular Parliament just to precipitate the fatal clash—and certainly, painful and bloody as it was, it ideally served the ultimate best ends of Parliamentary government in England.

Sir Heneage Finch's address to the King, following his election as Speaker, modestly emphasises the growing self-respect of the Commons who chose him. "Since," he said, "we all stand for hundreds and thousands, for figures and cyphers, as your Majesty, the supreme and sovereign auditor, shall please to place and value us, and, like coin to pass, are made current by your Royal stamp and impression only, *I shall neither disable nor undervalue* myself, but with a faithful and cheerful heart apply myself with the best of my strength and abilities to the performance of this weighty and public charge." Surely, though, neither Heneage Finch nor the worthy Sir John Glanville, who followed him, ever remotely contemplated presiding over a House whose sole business was to be the death of the King, champions though they were of the new spirit in the Commons. This sinister distinction was left to Glanville's successor, William Lenthall, who became Speaker in 1640.

Lenthall was a strange mixture of fearfulness and indecision— one wonders where on earth he found the courage to behave as he did on that one occasion by which history principally remembers him. This was when, in 1642, Charles I, having surrounded the House with soldiers, burst into the Chamber to demand the surrender of the "five Members" who were plotting against the Crown; having read out the names from a list in his hand, he ordered the Speaker to hand them over for justice (little knowing, of course, that the five had already escaped by boat via the Speaker's Stairs and were well on their way back to the City!). Lenthall's reply, under circumstance of great personal danger, was courageous and correct and "parliamentary" to a degree, and was to be remembered as almost the foundation exposition of the privilege of Parliament vis-à-vis the Crown.

"Sir," he said, "I have ears to hear and lips to speak only that the *people* shall command me!"

Charles baffled and furious, retired empty-handed, and it is interesting to note that from that day to this no Member is ever addressed *by name* in the Chamber except for disciplinary reasons, and that no Monarch has been allowed to set foot inside the House. So Lenthall's gesture was a considerable one and deserves to be remembered to his credit, but his subsequent actions brought him nothing but dishonour. One remembers the occasion in 1647, when the Army and Parliament had come to loggerheads over the conduct of the war; Presbyterian apprentices from the City, Army supporters of course, burst into the House and forced the Commons to rescind decisions they had just voted on. Lenthall, terrified, not only permitted and abetted this gross abuse but even allowed himself to be dragged back into the Chair afterwards to propose that the King be brought back to London. It cannot be denied that he was in danger from the violence of the apprentices, but he was not alone in that and the spectacle of the Speaker of the Commons of England being hauled around and browbeaten by a pack of teenagers must have been a sorry one. Shall wonder Cromwell and his friends felt themselves on safe ground with such a House to handle!

Lenthall it was who put the fatal Question to the hand-picked House that debated the trial of the King; and when the King was dead, it was Lenthall who still presided over Cromwell's Interregnum Parliament, accepting with sickening alacrity from his new master one of those strange patents of nobility which the Protector was so fond of handing out to those he considered useful to his ends. And when the Interregnum began to age and totter, and the cracks in its clay foundations yawned ever more gaping for all to see, it was the time-serving Lenthall who was at the forefront of those who worked for the Restoration, seeking by a positive frenzy of pro-Royalist busyness to bury his shameful history and to ingratiate himself with yet another new master. But it was not only the Monarchy he had offended; Parliament itself could not forgive him either, and by their order he was personally excluded from the Act of Indemnity which was extended to many of his lesser colleagues.

He was fortunate to escape with his life, though he was disbarred from ever again holding public office, his evidence at the trials of the regicides—all of it a most grievous breach of privilege—notwithstanding. He died, almost unnoticed, in 1662, and his deathbed testimony is not without interest. "I confess with Saul," he said, "I held their clothes while they murdered him; but herein I was not so criminal as Saul, for I never consented to his death. No excuse can be made for me, that I proposed the bloody question for trying the King; but I hoped even then when I put the question, the very putting the question would have cleared him, because I believed they were four to one against it—Cromwell and his agents deceived me." So Lenthall died, as he had lived for most of his life, less than a man; and it is one of those odd quirks of history that for one single act of courage, in a career of many-sided hypocrisy, he should be remembered as one of the great ones of Parliament.

Lenthall was not the only Speaker to serve under Cromwell, however, though none of the others had anything like his staying-power (Lenthall lasted thirteen years). Between 1653 and 1659, no less than five Speakers occupied the Chair, and the last of these—the last pre-Restoration Speaker—was Thomas Bamfield, the noted hater of Puritans, who will be remembered principally for the part he played as Chairman of the Committee that "tried" James Naylor for blasphemy.*

With the return of the Monarchy in 1660 a new, military, element became ascendant in the Commons and the benches were filled with score upon score of redundant Colonels, newly emerged from hiding, most of them, or from banishment overseas with the Stuarts, and the position of the Speaker took a

* See Marsden : *In Peril Before Parliament*, 1965.

definite turn for the worse. Disorder was general; the high spirits of men with no more wars to fight were turned upon anyone bold enough to even suggest controlling them, and the Speaker was openly mocked and laughed at whenever he attempted to bring some order into the proceedings of the House. It was not until 1673, when the reign of Charles II was already thirteen years old, that a man was found with fibre enough to redeem the Speaker's position from the abyss into which it had been thrust by the turbulent Royalists. Edward Seymour, proud of his descent from the Protector Somerset, was a man of haughty pride who imposed his will upon a startled Commons by sheer force of personality and a determination to *lead* where his predecessors had been content merely to follow. It is recorded of him (by Lord Dartmouth, a contemporary) that when he was out riding one day and his carriage broke down somewhere near Charing Cross, he ordered his men to stop the next gentlemen's coach to pass by and to bring it to him. When the unfortunate owner found himself ejected willy-nilly from his own carriage and ventured to ask the reason why, "Sir Edward told him it was more proper for *him* to walk the streets than the Speaker of the House of Commons and left him so to do without further apology".

Seymour, however, was no lickspittle, and showed himself just as uncompromising towards his superiors as he ever was towards subordinates. There was a famous occasion when a message was brought in from the Lords to say that the King was already on the Throne and was waiting for the Speaker's attendance so that he could announce the prorogation of Parliament. Upon Seymour refusing to budge until the Bill of Supply had been brought back from the Lords to the Commons (as it should have been) he received a stern warning of the King's mounting displeasure—a warning which apparently bothered him not at all. He would sooner be torn by wild horses, he said, than quit the Chair in circumstances that would be not only improper but unconstitutional. The Lords had no option but to submit; the Bill was duly returned and Seymour attended upon the King— but his defiance cost him his office. When he came up for re-election in the following Parliament the King flatly refused to sanction the appointment, and that was the end of a career that might well have become remarkable.

The first Speaker of William III's first Parliament, Sir John Trevor (elected in 1685) is worth attention, if only as a prime example of what Speakers ought not to be. He was perhaps the most repulsive-looking Speaker ever to occupy the Chair. His hulking figure was uncouth and shambling, his scowling face was made even more villainous by a ferocious squint, and his inner self complemented his outer appearance to perfection. After he had been five years in the Chair, word began to go round that the Commons' Speaker was taking bribes from the City in respect of a Bill before the House relating to the public care of orphans, and from the East India Company in respect of a Bill which affected their business interests abroad. Venal though the age undoubtedly was, the rumours were much too circumstantial for the House to ignore, and a Committee was set up under Mr. Patrick Foley to enquire into their sources. Unfortunately for the Speaker, the sources were only too clear; both the City of London and the East India Company had kept written accounts of the transaction concerned, with the dates on which the payments were made and the reason *why* they were made, and they were soon in the hands of the Committee. The House then drafted a Motion, "That Sir John Trevor, Speaker of this House, receiving a gratuity of 1,000 guineas from the City of London, after passing of the Orphans Bill, is guilty of high crime and misdemeanour". And the Motion was put to the House by—the Speaker himself! Did he for one mad moment believe, one wonders, that the Motion might be rejected? Whether he did or not, however, the fact that he himself should put the question (unthinkable in modern times) was typical; not only was Trevor an out-and-out villain, he was a thick-skinned one too.

Unfortunately for him, the House was well-nigh unanimous in its verdict, and a shaken Trevor rushed from the Chair to hide his head, with at least the appearance of shame, at home, and the day's sitting closed abruptly in uproar. The House met again on the morrow agog to see what his reaction would be, but their Speaker did not appear; instead, a note was handed in to say that "after rising this morning he was taken suddenly ill with a violent colic"—he would attend next day, however, he said. Once more the House adjourned without taking business, and when, on the following day, only a further note was forthcoming from the guilty Speaker, they expelled him unanimously both from the Chair he had dishonoured and from the House he had disgraced. It is a reasonable reflection, though, that if the Foley Committee's terms of reference had been wide enough to cover the activities of the whole House a good many Members at that time would have followed Trevor into the wilderness.

This wretched man, did, however, leave behind him one convention which persists in the Commons to this day. One of the Speaker's duties is to designate the Member he has chosen to speak next in debate—i.e. to "catch the Speaker's eye", to use the Parliamentary phrase. Now prior to Trevor's time it was usual for the Speaker to catch the *Member's* eye and then to bow his head in the Member's direction as an indication of his selection, no words being spoken. But Trevor, of course, was burdened with that terrible squint—and it frequently happened that when he was in the Chair *two* Members became simultaneously convinced that they had "caught the Speaker's eye", and when both rose and insisted on speaking the result was often acrimonious. For the sake of peace and goodwill, therefore, Trevor introduced the practice of calling out the appropriate *name* as he inclined his head—and a new convention was born.

The Speakers of the seventeenth century were, on the whole, a sorry lot and did little to advance the dignity of the office, but as the new century was born a new line of Speakers began to appear, men whose presence in the Chair laid with certainty the foundations of today's great and respected office. The first of these, Sir Richard Onslow, was elected in 1708, and he quickly made a name for himself. By nature authoritarian and hot-tempered, he was also thoroughly expert in the precedents and proceedings of Parliament—both Commons and Lords—and these characteristics, combined with his unyielding insistence on the observation of proper protocol, notably increased the prestige of his office, both within the House and outside. One doubts very much whether his nickname, by which the whole House referred to him, was ever used to his face—they called him "Stiff Dick"!

If his attitude towards his colleagues in the Commons was

"stiff", towards the Lords it was rigid. There was the celebrated occasion when he led the House up to the Lords to demand judgment against Dr. Sacheverell; three times during the proceedings Black Rod (the Messenger of the Lords) was guilty of minor infringements of the traditional protocol—whether from sheer ignorance or lack of practice, or from some petty or malicious notion of asserting his own superiority over the Members of the Lower House it is impossible to decide—but on each occasion Onslow interrupted the proceedings to insist upon receiving the respect due to his office. Onslow's objections were so obviously well-founded that the Lord Chancellor had no alternative but to come to his support and to direct Black Rod to perform his duties in such a way that the Commons should not be affronted further, and the Lower House was never offended in a similar manner again.

Sir Richard Onslow may well be described as the first of the modern line of great Speakers. The respect for the Chair which he worked so hard to establish was not gained lightly, and when it was achieved it was established on the firmest of foundations —the honest self-respect of the Chair's occupant. Though there were to be weak Speakers after Onslow—and some so inept as to be positively *bad* ones—there was never again a corrupt one, and it is on this basis of personal honour and probity that the subsequent Speakership has grown and developed. The ascendency seized by Onslow was never relinquished by his successors, and the House accepted the new convention of strength in the Chair with surprising docility and calm.

Onslow's nephew, Arthur Onslow, who became Speaker in 1728 and held the appointment for nearly thirty-four years, so consolidated the authority of the Chair that it assumed despotic proportions; yet successive Houses loved him for it and re-elected him with enthusiasm on each of the five occasions upon which he was subsequently nominated for the appointment. His rule was absolutely firm and absolutely impartial and it was absolutely respected. Members of the day, so it is said, went in positive dread of being "named" in the Chamber by Speaker Onslow, and came quickly to order at the mere threat of such action. (When a Member is "named" by the Speaker—always for some offence against the rules of order—he is required to leave his seat and quit the premises until the next day's sitting. It costs him a day's pay.) That Onslow possessed in high degree that priceless asset of a good sense of humour—without which no Speaker could survive even a day of Parliamentary pitfalls—was well illustrated by a story that was current in his day. He was asked, in all seriousness, what the consequence would be if a Member should be bold enough, and stubborn enough, to disregard a "naming", and Onslow's reply, "The Lord in heaven only knows", is one that will bear thinking about. To a good Speaker, the door is ever open to compromise!

Another story about Onslow, vouched for by Horace Walpole in a letter to Sir Horace Mann in 1758, illustrates the strange fact that even as late as the mid-eighteenth century Speakers still took part in Commons debates—though how they could do that and still maintain an absolutely impartial control over the House (which they most certainly did) "the Lord in heaven only knows". On this occasion the House was in Committee, with the Chairman of Ways and Means in the Chair, the Mace *below* the Table and the Speaker—as was often the way—listening from a seat in the gallery. New taxes were being debated, and it seems that Lord Strange, having made some sort of wager with his friends that "he would bring the Speaker down from the gallery", got up and proposed that Mr. Speaker be personally exempted from the tax under discussion. On a man with the high probity of Onslow, it worked like a charm, and the Speaker hurried down from his place to insist that he should be as subject to the tax as everyone else. Strange argued his case vigorously and Onslow replied with equal insistence and the debate was long and closely fought. When it was over, Strange, who had had the last laugh in spite of the defeat of his motion said, "Well, did I not show my dromedary well?" a reference to a popular London entertainment that winter in which a camel or drome-dary was put through its paces by an animal trainer, and was drawing great crowds.

But Onslow was unsparing of himself in the service of the House and nothing was too much trouble to him if it would enhance the honour and prestige of the Chair. Though he was stern, his patience was endless; though often severe, the justness of his rulings was so manifest that they were invariably accepted

—and by a House that was itself becoming more aware of its own dignity and importance than it had been since the days of Cromwell. The wonder was that he could stand up to it as long as he did; it was not until 1761, in fact, that his health began to fail and he was forced to resign the post he had adorned for so long. His departure was marked by the bestowal of signal honours—and not only from Parliament whose cause he had fostered into greatness. The City of London made him a Freeman "as a grateful and lasting testimony of the respectful love and veneration" which the Corporation felt "for the unwearied and disinterested labours he bestowed, and the impartial and judicious conduct he maintained in the execution of his important office". The King himself at the specific request of the Commons, granted an annuity of £3,000 for the lives of both Onslow and his son George—a happy precedent that was to become established by Act of Parliament to the great advantage of subsequent Speakers.

The two Speakers who followed Onslow, Sir John Cust and Sir Fletcher Norton, continued his great work—Norton, in fact, even managed to improve on it, for he was very stiff in his attitude towards the Lords and seemed determined to cut them down to size. His most memorable display of contempt towards the Upper House was an occasion in 1772, when he had been Speaker for a mere two years. Burke, having taken a Bill up to the Lords from the Commons in the normal way, had been kept waiting for *three hours* at the door of the Upper Chamber, and it was small wonder that on his return to the Commons he complained long and bitterly to the Speaker regarding the treatment he had received. The whole House, incensed beyond measure, at once unanimously rejected a Bill which had just been brought down from the Lords, and the vote having been taken, Norton flung the document contemptuously across the Table and on to the floor between the two front Benches. Then, with the Speaker's unspoken approval, the despised Measure was literally kicked out of the chamber and into the Lobby, after which —revenge taken and honour satisfied—the House resumed its sitting. What a sight *that* must have been . . . !

But it was not only the Upper House that attracted Norton's censure; even the King was not safe from his candour. There was a time in 1777 when George had come once again to the House for more money and the Commons had passed an Act to augment the Royal revenue by £100,000 a year—no mean sum, and one with which the irate Norton disagreed profoundly. On handing the Commons Bill in to the Lords, Norton was apparently so overcome by disapproval that he launched into a speech aimed directly at the monarch—"The faithful Commons," he said, "have, in a time of public distress, full of difficulty and danger, and labouring under burdens almost too heavy to be borne, granted him a supply and great additional revenue, great beyond example, great beyond his Majesty's highest wants, but hoping that what they had contributed so liberally would be employed wisely."

It is a fair indication of the heights to which a Speaker's prestige had risen when such a bold statement could be made by a commoner in the Upper House without fear of reprisal—but it is hardly surprising to find that the King was not amused. A few days later—at George's instigation, so it was said—a Member called Rigby delivered himself of a speech in the Commons attacking Norton's "impertinence" towards the Crown —a speech so hostile that Norton, brought almost to the verge of apoplexy by this onslaught from so unexpected a direction as the back benches of his own House, threatened to resign. He would almost certainly have done so had not Lord North "prevailed upon" Rigby to apologise—one shudders to think what the wretched man must have gone through before he agreed! Norton's wounded feelings, however, were admirably healed when the whole House passed a resolution approving the course he had adopted.

But Norton's intemperate outspokenness was to prove his own worst enemy. Only three years later, in 1780, while the House was in Committee discussing the Royal revenue, Norton came down from his place in the gallery to launch a bitter tirade against the "increasing influence" of the Crown; and not content with this, he widened his attack to embrace both the Duke of Grafton and Lord North, whom he accused of place-fixing. North repudiated the charges with equal ferocity and the clash soon deteriorated into what someone described at the time as "pure Billingsgate"—a disgraceful scene which the House was not easily to forget. Although Norton offered a qualified apology a few days later (prodded by a spate of extremely hostile criticism in the Press) the House felt that his outbreak, though perhaps acceptable from a backbencher in the heat of a debate, was inexcusable from a Speaker, and when he came up for re-election shortly after he was opposed. The opposition went to a division, and when the votes were counted Norton was defeated by 203 votes to 175. He was subsequently elevated to the peerage as Baron Grantly.

This stern action by the Commons is interesting. Less than a century previously (disregarding the fact that no Speaker would then have had either the authority or the courage to behave as Norton did) the House itself was so careless of its honour that misbehaviour by the Speaker—or anyone else, for that matter—would have become the subject of no more than momentary comment or a little private head-shaking by the more strait-laced older Members, whose views were in any case inconsiderable. But in 1780 the Commons were possessed of enough dignity and self-respect not only to be capable of taking offence but to discipline the offender—and not only to discipline him, but to actually throw him out of office. The example of successive Speakers since 1708 had borne fruit; the Commons had been set an example from which they had profited well, and from which they were thenceforward to set the very high standards of both professional and personal comportment which we take for granted in our Speakers today. Having learned first to *obey* authority, the House now essayed to assert it, and in doing so they invested the Chair of their Speaker with even greater power and respect than its occupant could ever have commanded on his own, however "stiff" his attitude.

The man who replaced Norton, Charles Wolfram Cornwall, was a Speaker of no particular brilliance and his only mark upon history is a verse in the *Rolliad* (a well-known collection of Whig skits):

> There Cornwall sits, and, oh! unhappy fate,
> Must sit forever through the long debate.
> Painful pre-eminence! He hears, 'tis true,
> Fox, North and Burke—but hears Sir Joseph too.

(The closing reference was to Sir Joseph Mawby, who might be described as the most renowned bore of the century.)

Cornwall was succeeded in turn by William Wyndham Grenville and Henry Addington, both of whom went on to become Prime Minister—another interesting reminder that even so recently as the early nineteenth century Speakers were still party politicians. Grenville occupied the Chair for only a few months before moving back into full-time politics (he became Prime Minister in the "Ministry of all the Talents" of 1806–1807), but Addington was Speaker for twelve years, 1789–1801, and he was a good one. His rulings were quick and sound, and absolutely firm, but were always in a spirit of such good humour and apparent willingness to compromise that the House never found any difficulty in accepting them—this is the hallmark of a really capable Speaker. Addington would almost certainly have become one of the great ones had he remained in office, but when Pitt resigned the Premiership over the Catholic Question in 1801 and Addington accepted the King's invitation to form a new administration he found himself translated into a sphere he was quite unequipped to cope with. For all his powers of tact and conciliation, his profound understanding of men and his un-doubted talent for the smooth prosecution of public business in the Commons, Addington was no politician and his tenure of the Premier's office ended in complete disaster. It has been said of him that he was the best of Speakers and the worst of Prime Ministers—a judgment with which it would be impossible to disagree.

The first Speaker to be elected in the nineteenth century, Sir John Freeman-Mitford (1801–1802) will be remembered for two things—neither of them, unfortunately, being his distinction in the Chair, for he was a mediocre Speaker. He presided over the first House of Commons to sit after the Union with Ireland in 1800; and as students of political history will be only too well aware, the advent of Irish Members into the central Parliament brought problems undreamed of by earlier Houses—problems with which, apparently, Freeman-Mitford was unable to deal. The second thing he is remembered for is that he was the first Speaker to be ennobled directly for his service to the House, a precedent which, once set, has been followed ever since.

Freeman-Mitford went from the Chair into the Lords as Lord Redesdale.

His place was taken by one who, from the point of view of the officers of the House, was probably one of the most significant figures to occupy the chair, since he was the first Speaker to really concentrate an informed attention upon the domestic machinery of Parliament. Reference to Speaker Charles Abbot's work in this sphere has already been made in the chapter dealing with the offices of the Clerk and it need not be pursued further here, except to say that—whatever Abbot's impact on the House itself and the world outside might have been—his influence upon the staff and their conditions of work was considerable. He was elected in 1802 and held office for fifteen interesting and strenuous years, and it was largely upon the foundations which he began to lay that the 1833 Committee was able to operate years after his retirement.

But his rule in the Commons was a distinguished one. Like all good Speakers, he was firm but not hectoring; his judgments —and he had many difficult ones to make in the face of the still "new" Irish Members—were inevitably sound and were enforced with a courtesy that was acknowledged even by his opponents as impeccable. He is associated with an event that has been described as the most dramatic ever to occur in the House of Commons—certainly the tension and emotion of the day can never have been exceeded, before or since, and certainly no other Speaker was ever thrust into so intolerable a dilemma by virtue of his office.

The occasion was a debate on a resolution for the impeachment of Lord Melville on the grounds of corruption in office. It was alleged that when he had held the post of Treasurer of the Navy, a short time previously, huge sums of public money had been drawn from the Bank of England and lodged in a private account, the accrued interest being diverted into unofficial channels—and the evidence in support of the charge appeared conclusive. The only aspect that remained at all debatable was the question of Melville's personal involvement, and this his Lordship fiercely denied; as head of a public department he was of course prepared to accept official responsibility for any malpractices which may have taken place in his office, but to a charge of personal corruption he would not submit. Public opinion was heavily, and noisily, against him, and the Commons had been left with no alternative but to order a probe. In April 1805, the Motion for Melville's impeachment was brought formally before the House, and one of its most prominent prosecutors was William Wilberforce—a man whose known probity and sense of social duty lent added weight and solemnity to the indictment.

Pitt, however, both as Prime Minister and personal friend of Melville, was absolutely convinced of the accused man's innocence and defended him powerfully during the debate, convincing many of the more influential Members of the House that the passing of the Motion could only result in the infliction of a grave injustice on one whose sole offence had been lack of sufficiently close supervision over the work of his subordinates. But general feeling, fanned by the Press and by public expression outside the House, was very strong against Melville, and the debate raged back and forth fiercely all day, being brought to an end only by a division at the close of the sitting. There were 432 Members present; when the vote was taken, 216 of them were Ayes, 216 Noes; the House had not arrived at a decision, and Melville's agony was to be further prolonged.

And not only Melville's. It had long been the rule in the House that when the Ayes and the Noes are equal it should devolve upon the Speaker to record his casting vote (under modern procedures, this is the only time he does vote), and in divisions involving legislative or procedural matters this duty need not prove too embarrassing. But when the question of the personal fate of an individual is concerned, as in the Melville case, the position of the Speaker must become well-nigh intolerable. As will be explained later, there are precedents to guide a Speaker to the decision he should make on these occasions, precedents which assist admirably when ordinary business is under question, but in the present dilemma the precedents could have offered precious little comfort to Speaker Abbot.

As the House became aware of the position into which the Speaker had been thrust by the vote the Chamber grew suddenly silent and every eye was turned towards the Chair. "Yet it was long," records Mr. Mark Boyd, who was present at the time, "before the Speaker gave his vote; agitation overcame him, his face grew white as a sheet. Terrible as was the distress to all who awaited the decision from the Chair, terrible as was the Speaker's distress, this moment of suspense lasted ten long minutes. There the Speaker sat in silence; all were silent. At length his voice was heard; he gave his vote, and he condemned Lord Melville."

The effect upon Pitt was catastrophic. "At the sound of the Speaker's voice," records Boyd, "the Prime Minister crushed his hat over his brows to hide the tears that poured over his cheeks. He pushed in haste out of the House. Some of his opponents, I am ashamed to say, thrust themselves near 'to see how Billy looked'. His friends gathered in defence around and screened him from rude glances." He was never to recover. So certain was he of Melville's honour and integrity, and so constant in his friendship, that he felt Melville's condemnation as keenly as if it had been delivered against himself; and not long afterwards—long before Melville was acquitted completely by the Lords in April 1806, the Great Commoner was carried to his grave in the Abbey.

What the strain of the occasion did to Abbot, however, though not recorded, can be imagined. But the courage that enabled him to pronounce that fatal "Aye" sustained him in office and in authority for a further twelve years, and it was not until 1817 that ill-health compelled his resignation from the Chair and caused his elevation to the Upper House as Lord Colchester, bringing to the Chair the last Speaker to be considered in this section—the Speaker who was in office during the investigations of the 1833 Committee.

This was Sir Charles Manners Sutton, whose service covered five successive Parliaments and was to last for eighteen years, a period during which great changes were to be made in the machinery of the House—not least in the Speaker's own Department. The fact that five different Houses thought well enough of Sutton to elect him their Speaker is perhaps sufficient testimony to his quality, but the following picture from Grant's *Random Recollections of the House of Commons*, florid and longwinded though it may be, is worth restating:

"A man of more conciliating, bland and gentlemanly manners," says Grant, "never crossed the threshold of St.

Stephen's. . . . He never suffered his political prejudices, strong as they were, to interfere with the amenities of gentlemanly intercourse. The perfect gentleman was visible in everything he said and did; nay, it was visible in his very person, whether you saw him walking in the streets or filling the Chair in the House of Commons. There was a mildness and good nature in his features which could not fail to strike the stranger the moment he saw him, and which was certain of prepossessing everyone in his favour. With these softer and more amiable features there were blended a dignity and energy of character which invariably secured the respect of Members. . . . His voice was, without exception, the most sonorous, powerful and melodious I ever heard. . . ."

So the eulogy continues, and for some length, though towards its end a note of caution appears—even to Mr. Grant, apparently, undoubted fan though he was of Speaker Sutton, facts were undeniable. Though the Speaker enjoyed a great and deserved reputation for impartiality, he says, "it was sometimes thought by the Liberals that he did not exercise his powers with absolute fairness". The Liberals thought—and said loudly—that "when several members rose to reply to a Tory speech of ability, he took care to fix his eye on the least talented of Members; and conversely, when a number of Tories got up to answer a Liberal speech, he invariably took particular pains to ensure that the ablest of the group should address the House". And, not unnaturally, the time arrived when the disgruntled Whigs felt they had had enough. When the new Parliament met on the 19th February 1835 Mr. Speaker Sutton found himself opposed by a Whig nominee, and when the voices were gathered Mr. James Abercromby, Member for Edinburgh, found himself in the Chair by a majority of six votes. Sutton, in receipt of the now customary pension, took his seat in the Lords as Viscount Canterbury.

This reminiscent glance over the earlier history of the Speakership, brief and selective as it must necessarily be, brings forward an interesting point—"the Speaker" has arrived at respectability by a devious and roundabout route! In the case of the Clerks, it will be remembered, the development of their office showed a steady and continuing progress from early obscurity, through gradually increasing professional skill and wider acceptance of responsibility, to a position where their authority inside the Commons was almost unquestioned on domestic matters and was universally respected on questions of precedent and procedure. Even as early as 1768, when Hatsell was appointed, the Clerk was already a figure of great authority in Parliament, and there has not been a Clerk since that time who has not added to the stature of the office.

Speakers, however, have varied tremendously over the centuries, and the great respect which is rightly accorded to the office today is something which is, historically speaking, of fairly recent origin. There have been good Speakers in days gone by, and there have been bad ones—some just weak and some just stupid, and these can be forgiven by history since it is not given to all men to be brilliant in high office. But there have also been corrupt Speakers who will reflect shame for ever on the Houses that elected them—and not only elected them, but often maintained them in office even when their corruption was known. Two reasons may be suggested to account for this erratic, "stop-go" development of the Speaker's status. First, the House itself was, at times venal to a degree unimaginable today. Earlier Parliaments, terrified and browbeaten by bloodthirsty and tyrannical monarchs, have betrayed their own standards simply through fear-induced weakness and inertia; others, perhaps with too *much* power rather than too little, abused their strength and became corrupt—though always, of course, "in the name of the people". It was natural that the man they selected from their own ranks to preside over their sittings should reflect the spirit of the day, and it is small wonder, looking back on some of the Parliaments that have sat in Westminster, that some strange men should have sat in the Chair.

The second factor that certain militated against a *progressive* development of the Speakership was the short tenure of office that was the general rule in earlier times. As we have seen, it was not uncommon to have two, or even three, Speakers in the course of a single year, and even an outstanding man could hardly be expected to assert his personality and establish a sound authority in the short time usually available. Indeed, it was clearly not worth his while even to consider plans for long-term improvements, since he could be quite certain of not being in office long enough to put them into effect. Thus long-term considerations became increasingly matters for the Clerk, whose appointment was for life; and as the real power of the Clerk increased in consequence, that of the Speaker became less and less and might well have resulted in reducing him to the status of a mere chairman of debates had the system continued. However, by the early eighteenth century the position was beginning to right itself when Speakers were found with influence enough over the House to last through several Parliaments in succession (Arthur Onslow, for example, occupied the Chair from 1728–1761—thirty-three years, no less!) and with a new sense of authority and responsibility they began the long ascent to the level of high eminence which the Speaker's office enjoys today.

Prior to our 1833 dividing-line the Speaker could hardly be described as having a "Department" in the machinery of the House, certainly not in the sense of the executive offices for which he is now responsible. He had, of necessity, one or two personal assistants to help with the day-to-day running of his own office, but it was not until towards the middle of the century that "the Speaker's Department" began to assume real importance outside the Chamber. After 1833, as will be seen, its growth was rapid.

Part Two

The 1833 Committee (Findings)

CHAPTER 5

The Clerk of the House

It would be inaccurate to say that the findings of the Select Committee on the Establishment of the House of Commons came as a complete surprise to Members—it had, after all, only been set up because of the House's own desire to remedy a situation generally acknowledged to be both unsatisfactory and undesirable—but when the evidence was sifted and committed to cold print it certainly created a stir. The Committee, under the chairmanship of Josiah Guest, was a strong one, and their searching examination of the witnesses threw the spotlight of enquiry into some strange and shadowy corners of the House's domestic machinery.

On the 19th March 1833 the House ordered:
"That a Select Committee be appointed to take into consideration the Fees, Salaries and Emoluments received by the Officers and Public Servants of the House of Commons, and the Fees, Charges and Expenses of passing Bills through Parliament, and to report their Opinion thereon to the House. . . ."

The Committee selected consisted of twenty-nine Members, with power to "send for Persons, Papers and Records".

With a weak Committee, or a disinterested one, these terms of reference were permissive enough to allow the production of an inconclusive and meaningless Report; but the Guest Committee was neither weak nor disinterested, and the Report which they eventually published on the 12th August following was exhaustive. It is fair to say that modern practice in the Commons still follows, in general, the recommendations of this Committee, whose thoughtful proposals have survived successfully through over 130 years of cataclysmic change, and that what alterations *may* have been made have been alterations of degree rather than of kind.

The complete reorganisation of the Commons machinery, of course, was not accomplished overnight. No less than four Committees reported before the job was finished, but since those of 1834, 1835 and 1836 were largely devoted to ensuring that the requirements of the parent Committee were actually being met (some of them most certainly were not!) and tidying up the loose ends, it is the 1833 Committee which must be given chief credit for the re-shaping of the Commons' internal economy.

The background against which the Committee sat is an astonishing one. Whole families, it seemed, could occupy the top appointments in the Commons and hold on to them tenaciously for years on end; officers with mere token salaries and no private income appeared to lead the lives of wealthy aristocrats; with only a negligible outlay by the Treasury, fortunes were made among the Parliamentary staff. Small wonder, then, that there was irritation among Members and other users of the Commons' facilities, for it was from their pockets that the money came to swell the private fortunes of the Commons' officers. Yet, contradictory though it may seem, while Members of Parliament and a large section of the public were certainly being mulcted unmercifully in their dealings with their servants in the Commons, it was not because of any dishonesty—or even undue avarice—on the part of the latter. It was because of the system—or rather the chaotic *lack* of system—under which the machinery of the Commons had evolved over the centuries, and the 1833 Committee went out of its way to acknowledge this fact (and it is an important one) in their Report:

> "The Committee deem it an act of justice to the Clerk and Officers, to express the gratification they have felt in witnessing the open and candid manner in which their enquiries have been met; and if in the course of this Report they have appeared to reflect upon any of the Emoluments now derived, as it appears to the Committee, from improper sources, and in improper modes, they desire to be considered as having disapproved of the system, not of the conduct of individuals, who, as they are aware, succeeded to Offices in which the same line of conduct had long been pursued. . . ."

The "improper sources and improper modes" referred to must be looked at and their origins understood if we are to appreciate fully the Committee's impact on the Commons machinery, and to do so properly means going back a very long way into the history of Parliament. The abuses which the Committee set out to rectify had roots four centuries deep and their practice had become hallowed by time and tradition.

It will be remembered that when the first "Under-Clerk to the Parliaments" was appointed by letters patent in the fourteenth century he was granted a yearly allowance of £10 from the Treasury; but that was not to be the whole of his income, and it was not intended to be. His letters patent went on to say that he should also have "all rewards, dues, rights, profits, commodities, advantages and emoluments whatsoever to the said office ... appertaining", and it was from these additional items that he made his living. They came under a variety of heads, and though many of them would be frowned on today it should not be forgotten that every action the Clerk did to make money, and every charge he raised, was done only under the authority of the House and at their express command. All the officers of Parliament, no matter how illustrious, are the servants of their House and always have been, and not even the authoritarian Clerks of past ages could start fund-raising schemes on their own initiative. The fact that things began to get out of hand as the centuries went by can hardly be blamed on the officers themselves who were, after all, merely human, with families to support and a living to make.

The Clerks were not *always* financially enviable, at least as far as their Commons incomes were concerned, principally because the earlier ones were generally Clerks in Chancery who took on the Parliamentary work as an extra to their real employment and never saw it as anything resembling an actual career. Also, since they used their own office staffs for the clerical work involved in the appointment, the Treasury was never called upon to provide salaries, and the status of the public servants in the Commons long remained insignificant. When the Clerks *did* begin to become more professional—in the sense that they visualised a career at the Table, and appointed officers to supervise the developing branches of the Parliamentary machinery under their own control—they fell on bad times. Towards the end of the 1500s the Clerk's financial position became actually critical and he was only kept in office through the generosity of the Members of the House, who passed the hat round annually on behalf of their principal officers. From the famous D'Ewes Journal we learn that a collection of twelve pence a head in 1601 netted the Clerk about £25; by 1604, according to the Commons Journal, the collection had become customary and had increased to five shillings a head from every knight and half-a-crown from every burgess. By 1625 the sum had grown to £1 per Member, and the Clerk received £30; his son (who had probably been assisting in the Clerk's duties) was given £10 and the Serjeant at Arms £20. Two years later the "collection" was increased again by 2s. a head, and the Clerk received £100. It is plain to see from the Journal entries that this "collection" system, which began as a piece of openhearted kindliness on the part of the Members, developed into a seemingly permanent feature of life in Parliament and no one would be surprised if Members began, at length, to resent it. Compulsory charity is without virtue to all of us.

Fortunately for the Clerk's dignity, however, and for the eventual good of the House itself, the collection system was brought to an end by the Commonwealth Parliament under Cromwell. In 1648, while Charles was still, nominally at least, the Head of State, Parliament had appointed a Committee to look into the Clerk's remuneration, and this Committee apparently proceeded with its domestic task in spite of the worldshaking events going on around it. They reported on the 30th August 1649, and the Clerk was voted an official salary of £500 a year for life—a salary which was probably paid during the whole period of the Interregnum and was almost certainly "in lieu of fees".

Now these "fees" were a curious institution, and they provided the basis of the 1833 Committee's comment about "improper sources" though their original introduction had been brought about from very proper motives indeed. It will be remembered that the majority of the earliest legislation was based upon "petitions" from private sources, personal or corporate, outside of Parliament itself, and that the number of petitions received was very large. It must have been a great temptation to people who considered themselves aggrieved, or who were seeking favourable treatment, to take their plea straight to the fountain-head of government rather than to submit it to the lower courts whose functionings were often erratic, tardy or devious, and the Commons soon found it necessary to protect themselves from frivolous applications for legislative action. And to this end the House drew up a Table of Fees, outlining the sums applicants must necessarily pay in respect of any business brought before the House on their behalf.

There was, of course, no official "organisation" of the Commons machinery as we know it more recently, and the charges laid down in the Table of Fees were collected personally by the Clerk who used the proceeds to defray his own expenses and those of whatever assistance he was obliged to employ. As will be seen from the Table, the fees chargeable were fairly comprehensive, though it should be said here that later Tables extended them even further and raised new charges—all of them, of course, by Order of the House itself.

TABLE OF FEES PAYABLE TO THE CLERKS AND OTHER OFFICERS OF THE HOUSE

(From the Commons Journal of 31st August 1649)

	£	s	d
Of every private person taking benefit of any private act	2	0	0
Of any private person taking benefit of any proviso in any act public, or private, and being named therein	2	0	0
Of every corporation, town, company, society, several shire or place taking benefit of any private act or of any proviso, etc. (as above)	4	0	0
Of every Knight of the shire returned by certificate from the Clerk of the Crown after the first day of every session		5	0
Of every Burgess returned as above		2	6
For the entry and copy of every private order taken out by a party		6	8

	£	s	d
For every copy of the names of a private committee taken forth for the party itself		2	6
For writing copywise, 16 lines in the sheet		1	0
For ingrossing every private bill, for every press		10	0
For every one that is to be naturalised		13	4
For the Clerk's hand, for signing business		2	0
For every discharge of a prisoner committeed by this House as a delinquent		18	4
For a search in the old records before this Parliament		10	0
The under-clerks for every private bill		10	0

It would be tedious to detail the provisions of subsequent Tables, since there were many of them, but the foregoing list of the 1649 charges will suffice to show what *kind* of fees were payable.

Not unnaturally, the Clerk came off best under this system. Once it was fairly established, his income began to increase almost astronomically, and as time went by the Table of Fees was gradually extended to provide quite nice perquisites for a whole new range of officers, until, by the time the 1833 Committee carried out its probe, every officer in the House was receiving money in respect of daily business. In addition, nearly all the clerks were acting as Agents for private legislation and drawing large fees from either the promoters or the opposers of private bills. Appointments in the House were bought and sold for large sums (it will be remembered that Jeremiah Dyson paid Hardinge £6,000 in 1748 for the Clerkship when the latter decided to go into politics), and junior posts were often "farmed out" by the top officials.

The incomes of the Clerk and the two Clerks Assistant had been tentatively dealt with by Act of Parliament at the end of the eighteenth century (52 Geo. III c.11 of 1800) under which, on the expiration of Hatsell's patent (he died in 1820) all the Clerk's fees were to be paid into the newly established Fee Fund. The salary of the Clerk, to be paid by the Treasury, was set at £3,000 per annum increasing to £3,500 after five years, and his relinquished fees were to be paid into a Fee Fund and to come under the control of the Commissioners for the House of Commons Offices (first appointed under the same Act). From them, the Commissioners were empowered to authorise a variety of payments to most of the subordinate officers—the majority of whom, of course, received little or nothing in the way of official salary.

The Clerk and his officers were the first to come under the scrutiny of the Committee and John Henry Ley, the Clerk, submitted a written statement about his salary.

During the nine years prior to 1800 (when the Clerk's office had last been regulated), he said, the Clerk's fees averaged between £8,000 and £10,000 a year; from 1800 to 1820, when Hatsell's patent expired, the income from fees remained consistently *over* £10,000 a year. Yet his own income, under the new arrangement, was simply £3,500 a year salary with no extras apart from the enjoyment of an official residence on the premises, which he valued at £500 per annum. "Since I have held the office," he added wistfully, "the fatigue and labour of attending to the duties of it have been nearly doubled."

But the Clerk did not come under really heavy fire in respect of his own salary—which was, after all, duly fixed by Act of Parliament, as was that of the two Clerk Assistants. Certainly, as recently as 1809 Hatsell had grossed the startling sum of £15,365 13s. 10½d. (Hatsell was nothing if not precise!) in the way of fees and other emoluments and had not regarded this as by any means extraordinary, but with his death in 1820 and the application of the Act of 1800 the bulk of these vast sums had been channelled away into the Fee Fund. So the three Clerks at the Table had already been "tamed", and their salaries of £3,500, £2,000 and £1,500 respectively were easy to see and deal with; but the rest of the Clerk's department was not quite so simple.

CHAPTER 6

The Clerk's Offices

THE FEES OFFICE

The staff of this office consisted of John E. Dorington (the Clerk of the Fees) and four assistant clerks, whose duties have already been outlined in an earlier chapter (see p. 59); their incomes presented a veritable maze to the Committee, coming as they did from such a variety of sources.

Dorington himself occupied a position that really amounted to that of Parliamentary Agent for Treasury business (i.e. Government legislation) passing through the House, and for this he was paid a flat salary of £1,100 a year from the Treasury. He received, in addition, £35 a year in lieu of stationery ("but I cannot tell in lieu of, or for, what," he said when giving evidence); forty guineas and twenty-five guineas from the War Office and Admiralty respectively for supervising the passage of the annual Mutiny Acts: and he acted as agent for Members who introduced public bills, charging the clerical costs to the Treasury at 3s. an hour. This, he explained, is what he paid to his clerks for copying, ingrossing, etc., and contained no element of profit to himself.

Treasury business was an income item that increased steadily over the years. The account rendered to the Treasury by the Clerk of the Fees in 1777 was £190 7s. 3d.; forty years later, in 1817, it was no less than £1,365 18s. 3d. and obviously still rising.

Dorington had one more "official" source of revenue—his charges for collecting the fees on private bills (one is almost apt to forget that his appointment *was*, after all, as "Clerk of the

Fees"!) Dorington was entitled to charge for himself 10s. on every fee collected in respect of a private bill or petition, and to double or treble this charge according to the number of interests involved in the legislation. Thus, for example, a single individual might present a petition for his own naturalisation—and the charge raised by Dorington (over and above the normal Parliamentary fees, of course) would be ten shillings. If two parties were involved, as might be the case where adjacent counties sought authority to construct a railway-line the charge would be double, ten shillings each. But if these two counties wanted to build not only a railway, but a bridge to carry it and a canal to run alongside the charge would be £3. Whether or not a multiple charge should be raised was Dorington's own decision, though he could be appealed against to the Speaker in cases of dispute.

So here was the Clerk of the Fees, spending only a few hours a week on the work of the Fees Office, but making quite a nice income "on the side" as it were, looking after Treasury business in Parliament and drawing his salary from that outside source —1832 it amounted to £1,388 5s. 0d. And this was by far the least of his revenue! John Dorington had followed his father into the lucrative business of Private Bill Agency, and in partnership with his brother and two of his own clerks (Arthur Jones and George Ellicomb) ran the largest and most profitable agency then operating. In 1832 the firm of Dorington and Jones handled no less than thirty-four private bills and petitions in Parliament (there is no record of how many they had which did not reach the stage of formal presentation) and their income in respect of these is anybody's guess.

It cannot be too often emphasised, however, that Dorington was doing nothing wrong or dishonourable in all this. The practice had been sanctioned for generations and its origins lost in time; all the fees he charged were only charged under the authority of Parliament itself, and it was only the *size* of the operation which, increasing almost unnoticed, had got out of hand. The Clerk, Ley, in fact asserted to the Committee that in his opinion it should continue unchanged, as best serving the interests of the House.

Of Dorington's four assistants, George Dyson received a salary of £50. He was also paid the following from the Fee Fund: £200 for preparing business and order books for the Table of the House; £100 for compiling proceedings of Committees of the Whole House for the fair copy of the Minute Book and arranging and transcribing amendments in Committee Bills; £100 for arranging and transcribing Reports from Committees of the Whole House; £50 special allowance "on account of the great length of the Session"; ten guineas for making out a list for Committees on Private Business. He received £171 12s. 0d. for business done for the Treasury and Members and £50 for compiling and examining the business of Committees of the Whole House to be entered in the Journal. A total of £732 2s. 0d.

This hotch-potch of payments is typical of the way the three other clerks' incomes were made up, and it would be tedious to itemise them here—sufficient to say that Arthur Jones made £447 18s. 0d., Henry Ley £268 7s. 6d., and George Ellicombe £263 11s. 1d. in 1852 in the way of official payments. But once again, their revenue from private business was not disclosed; it was not, of course, really relevant to the enquiry.

THE JOURNAL OFFICE

John Bull, Clerk of the Journals and Papers, came under very close scrutiny from the Committee. They were interested, first of all, in the cost of printing for the House (i.e. of the Journal, Votes and papers) and the Journal Office was the obvious place to look for answers in this connection. Secondly, the Committee wanted to know more about the comparatively high salaries quoted by Bull and his seven clerks in their written submissions.

Bull's own salary came from a wide variety of sources, but since they were all fixed regular sums they were easy to follow. His £1,662 6s. 4d. was made up as follows: (a) £1,000 paid by the Commissioners out of the £4,300 voted by Parliament in lieu of copy money. (In the days before papers were *printed* the Clerk had allowed members of his staff to copy reports, bills, etc., for Members and the public at a regular fee. Since 1800, copy money had brought in something like £6,000 a year and as the number of Parliamentary papers was increasing annually it had become clear to Hatsell and his deputy, Ley, that the income from that source was going to reach unmanageable proportions. The problem was eventually solved in 1807 by doing away with copy-money altogether and substituting a fixed annual sum of £4,300 from the Treasury in lieu, to be divided proportionally among those officers who prepared the papers for printing.) (*b*) £400 sessional allowance from the Treasury; (*c*) £201 for super-intending the production and delivery of the Journals; and (*d*) £61 6s. 4d., being one-quarter share of the total fees received from Members and the public in respect of certain copying work still performed for special occasions.

The seven clerks, whose incomes ranged from £1,081 0s. 11d. to £154 8s. 10d. and whose Treasury salaries varied from only £100 to £10, made up the balance by doing an enormous variety of odd jobs connected with the production of the Journal, the Vote, and Sessional papers, and they had the disadvantage of being paid only for actual work done—i.e. they were on piece rates. If one of them should be absent through illness he got no pay; and if, as was sometimes the case, a man's health could not stand the strain imposed by long nights on duty, he lost his night allowance (which ranged from £60–£140).

Ley defended this system. To introduce fixed salaries, he told the Committee, would necessitate the introduction of fixed hours —and that would mean the employment of three extra clerks to cover the duty (!). Bull agreed with Ley. His clerks, he said, "work extremely hard, much harder than I think they ought, but they know that if they do the business they will get paid for it; they sometimes work all night". They had to, poor devils. Bull's previous first assistant, Dickinson, had died under the strain at the age of forty-three, having been unable to heed his doctor's advice; and Bull himself, when principal assistant, found himself averaging a mere four hours a night in his bed. Speaking of his present staff, he said, "I have known them come here (i.e. to the House) at five o'clock in the morning; in fact they almost live here, and it very often happens that they do not get a walk for relaxation for a whole week together". But hard as the life might be, Bull certainly preferred it to being put on a fixed salary— which, he shrewdly judged, was likely to offer a much smaller income than the one he presently enjoyed.

Most of the clerks had, in addition, the usual interests in the promotion of private legislation.

THE COMMITTEE OFFICE

The officers of this department, who were, of course, the cream of the establishment in the professional sense, reflected their status in their incomes, most of which topped £1,000 a year in addition to private enterprise extras from private business. It will be remembered that the four senior posts in this office had been those of "clerks without doors' and that they had become, in time, simple sinecures to provide "pensions" for clerks who became too old for active employment, the actual work of the office being done by the four deputies. In 1833 only three principal clerks remained on the establishment, the previous vacancy (occuring in 1830) not having been filled by Ley as he wanted to use the money for something else. (He used part of it, in fact, to "pension off" a certain David Jones, an elderly ingrossing clerk who would have succeeded to the sinecure post under normal circumstances, but who had become so inefficient through age and ill-health that he no longer justified promotion. The rest of the money was put aside and earmarked towards retirements pensions for other deserving cases that must certainly occur from time to time.) Of the three Principals, only W. G. Rose was actually effective; the other two, Stracey and Gunwell being sinecurists.

The four "deputies", of course, were still in existence, though they had now become simply Committee Clerks, while the four junior Clerks—who had been first appointed around the 1820's—had become recognised as established officers under the title of Clerks in the Committee Clerk's Office.

The active Principal, William Grant Rose, though described before the Committee as simply "one of the principal Committee Clerks" was in fact running the office single-handed, and since his evidence was so informative, I propose to include a good deal of it. He outlined his duties in reply to Question 443.

A : I am in daily attendance from half past ten in the morning till five in the evening, and I generally attend at night to see that some of the Committee Clerks are present to do the duties of the office; and in case a Clerk is wanted I attend Committees; but my principal duty is to see the Clerks are there, and also to check all the accounts, both public and private, and keep the accounts of the office. I also receive all the money for the office. It was understood when I was appointed a principal Committee Clerk, that I should be placed at the head of the Committee Clerks' Office, it being at that time the only office in the House that had not a principal; the consequence of which was, every gentleman in the office was his own master, and left the office whenever he thought proper, without making application to anyone.

Q 454 : Do not the persons who are Clerks actually attending the Committees receive (only) one-third of the Committee fees, and the principals receive the other two-thirds?

A : Yes, it was always so; those offices were considered as a remuneration for past services; when I was a Deputy Clerk I used to receive a third; and I was obliged to pay all the expenses, if I had a person to assist me, out of my third; the Deputy Clerks (now called Committee Clerks) used also to receive for the Public Committees, with which the principal Committee Clerks had nothing to do, and there are certain gratuities given to the deputies.

Q 455 : Have the Public any interest in any part of the money received by you?

A : No; it is divided among the clerks of the office.

Q 456 : It is not out of the Fee Fund?

A : No.

Rose went on to say that he was in complete charge of the staff of the office, the allocation of duties, maintenance of discipline and the proper sharing of fees amongst them.

Q 464 : Are you at all cognizant of the fact of gratuities being received by the Committee Clerks?

A : Yes, I received them many years myself.

Q 465 : On what scale are they received?

A : At one time it was according to their own judgment; a guinea was the usual gratuity; but there were other emoluments received by the Deputy Committee Clerks, which were settled by Mr. Abbot, when Speaker, these were respecting the newspapers delivered in at the Committee when the Standing Orders required them; there was a dispute on this matter, and a complaint made by an agent to Mr. Abbot; the Committee Clerk demanding a guinea for the delivery of newspapers to

be produced before the House of Lords; Mr. Abbot was of
opinion that they ought not to deliver them up without their
guinea, or that they might retain them and produce them in
the House of Lords; therefore I do not consider that in the
nature of a gratuity. Another guinea was also given by Agents
to the Committee Clerks for making out a special Report;
another guinea was given for making out the Report the same
day; another was given for making out a Report the last week
for receiving Reports; but two years ago the Agents for Private
Bills met together, and they agreed upon a scale of gratuities
that should be given hereafter—which I understand is now
before the Committee.

Clearly, even before the Select Committee the Parliamentary
Agents had become alarmed by what their business was costing
them in the House and had begun to take steps to protect themselves. "Gratuities", however—though reduced in size, had continued to be paid as a matter of course.

Q 466 : Those gratuities are given in order to remunerate the
working Committee Clerks for the duty performed by them in
consequence of the one-third not being sufficient?
A : No, it was never considered as such. We considered it done
for the accommodation we gave to Agents, and also as a
remuneration for the expense we were put to when we paid for
assistance out of the one-third we received.
Q 467 : Was it not your duty as Committee Clerks to give
every accommodation to the Agents?
A : No—not to attend at nine o'clock, and to sit up the best
part of the night to make out Reports, or to pay others out of
our own pockets for copying them.
Q 470 : When did the period of permitting persons to act as
agents for private business, when Committee Clerks, com-
mence?
A : Long before I can remember; I found them all acting as
such on my appointment in 1791.
Q 476 : Before the appointment of yourself as one of the
principal Committee Clerks having charge of the office (about
1827) was not the duty of the acting (i.e. *active*) Committee
Clerks well performed by themselves, without any control?
A : No, it was not.
Q 477 : *You* were one of them?
A : I was; and the greatest part of the business fell upon me;

the principal Committee Clerks never used to give themselves much trouble.

Q 492 : Are you aware that the Committee Clerks are employed in private business?

A : **Yes.**

Q 493 : Do you think that a proper arrangement?

A : I do not see that it is improper.

Certainly, there was no improper *conduct* in the system, for the people who did the work were entitled to payment for it; and since their official salary from the Treasury was a mere £50 a year, the money had to come from somewhere. Further, Ley (the Clerk) had expressly ordered that any Committee Clerk who had a personal financial interest in a bill—public or private—should on no account become involved in the Committee work connected with it, so there was no suggestion of malpractice or corruption in the fact that the Clerks were drawing money from outside interested parties. But the system itself was clearly deplorable and simply invited suspicion; also, it meant that the Clerks concerned in it had perforce to work themselves half to death to bring in a reasonable income and this was by no means beneficial to the general efficiency of the machine.

A breakdown of the income of all the Clerks in the Committee Office will show just how much each received (i.e. in 1832) and where it came from. First, the three Principals—among whom, of course were Edward Stracey, the absolute sinecurist, and S. R. Gunnell who, though still on the establishment, was for all practical purposes a sinecurist too. Stracey, who had been appointed by Hatsell in 1789 for life and who was also —nominally—the Ingrossing Clerk, drew £918 3s. 7d. as his share of office fees on private business, plus £278 8s. 6d. as Ingrossing Clerk; a total of £1,196 12s. 1d. for officially doing precisely nothing at all. He had, in addition, a full set of Parliamentary Papers (cost value about 12 guineas) but remarked that "except for the above Fees, I receive nothing; no salary, no Stationery, no House, no House Rent, nor any Emoluments or Perquisites of any nature or kind whatsoever". Poor, poor Stracey!

W. G. Rose, also appointed by Hatsell (in 1791) had come from the Journal Office to take charge of the Committee Office.

He received his salary of £50; his £918 3s. 7d. share of fees on private business; £30 from the Recognizance Office; £129 14s. 0d. from the Treasury in respect of Public Committees, less £83 10s. 0d. expenses incurred in connection with the East India Military Committee; a net figure of £1,044 7s. 7d.—plus, of course, the usual set of printed papers.

S. R. Gunnell, originally appointed by Hatsell in 1776, had become a Deputy Clerk in 1803 and had been promoted to Principal Committee Clerk by Ley in 1827—a special appointment, this, in recognition of his fifty-one years of service. His income consisted of £50 Treasury salary, £918 3s. 6d. share of Private Bill fees and £200 for acting as Parliamentary Agent to the Irish Office—total, £1,168 3s. 6d. plus a set of printed papers and Journal. But no one grudged old Gunnell his handsome income—he had spent a lifetime qualifying for it.

Thomas Beeby, Committee Clerk, had a salary of £50 (less Land Tax of £1 12s. 5d.); Treasury allowances totalling £370 9s. 11d. for attending Public Committees; £459 1s. 9d. share of fees on Private Committees; gratuities from Private Bill Agents £106 16s. 0d.; total, £984 15s. 3d., plus a set of papers.

Robert Chalmers, another Committee Clerk, had no salary at all; but fees on Private Bills brought him in £459 1s. 9d., Public Committees £257 5s. 0d., gratuities from Agents £91 7s. 0d. and a further £200 for abstracting the Poor Returns. His total was £1,007 13s. 9d., plus papers.

Both Chalmers and Beeby had been in the service of the House since 1802, having been appointed to the Journal Office by J. Ley (Senior) and transferred to the Committee Office by the present Clerk, J. H. Ley, in 1822 and 1823 respectively.

George Whittam's income was £990 3s. 6½d. (the total included £93 12s. 0d. in gratuities), and George White made £793 16s. 0d. (including gratuities of £58 16s. 0d.).

The four Junior Clerks—of whom three had been appointed in 1823 and the fourth in 1830—naturally did less well than their long-service superiors and had to take on a variety of duties to make up their incomes, but they still made a very comfortable living according to contemporary standards. Each was paid a salary of £25 a year by Ley, who—it will be remembered—had not filled up the fourth desk at the top end of the Committee

Office hierarchy so that he could apply its income for just this kind of purpose. The bulk of the remainder of their incomes came from copying, work which seemed to keep them up most of the night but which they were glad to do since it was regarded as a definite apprenticeship towards higher things later.

J. B. Rose (who was the son of W. G. Rose and who had been appointed at the age of fourteen) made £209 7s. 8d.; C. M. Gunnell £227 7s. 4d.; C. W. Pole £253 19s. 10d. and C. Frere £166 exactly. They had no sets of papers or Journals.

The Committee Office was not a pleasant place to work in. According to Rose's evidence before the 1835 Committee on Rebuilding the Houses of Parliament (i.e. after the fire of 1834) the room was a mere thirty feet long by thirteen feet wide, with a low ceiling, divided into its four "desks" by wooden partitions. Behind each "desk" a large press or cupboard encroached seriously upon the limited floor-space and into this dark, hot and stuffy corridor the Parliamentary Agents and other interested parties were packed around the respective clerks in a continual welter of worried busyness which Rose described as "very unhealthy".

Ley himself was not happy at the way the Committee Office functioned :

"The only office which is not in exactly a satisfactory state," he told the Committee (Q. 3098), "is the Committee Clerks' Office, but this arises more from the irregular manner in which the Committees conduct their business, than from the fault of the Clerks, and from the business of each Committee being perfectly distinct and separate from any other. It would be desirable that *every* Committee be attended by a Clerk, whereas now the same clerk may have to look after three Committees, sitting at the same time; the Committee Clerks being now paid for each Committee, the Principals attend as many as they can; if the salary system is adopted, the head Clerks will give as much as they can [i.e. *of the work*!] to the juniors, and relieve themselves; they will get into the old system of 'Committee Clerks and deputies', according to which ... the deputies or assistants will do the duties. If this system of salaries is adopted the Committee Clerks ought not to have any assistance but what they may pay for themselves; and instead of five Committee Clerks and five

assistants, there should be ten Committee Clerks, all capable of
attending Committees, each doing the whole business of the
respective Committees to which they may be appointed. The
private business of the Committees is well paid for, it is the public
business which is badly paid for. The whole sum now due from
Public Committees is not more than £1,300."

Perhaps Ley's own experience of going on to a fixed salary had
soured him—he must certainly have had some wistful memories
of the fortune made by his predecessor while he himself was still
the Clerk Assistant—and he certainly did all he could to keep his
subordinates on a private enterprise footing. Asked about
"gratuities", and whether it was perhaps desirable to abolish
them (Q. 3089) he replied:

"The gratuities now paid in the Committee Clerk's Office and
in the Ingrossing Office are in the nature of fees paid to the
person who actually does the business; they would be highly
objectionable if they were paid by some (Agents) and not by all,
because then they would act as expedition money in favour of
those that paid them; the Clerk attending a Committee has, in
truth, nothing to do but to take minutes of the proceedings and
see that the solicitor does his business regularly (i.e. in accordance
with the regulations): it is not his business to instruct the solicitor
how he is to do his business: at any rate, a personal fee insures
attention. The only objection to these gratuities is that they are
not exactly recognised by the House (they were not 'recognised'
in the sense that the Agent was not permitted to claim them as
legitimate expenses when his Bill came up for taxing) although
they have been paid time out of mind; instead of being abolished,
it would be better for all parties that they should be recognised,
at the same time perhaps giving the solicitor an option of not
paying them in case of incivility or inattention."

Conditions in the Committee Office, in fact, were chaotic.
Each Clerk was responsible for every aspect of the work of whatever Committees he was handing; he kept all the papers, reports,
petitions and Bills within his own "desk", received and served
the various Agents, collected his own fees from both private and
Treasury sources and kept his own accounts. The amount of
work involved was enormous, and because of this, said Ley
(Q. 3104), "Very great irregularity, even now, takes place in

respect of the printing of Reports of Committees, which are frequently presented to the House in a most imperfect state. . . ."

THE PRIVATE BILL OFFICE

As has been seen, this office was a fairly new establishment, having been created as recently as 1811 by Speaker Abbot specially to handle the affairs of Private Business, and it had worked well. The staff, all of whom were debarred from acting as Agents for private business, consisted of one Principal Clerk (Edward Johnson), two Clerks (W. Hawes and R. Gibbons) and one "extra clerk" (W. Hodgkin), all of whose excellent services to the House appear to have been very poorly rewarded. The office was self-supporting, since at its inception appropriate fees had been fixed for its services to maintain the necessary staff, but though the scale of fees had been revised in 1830 the income derived in 1832 was still pitifully small—providing, in fact, an excellent argument in support of Ley's objection to a system of fixed salaries. No matter how hard or conscientiously the men worked, and work hard they certainly did, the fees were fixed by Standing Order and their incomes were disgracefully meagre compared with those of some of their colleagues in other departments. Johnson, for example, received only £731 from fees— which Ley himself stated was a good £200 less than a man might reasonably have expected *"after thirty-three years of service"*(!). He received a further £50 from the Treasury and £10 from the Commissioners for keeping a list of progress of Private Bills— total income £791.

Johnson's assistant, Hawes, received a mere £387 from fees and his only other income was £10 a year for correcting Private Bill Lists nightly for inclusion in the Vote. Thus, after over twenty-two years of service his total income was only £397. Robert Gibbons, the Third Clerk received a total of £311 after sixteen years' service in the House—an income which, when compared with the £1,006 9s. 6d. made by the Third Clerk in the Journal Office after only ten years' service, tells its own story. The Extra Clerk, Hodgkin, had only been in the House since 1827; he received £94 7s. od. in the way of Office Fees and was

obliged to make up his income by doing extra work—£100 from
the Poor Returns Office and £10 from the Committee Office.

THE INGROSSING OFFICE

The post of Clerk of Ingrossments was held officially by the
ubiquitous Sir Edward Stracey, but the actual work was done by
three clerks under the general supervision of Samuel Gunnell
(junior), an experienced clerk with twenty-one years of service
behind him. As First Clerk, he was authorised by Ley to share
equally with the sinecurist Stracey the one shilling per press
allowed to the Office in respect of ingrossing, and in 1832 his
income from this source was £278 8s. 6d. For other copying
work he received £209 17s. 11d.; his share of gratuities was
£190 10s. od.; for drawing up Briefs on Private Bills the Agents
paid him £68 5s. od.—a total income of £748 1s. 5d. But since
this amount was generally conceded to be quite inadequate, it
was supplemented by an allowance from the Treasury (disguised
as a fee for amending and examining Public Bills on third reading) to bring his total up to £800 so that he was drawing, in
effect, what really amounted to a regular annual salary—though
not all of it from the Treasury.

In the same way the two other clerks, G. Gunnell and
W. Ginger, had regular "salaries" of £500 and £150 respectively
—though it should be remembered that these were not recognised as salaries officially and that they were made up from a
variety of small components with only a small and varying
contribution from the Treasury each year The Treasury element
in 1832 was £34 11s. od. and £11 15s. 8d. to Gunnell and
Ginger.

PRIVILEGES AND ELECTIONS

The Committee of Privileges sat very rarely and made practically
no demands on the time of the Clerk who became therefore to
all intents and purposes simply the Clerk to the Committee which
dealt with *controverted* elections. In the year following a General
Election the office was kept employed almost day and night, so
great was the press of work, and clerks had to be "borrowed"

from other offices which might be able to spare their services. Thomas Dyson, who was in charge of the office, received a Treasury salary of £100 a year, and in 1832 drew a further £115 4s. 5d. in respect of House fees—an apparently paltry income for a man who had been head of his department for over thirteen years. But Dyson was also able to charge his own set of fees on the business that went through his office, and these were heavy; as was shown in an earlier chapter, they amounted to over £2,000 in 1835, while in 1831 they were £1,759 8s. 3d. (It must be admitted, however, that in 1829 they were a mere £29 15s. od.)

Out of these fees he maintained such assistance as he considered necessary to the job, though he was allowed only one assistant officially "on the strength". This was Richard Jones, whose written return of income to the Committee was obviously compiled very tongue-in-cheek :

Amount of salary	None
Fees from the Treasury	None
From Private Bills	None
From the Fee Fund	None
Allowance of House Rent	None
Perquisites of Stationery	None
Perquisites of Printed Papers	None
Journals or other Parliamentary Papers	A set of Public Reports and Papers from the Vote Office, but not Journals.

To underline his seemingly sorry plight, a note was appended by Ley :

"There were not any Election Committees this year from the fees of which Mr. Jones is paid as Assistant to the Clerk of Elections Committees."

A thoroughly bankrupt office, it would seem, yet in addition to Jones Dyson maintained two more full-time clerks who were not on the establishment at all—Hall and Walmisley ! The fact was, of course—as has been mentioned earlier—that they were all engaged up to the eyes as Agents for private business and drew their main incomes from that source. And except for Dyson himself, they were all permitted to act as agents even in election cases providing they did not actually serve the Committee dealing with the particular petition they represented.

This brought to an end the Committee's exploration into the affairs of the Clerk and his department and uncovered a veritable jungle of moss-covered conventions among which men had spent their lives in the service of the House. Some of them, like Stracey, made five incomes without so much as setting foot in the building; others, like most of the "junior" officers, worked incredibly hard for unbelievable hours for a mere pittance, year in and year out, very often not living long enough to inherit one of the senior posts with its decent emolument. Incomes came from at least nine recognised sources:

The Treasury (by far the smallest); the Fee Fund; copy money; for work on the Journal; work on the Votes; committee fees on private bills; Private Bill Office fees; attendance on public committees; and gratuities (most of which seemed to have become compulsory on the donors!).

Apart from the Clerk and the two Clerk Assistants, there were thirty active clerks on the establishment (not counting, of course, the two sinecurists, three "extra" clerks and the Assistant to the Clerk of Elections who, though on the establishment, was paid personally by Dyson from his own fees). And it is interesting to note that in the department there were four Leys, four Gunnells, two Dysons, two Joneses and two Whites; the similarity in names *was by no means coincidental!*

CHAPTER 7

The Serjeant at Arms's Department

As was mentioned in the chapter on the Serjeant's duties, much
of the income of the various members of his staff derived from
gratuities, but when the actual figure of "gratuities" received
was produced to the Committee it shook them. (It should be
remembered, too, that the officials only included in their returns
those gratuities that could be traced—i.e. those official payments
that had become virtual *fees*; what they made in the way of
simple friendly backhanders is anybody's guess.)

The Serjeant himself, Henry Seymour, was naturally the first
to face the Committee and it must be conceded that he faced
them with considerable aplomb considering the sort of questions
that were certain to be asked. After establishing that Seymour's
doorkeepers and messengers were in receipt of a small salary
from the Treasury and that they shared in the official fees raised
under the appropriate Table, the Committee cut right into the
meat of the "gratuity" situation—and one can be sure that quite
a few private axes were brought out for grinding:

Q 1170 : There are large sums returned as gratuities and
emoluments—from what do they arise?
A : They arise entirely from presents, I suppose; a regular
present from Members to them in the course of the Session,
which is what they ask for.
Q 1180 : Are they justified in asking for that?
A : I suppose they are, because it has always been understood
so. This constitutes the principal part of their income.
Q 1181 : It appears, upon the Return you have made to the
Committee, that the sum of £6,950 11s. 4d. is received by

different parties in your department for gratuities and emoluments; is there any authority for this payment?

A: No, none whatever, I believe.

Q 1182: Are the parties who pay these emoluments at all obliged by any Order of the House, or any Act of Parliament or direction of the House, to any part of those?

A: Certainly not; all which can be said, I believe, is that they have been so paid as long or much longer than anybody about the House can remember.

When he was asked whether he knew these gratuities were being asked for by his staff, the Serjeant made the odd distinction that though they were certainly *asked* for he "found that they were not *demanded*"(!). The Committee pointed out that although the Table of Fees authorised a charge of two and a half guineas for the delivery of the Vote, Members were actually paying something like £9 a head in "tips" to people in the Serjeant's department, and this, they said, was considered by many to be highly objectionable. Almost all of the Messengers and Doorkeepers (who had until quite recently purchased their appointments from the Serjeant, for large sums) were former domestic servants, placed into the service of the House by the influence of their aristocratic employers, yet they were making regular incomes of between £600 and £800 a year, mostly from gratuities.

The First Doorkeeper, Mr. Pratt, enjoyed a salary of £12 13s. 6d. but returned a total income of £892 14s. od.—of which no less than £631 8s. 6d. came from "gratuitous emoluments". Of the Second Doorkeeper's income of £808 4s. od. the proportion of tips was £584 8s. 6d. The four Messengers, who divided all their fees and tips equally among themselves, showed incomes of £557 10s. 1d., of which £112 1s. 7d. was from fees and £350 0s. od. from gratuities. It must have been very frustrating for the less privileged servants of the Serjeant, like Benjamin Riches who "had the care of the Ventilators and Stove for warming the House", for a mere £105 per annum—no tips for *him*, imprisoned in his boiler-room. Or for the two Day Porters and two Night Watchmen, who drew a meagre £37 10s. od. from the Treasury; or for John Elliott, the Fire-lighter, and his Assistant John Cooke, whose salaries were £50 and £45 respectively. How they must have envied their more fortunate colleagues!

It was typical of the hotch-potch system then in operation that the Deputy Housekeeper, Bellamy, who drew the largest salary of all the Serjeant's officers (£15 6s. 6d.) should have shown the smallest income on his Return. His total of £641 19s. 0d. was derived from no less than ten assorted sources and his fees and gratuities amounted to a mere £327 2s. 6d. (compared to the First Doorkeeper's £631 in tips alone); and what seemed even harder on him was the fact that he paid out in "necessary wages" £212 14s. 6d., leaving only £429 4s. 6d. for himself. His duties were varied. In addition to being responsible for the cleaning and furnishing of the whole of the Commons' accommodation and the allocation of rooms for Committees and so on, he was also the collector of the Serjeant's and Housekeeper's fees, which were paid into the Fee Fund and upon which he was authorised to charge a poundage (£41 15s. 0d. in 1832). He had also complete charge of all the stationery, and though this was a fiddling and onerous task it was a valuable perquisite to have since he was allowed to sell off old stocks and made something like £40 a year from it. He earned another £30 or so a year by making up the daily "Twopenny Post" on behalf of the Post Office.

The Deputy Housekeeper's own staff comprised a cook, a kitchen-maid, four housemaids, two manservants and such casual help as he should from time to time require, some of these being "lent" to the Speaker for daily domestic chores in his residence—on repayment, of course. All in all, Bellamy was a very busy man. In fact, reading his evidence, it is difficult to imagine how the House could have functioned without him—and all for a paltry £429 4s. 6d. per annum!

But what did not appear in his Return to the Committee were his *private* sources of income—which many a Member might well have envied. Bellamy, in fact, was a rich man and could well afford to be complacent about his relatively small official income. Like his father before him (and who he had succeeded in his Commons appointment), Bellamy was a thriving wine merchant outside the House. Add to this that he also ran all the catering *inside* the House—in a day when men drank beer or wine with their meals rather than tea or coffee—and it will be seen that he was in the perfect position for making a fortune, which, in fact, he did, since he paid no rent for premises or staff, and furniture, coals and candles were provided. Neither were his prices cheap, by contemporary standards.

Q 1429 : What is the mode of charge established in the Coffee-room?

A : They are established on a Table. I believe a sandwich is one shilling; cold meat with bread, beer and cheese, 2s. 6d.; cold meat with salad and tart, 3s. 6d.; the most expensive dinner that can be had is of steaks, veal-pie, mutton-chops to any extent, with tarts, salad, pickles, beer, toasted cheese, etc.; and can never exceed 5s. 6d. and that without regard to quantity.

Q 1430 : The wine of course is extra?

A : Yes, of course, that is extra; a glass of wine and water, or negus, is 1s. 6d.; port wine and sherry at 6 shillings a bottle; claret 10 shillings; Madeira 8 shillings; and all other wines in proportion. Those wines are of the best quality that can be procured.

No doubt Bellamy can be forgiven for getting in his plug; but the fact remains that he had a large daily clientele for his wines and beers and that he did remarkably well out of it.

The last of the Serjeant's officers was the Deliverer of the Vote, whose duties and emoluments attracted very close scrutiny from the Committee. The Deliverer's task, then as now, was far from being a sinecure, since his main function was to order appropriate numbers of all Parliamentary Papers, Bills, Acts and Orders required for the Work of the Commons, to deliver them to Members and to keep a sufficient quantity always in stock so that he could produce practically any Government document on demand. He also was the sole vendor of Parliamentary papers to the public, whose demands far exceeded what he could supply, and since he had to pay for what papers he ordered—and account for his transactions—his job was tricky as well as arduous. This fact was acknowledged by both the Committee and other staff in the House, as the Serjeant himself indicated in his evidence :

Q 1206: Upon referring to the salary and duties of Mr. Paskin [the Deputy Deliverer], who was paid last year £600 ... and comparing his fees and emoluments with those of the Doorkeepers, do you think they bear any sort of proportion?

A: No, I think they do not; I think there is a great deal of responsibility attached to Mr. Mitchell's [the Deliverer] office, and that his labour is quite out of proportion; his duties are more confidential; they are quite of a different sort; they are entrusted with papers of value, and to take care of Ministers' boxes and confidential papers, which renders their situation superior to any of the others.

His duties, in fact, had had a disastrous effect on Mitchell's health, obliging him to be absent from duty for most of the preceding twelve months; the work of the office had been carried out by poor Paskin on his own—though, since Paskin was described as "a near relation" of Mitchell's, he no doubt soldiered on without bitterness. The office was self-supporting, except for the Deliverer's official salary of £14 12s. 6d., and any profits it made went to the Deliverer. Income came both from Members and the public, the delivery charge for the Vote being £2 12s. 6d. per Member (official fee), many Members giving a handsome tip in addition to the authorised charge. And although Members paid the two and a half guineas fee as a matter of course, they did not have their papers delivered to them unless they entered a specific request in the Vote Office; unclaimed papers and Votes, of which there were many, went to swell the Deliverer's sales to the public. So, too, did those papers which had been allocated to former offices and departments now defunct; in 1832 Mitchell had netted no less than £1,547 17s. od. from this source alone. Under the heading of delivery fees and gratuities he returned a further £1,956 17s. od. which, with his salary of £14 12s. 6d., brought his total income up to £3,519 6s. 6d.

Out of this sum, however, the Deliverer paid the entire expenses of his office. Paskin, who had been appointed as an ordinary clerk in the Vote Office in 1818, had been promoted to Deputy Deliverer in 1825 and with the sanction of the Serjeant had been put on a fixed salary of £600 per annum. The three

office clerks also had fixed salaries of £250, £100 and £50
respectively, and a gratuitous allowance of £200 a year was paid
to Paskin's predecessor, George Eastaff, whose health had broken
down completely after thirty years in the position of Mitchell's
assistant. (Mitchell himself, by 1833, had completed fifty years'
service in the Vote Office, and it can hardly be wondered at that
he too was having to absent himself more and more frequently
from duty because of ill-health. In fact, only a few months after
the Committee sat he retired for good, leaving the way open for
promotion to the long-suffering Paskin.)

Another expense on Mitchell's account was the payment of
the part-time Porters who actually delivered the Vote and papers
to Members who lived in London and to the various Ministries
in and around Whitehall. There were ten of these, and their
wages varied between fifteen and twenty-four shillings a week,
according to the length of their "walk", or the number of
addresses it covered. It was occasionally necessary to employ extra
men when there were a lot of papers to go out, and at these times
a horse and cart was hired to carry the bulky load to strategic
spots where the Porters could pick up their own bundles for
delivery. In all, Mitchell, estimated his total expenses at
£1,694 12s. 6d., leaving him a net profit of £1,824 14s. 0d. a
year—which, since he also owned and ran a large and profitable
coal-merchant's business in Westminster, was not bad going.
(The Report makes no mention of it, but we can guess where
the Serjeant bought the House's coal, Mitchell being the
Serjeant's appointee!)

It should be noted that while Members were obliged to pay
for the *delivery* of their Votes and papers the documents themselves were issued free, each Member being entitled to one copy
of every Parliamentary paper published. Estimating the number
to be printed was entirely Mitchell's responsibility, and if his
judgment went wrong on this it could cost him a lot of money.
The Committee asked Paskin whether, if Parliamentary papers
were offered for sale to the public at a fair profit over the printing
cost, he thought many sets might be sold? Paskin's cautious reply,
"I should think there might"—on the right lines though it was—
scarcely anticipated the present position, when all Parliamentary

papers are available for sale to the public by the Stationery Office and have proved to be a considerable source of revenue. In modern times, too, there is even a Sale Office in the House itself where Members may buy additional copies of papers and bills and Parliamentary Agents and others can buy both Parliamentary and non-Parliamentary papers.

CHAPTER 8

The Speaker and His Officers

By Act of Parliament, Mr. Speaker's salary had been fixed in
1790 at £6,000 a year "for the better support of the Dignity of
the Speaker of the House of Commons", since previously to that
time his income—averaged over a ten-year period had amounted
to a mere £3,000 per annum. He had, however, one or two
unique perquisites of office, as John Rickman testified when he
appeared before the Committee in place of Edward Phillips, the
then Speaker's Secretary who was absent through illness:

Q 1818 : You are Clerk Assistant?
A : I am.
Q 1819 : You filled the office of Speaker's Secretary for some
time, did you not?
A : Thirteen years.
Q 1820 : What is the sum allowed to the Speaker for his
outfit of plate?
A : About £1,400 in lieu of 4,000 ounces of plate, calculated
according to the current price of silver.
Q 1821 : How frequently is that given?
A : On every election of a Speaker.
Q 1822 : If he continues as Speaker, (i.e. if re-elected by a new
Parliament) the allowance is repeated?
A : Yes, according to the value of this plate; it is called White
Plate (not gilt) in the language of our ancestors.
Q 1823 : However short the Parliament, he gets the allow-
ance?
A : Yes.
Q 1824 : What proportion does it amount to of the plate
required by the Speaker for State Dinners?
A : About a fourth part; less, at present.

In addition to his salary and Plate Allowance, the Speaker had also an Outfit allowance of £1,000 payable every time he was elected and was provided with an official residence all found with coals and candles, and even though the post was a full-time one which left no opportunities for outside ventures no one could say it was badly paid. Speakers, in fact, were much better off in 1832 than they are even today.

At the time of the enquiry the Speaker's Department, if such it could be called, was insignificant, consisting simply of the Speaker's Secretary and the Speaker's Chaplain.

Some interesting evidence was given about the duties of the Speaker's Secretary by the invaluable John Rickman, the sick Phillips having apparently died since submitting his written Return of Income in April. (In it he showed a total income of £993 14s. 4d. made up of Fees, an allowance of £200 in lieu of house, a stationery allowance of £6 6s. 0d. paid by the Speaker himself and £250 from the Fee Fund for acting as Secretary to the Commissioners for regulating the Offices of the House of Commons.) Rickman, it appeared, had been much less well-off during his tenure of the office:

Q 1835: What was the average income of the Speaker's Secretary during the year you held that office?

A: It averaged at £550 a year.

Q 1836: What proportion of your time did that occupy?

A: During an election year, and especially in the first three months of that year, it occupied the whole time; perpetual attention being necessary on account of the recognizances and trials of Election Petitions. At other times the duty of the Secretary is at the discretion of the Speaker; it always occupies two or three hours in the beginning of the morning; after that the Speaker's Secretary is employed as the Speaker directs, till he attends the Speaker to the House. The miscellaneous duty of the Speaker's Secretary is not inconsiderable, the Speaker frequently desiring him to make investigations in the Journals, the Statute Book, and sometimes in general history, of which on some occasions the Speaker has need of more authentic knowledge than any other person.

Q 1837: It appears that the fees of the Speaker's Secretary

arise in a great measure from Election Petitions; of what nature are those fees?

A : The Secretary gets ten shillings fee on every postponement of Election Petition when the day of Ballot is altered; in fact, on every occasion when the Speaker's signature is necessary to a document prepared by his Secretary.

Q 1838 : What has he to do with the summons of the witness?

A : Before the Election Committee is actually appointed, the Chairman cannot summon a witness, because he does not exist; wherefore the House gives a power to the Speaker to send for persons, papers and records, in preparation for the trial of the Election Petition.

Q 1839 : Does he receive ten shillings for every witness summoned?

A : Yes, if in a separate summons.

Q 1840 : Does he write separate warrants?

A : Yes, he does at present; it was not so when I was Secretary, but I have understood that in consequence of some unpleasant disputes in summoning witnesses, that the summonses are all now written for a single witness.

Q 1841 : When you issued a summons for several witnesses, was ten shillings paid for every witness?

A : A scale was then in use by which four witnesses were considered to be the number that might be included in one warrant without increase of charge.

Q 1843 : You have stated, that when you was [sic] Secretary your emoluments amounted to £550 a year; had you not, in addition to that, an official residence?

A : Yes.

Q1844 : Did it include the £400 salary?

A : What you allude to did not exist in my time.

Q 1848 : The principal augmentation has been in the greater number of Election Petitions, has it not?

A : No, the augmentation of the office is virtually about £200 a year, in making good £400 a year from fees on Private Bills. I am not aware that Election Petitions have increased in number since I held the office.

After a few more questions, the Committee turned its attention to the Vote and the Journal—it will be remembered that Rickman had been the principal architect of the new style of Vote:

Q 1854: The Committee have before them the Vote of 30th April last and also the Journal of the same date; it is observed that the proceedings in respect of the Linlithgow and Salisbury Elections take in the Vote ten lines, and in the Journal forty-four lines; do not the proceedings in the Vote give as much information as the other in forty lines, with respect to the matter?

A: The difference arises from some parts that are essential, and some parts that are not so; one fourth, perhaps, may be a matter of form, but the rest is essential, because it contains a fuller description of the Petitions and of the proceedings which take place in the Ballot. The first difference is that the Journal states that "The Serjeant at Arms was sent with the Mace to the Places adjacent, to require the attendance of the Members on the business of the House"; that is not otherwise essential than as a matter of narrative. That "the Order of the Day for taking into consideration the Petition complaining of an undue Election for Linlithgow was read"; this must be inserted, to dispose of the Order of the Day. Then that "the names of the Members were drawn in the usual manner"; and there is a Note, that "In the course of the drawing of the names of the Members, some Members were excused as being above sixty years of age, or as having served on previous Election Committees". Such particulars are inserted, *mutatis mutandis*, to show that we conform to the Act of Parliament.

Q 1855: Do you consider that as important?

A: Yes, to prove that the Ballot was conducted conformably to Act of Parliament.

Q 1856: Could not the Votes, without loss of time, be put into the same form as the Journal?

A: There would be no consistent narrative of proceedings. It is essential, in the Votes, that everything should be entered, or rather notified, as briefly as possible; and it is essential that the Journal should be kept according to form. Nor does it cost merely time, a moment of thought to transform the Vote into the Journal; while it is evident that if the Vote were lengthened, it could not be printed off and delivered to Members the next morning.

It was Rickman, too, who answered the Committee's questions about the Speaker's Chaplain. Every sitting of Parliament is opened by Prayers, and in the earliest days these were read by the Clerk; but in 1597 a "preacher" was appointed to attend daily to read the prayers. This move seems to have been resented by the then Clerk, Fulk Onslow, for a dry note in the Journal for 23rd March 1603 records that the prayers were read that day by the Clerk of the House *"to whose place the service anciently appertains"*. But the change having been made, stayed; and in the first Parliament of the Restoration a regular cleric was appointed with the title of Speaker's Chaplain. John Rickman described how the Chaplains were rewarded:

Q 1827: How is the Chaplain of the House remunerated?
A: The Chaplain of the House is remunerated by means of an Address of the House of Commons at the end of the Session, requesting His Majesty to confer some dignity in the Church on the Chaplain of the House of Commons.
Q 1828: Is that done?
A: Yes; and in order to guard against the contingency of Parliament being dissolved during the Recess, they annually vote the Address, but it is effectual only once for each Chaplain.
Q 1829: How long is it expected the Chaplain will serve?
A: Three years; or in other words, there are two Chaplains for a Parliament, if it endures more than three years; the usual consequence of the address is a Stall at Westminster, at Canterbury, at Windsor, or at Christchurch, Oxford.
Q 1830: Has he a salary for his services?
A: He has not; eight guineas a year are given as an allowance in lieu of stationery, and he has no other perquisites; this he receives from the Speaker, out of the Speaker's allowance, in lieu of stationery.
Q 1831: Are those four stalls reserved expressly for the Chaplain?
A: No; whichever happens to become vacant is given to him.
Q 1833: The recommendation of the House is always attended to?
A: Yes; I have traced it back as far as the reign of King William.
Q 1834: They remain on the list until there is a vacancy?
A: Yes.

In short, the Chaplain's position in the House was scarcely a dignified one. The job, unpaid, was necessarily done by some low-ranking cleric seeking advancement and merely served as a kind of apprenticeship for a better appointment—and the promotion itself was made as a matter of course whether or not the Chaplain was *worth* a stall at Westminster, etc. The system served the best interests of neither the House or the Church, and the Committee did not like it.

CHAPTER 9

The Committee's Recommendations

In seeking to bring order into the chaotic financial organisation of the Commons the Committee were faced with a double problem, and the solution of neither aspect was easy to find. First, they had to invent an entirely new pay structure, and for this there were no precedents. The structure had to be not only new; it had to be economical (for economy was, after all, one of the Committee's principal considerations), it had to be workable in practice, and it had to be sufficiently attractive to ensure a continuity of recruitment. Above all, a system had to be found that could be kept closely under the control of Parliament itself and not left merely to the private enterprise initiative of the officers concerned and the goodwill and long-suffering patience of those who hitherto had been required to put their hands continually into their pockets.

The other aspect of the problem was the position of the officers actually in service at the time of the change, and how they would react to it—the Committee were well aware that a mass desertion by the skilled and experienced clerks of the Commons would hamstring the whole work of government. They must have considered the comparatively easier methods of dating their proposed changes to take effect only on the retirement of the present office-holders, as had been done earlier in the case of Hatsell the Clerk, and so avoiding both unpleasantness and hardship as well as the possibility of large-scale defections, but they decided instead upon the bolder way. Indeed, the Committee's eventual recommendations might reasonably be described as the first outright "nationalisation" proposals in our history.

In the preamble to their Report the Committee said: "In

recommending to the House such arrangements and alterations in the duties and emoluments of its Officers, as upon attentive consideration of the subject referred to them they deem consistent with a due regard to a judicious economy of the Public Funds, they feel it at the same time of great importance that ample remuneration should be made to those officers, who from the arduous and responsible duties required of them, are entitled to the liberal consideration of Parliament."

Just how liberal that consideration turned out to be, will be seen.

The Committee went on to indicate its line of thinking: "The Official Establishment of the House of Commons is divided into two extensive Departments, that of the Under Clerk of the Parliaments, or, as he is usually called, the Clerk of the House of Commons, with the various Clerks of the different Offices appointed and regulated by him; and that of the Serjeant at Arms attending the House of Commons, with the Officers in the Vote Office, the Housekeeper, Doorkeeper, Messengers and some inferior Officers, who receive thir appointments from him, and are under his direction.

"In the year 1800 the attention of the House appears to have been directed to the large amount of the Fees and Emoluments of the Clerk attending the House, and an Act was passed to regulate the Salaries of the Clerk, the Clerk Assistant, and the Serjeant at Arms. By this Act, all the Fees of those officers were directed to be paid into one general Fee Fund, after the expiration of the then existing interests, to be under the management of the Speaker, the Chancellor of the Exchequer and other Commissioners named in the Act, who were directed to pay certain fixed salaries to those officers. This Act was repealed by the 52 Geo. III (1812) and re-enacted with additional provisions; which last mentioned Act has been fully in operation since the expiration of Mr. Hatsell's Patent in the year 1821.

"The emoluments of the Clerks in the different Offices under the Chief Clerk arise from various sources, and they are paid in a variety of modes, by Salaries from the Fee Fund and the Treasury, by payments for labour and for different services, and by Fees and Gratuities, rendering the income of each Clerk frequently dependent upon a variety of causes, and in general occasioning its amount, especially among the Junior Clerks, to vary according to the quantity of business executed by them. The present system is strongly supported by many of the Senior Clerks, as one best adapted to the peculiar nature of the business of the House of Commons; but, upon mature consideration, the Committee are of opinion, that as a general rule, fixed Salaries, dependent in amount upon the nature and importance of the services to be performed, would, as is the case in all the other Public Departments of the State, be the best mode of remuneration. They therefore recommend that the several payments heretofore made from the Treasury, should cease; that all the Fees now paid in different Offices should be carried to the general Fee Fund; that all the Expenses of the Establishment should be payable from that Fund; and that the Sum which may annually become necessary to make up the deficiency in it, should be provided for by a Vote of the House, in the same manner as is now the case in the Establishment of the Treasury, and several other Public Departments."

THE CLERK

As recently as the early part of the century the Clerk's emoluments from all sources had amounted to something like £15,000 per annum, but they had been severely cut in 1812. The Committee decided, however, that further retrenchment was desirable. In their own words:

". . . The Chief Clerk appoints the two Clerks who officiate at the Table, all the Clerks in the different Offices, the Librarian, and the Short-hand Writer; and he controls and regulates the whole of this extensive Department.

"By the Act of 52 Geo. III [i.e. of 1812] his salary was fixed at £3,500 per annum, after five years service; and he has also an official residence immediately adjoining to the House of Commons. The Committee are well aware of the importance of this office, and the necessity of its being filled by a person conversant with the constitutional law and practice of Parliament; but, having taken into their consideration the salaries assigned to other Officers in the State, of equal importance, they are of the opinion that the Salary of the Clerk of the House of Commons should be fixed at £2,000 per annum, together with an official residence, which appears to be necessary for this Office."

This must have come as a nasty shock to Ley; at a time when the duties of his offices were becoming steadily more complicated and onerous, his salary was almost halved! So much for the "liberal consideration of Parliament" as it affected its principal servants, and the fierce axe of the Committee bit no less sharply into the affairs of the subordinate Officers.

THE CLERK ASSISTANT

"His salary was by the Act established at £2,500 after five years service, and he has also an official residence. The Committee Recommend that the salary of the Clerk Assistant should be fixed at £1,500 per annum; and think that no official residence is necessary to be attached to the office."

The salary of the Second Clerk Assistant was reduced from £2,000 to £1,000 per annum, the clerkship to the Committee of Privileges was abolished, and the Clerk of Elections was given firm notice that he, too, must shortly disappear.

THE PUBLIC BILL AND FEE OFFICE

"The Offices of Agent to the Treasury for the management of Revenue and other Public Bills, and the Clerk of the Fees," said the Commitee, "have long been held by the same individual, and The Committee recommend that course still to be pursued, as a means of forming an equally beneficial and a more economical arrangement than if the two offices were separated. The duties to be performed in the Public Bill and Fee Office will be twofold:

"First, the conduct and management of the Treasury and Revenue Bills, and of those of the other Public Departments, and of all Public Bills brought in by individual Members of the House.

"Second, the transaction of the business in regard to Fees, and other duties of the Table, etc., now carried on in it,"

Under the Committee's recommendations the salary of the
Principal should be established at £1,000 per annum, a loss to
him of at least £388. His four clerks' incomes were docked by
£132, £47, £68 and £113 a year respectively to regular salaries
of £600, £400, £200 and £100, cuts which became even more
painful because of their inequality.

The Committee further proposed that the *mode* of charging
Fees should be altered and that whereas in the past the Fee on
each Bill, etc., had been calculated according to the number of
interests involved, henceforth the charges should be related to
the merits and importance of the measure itself. Also, they said,
the old system of paying the Fees piecemeal into the various
Offices should cease, and that they should henceforward be paid
directly to the Clerk of the Fees, who would also become the Paymaster and responsible for all salaries. He should be required to
deposit a security of £2,000 and to maintain a complete account
of all the Fee Fund transactions, to be certified by the Commissioners and laid before Parliament annually each February.

"For these (extra) duties," said the Committee, "the Clerk
should receive an allowance of £1 10s. 0d. per cent on the sums
received by him, so as, however, in no year to exceed £250."

This proportion was as lacking in "liberal consideration" as
what had gone before, since over the previous three years the
House Fees had averaged just over £20,000 a year, and $1\frac{1}{2}$ per
cent of that would have been £300!

THE JOURNAL OFFICE

"The fatiguing nature of the business executed in the Journal
Office," the Committee found, "requires a larger establishment
of Clerks than might otherwise appear necessary; the Committee
recommend that it should consist of:

Principal, at	£1,000 per annum
First Clerk	600 per annum
Second	
Third	
Clerks	500 per annum

Fourth
Fifth
      Clerks   300 per annum
Sixth
Seventh
      Clerks   150 per annum

The Committee do not deem an official residence to be requisite for the Principal of this Office."

In spite of the magnanimous opening to the Committee's remarks, the Journal Office suffered severely. John Bull, the Principal, already had an establishment of six clerks, but since he regularly employed an "extra clerk" (appointed by the Clerk on the authority of the Speaker) the enlargement of his staff was no more than a paper move. Moreover, both Bull and all his staff (with one exception) lost considerable slices of income under the proposals, Bull forfeiting not only £662 a year in hard cash but also his offices, store-room and apartments in Abingdon Street. The First Clerk lost £481 a year, the Second and Third just over £500, the Fourth and Fifth £190 and £142 respectively; and the extra Clerk, by coming on the establishment, suffered a pay cut of £4 8s. 10d. Only the sixth Clerk, whose salary jumped from £113 to £150 could have been in any way happy when the Recommendations were published—but since his name was Ley, perhaps his good luck might have been expected.

The Committee recommended finally—so far as the Journal Office was concerned—that the Manuscript Copy of the Journal should henceforth be discontinued, but that three copies should be printed on vellum "of a sufficiently large size to admit of any alterations which may be directed by the House".

THE COMMITTEE CLERKS

It will be remembered that this Office had begun as the office of the four Clerks-without-Doors and that its four senior appointments had degenerated into sinecures—two of which were presently occupied by W. G. Rose and his Deputy Sam Gunnell, one by the omnipresent Sir Edward Stracey, and one which was used to provide a retirement pension for an aged Clerk. These sinecures were abolished at once and *in toto* by the Committee, and one can almost hear the swish of their axe.

Following the recommendations offered in Ley's evidence, a new "desk" was established, consisting of one Committee Clerk and one Assistant, so that the Office now operated in five compartments instead of the historic four, and the salaries were slashed in the usual way. Rose himself, on a new salary of £1,000 a year, did quite well since the change cost him a mere £44, but his Clerks suffered disastrously. Sam Gunnell, the Deputy, as well as the four Committee Clerks, all showed Returns of more or less £1,000 a year; all were cut to a flat £600. The four Assistant Clerks, with incomes varying from £253 to £166, were put on a new salary of £100 each with permission to make a little extra by "copying such Papers as may be required by persons applying for them, which are to be paid for at a fair remunerating price".

Worst of all, however, from the human point of view of the staff, was the recommendation that all unofficial "fees" as well as all outright gratuities should be abolished forthwith.

THE PRIVATE BILL OFFICE

The staff of this office, one Principal and three Clerks, were of course paid from the Fees which they themselves collected and could be said to be self-supporting. Since, however, the Committee had recommended that *all* Fees should be carried direct into the Fee Fund, it became necessary to fix proper salaries for the Officers in the Private Bill Office, and the following scale was suggested:

Principal at £700 per annum (reduction of £91)
First Clerk at £350 per annum (reduction of £47)
Second Clerk at £250 per annum (reduction of £61)
Third Clerk at £150 per annum (reduction of £54)

Though these cuts themselves may appear fairly modest it must be remembered that the staff of this office were already the Cinderellas of the service and that their incomes compared very unfavourably with those of most of their colleagues of comparable status and responsibility.

THE LIBRARY

"The Committee have not thought it necessary," they said, "to direct their attention to the Establishment of the Library, as it was considered and reported upon by a Committee which reported as recently as 1832."

So the Librarian, Thomas Vardon, was left in peace to enjoy his £500 a year, and no doubt felt that he had come very well out of the purge that was engulfing everybody else around him.

THE INGROSSING OFFICE

The Clerkship of this Office, which was one of those comfortable sinecures held by Sir Edward Stracey, was abolished outright and a new establishment laid down to consist of:

> Principal at £600 per annum
> First Clerk at £350 per annum
> Extra Clerk at £150 per annum

Any ingrossing work in excess of what this staff might be expected to cope with, said the Committee, should be passed to outside stationers and paid for at standard rates.

Before leaving the Clerk's Department to report their recommendations concerning the Serjeant and his staff, the Committee had a word to say about House of Commons Officers participating in the business of private legislation:

"Having considered how far the employment of the Officers of the House in Private Parliamentary Business interferes with the efficient discharge of their official duties, the Committee are impressed with a sense of the inconvenience which may result from such employment, and strongly object to it. Feeling, however, much disinclination to interfere with the interests of Persons who, having been permitted for many years to devote their attention to private business, now derive considerable emoluments from this source, the Committee content themselves with recommending that the Clerks in the Private Bill Office, and the Committee Clerks (to whom objections to the practice in a peculiar manner apply,) be forthwith prohibited; and that every Officer hereafter to be appointed, or who is now so engaged, be prohibited from undertaking the solicitation of Private Bills, or engaging in the conduct of business before Election Committee."

This particular recommendation, though largely ignored at the time (as will be seen) nevertheless turned out to be the first peal in the death-knell on Private Bill Agency by Officers of Parliament. Of all the Committee's proposals, this one, perhaps, was more responsible than any of the others for bringing into being the highly specialised, disinterested and peculiarly *professional* service that exists in the House today, and though it caused considerable dismay at the time it is one we have cause to be grateful for.

THE DEPARTMENT OF THE SERJEANT AT ARMS

It was in this Department that some of the most spectacular cuts were suggested, and a couple of quick swishes of the axe disposed very summarily of the two senior Officers:

"The Serjeant at Arms. By the Act of the 52nd (1812) his salary was fixed at £2,500, after five years service, and an allowance of £300 per annum for a house. The Committee consider that this Officer would be sufficiently remunerated by a Salary of £1,500 per annum, without any allowance for a house.

"The salary of the Deputy Serjeant is also fixed at £800 by the Act, and an allowance of £200 for a house. The Committee recommend that a Salary of £700 per annum be paid to this Officer, without any allowance for a house."

A shrewd blow, this—and made more painful, one thinks, by the curt way it was delivered—but worse was to come.

Referring to "the Deputy Housekeeper, Messengers, Doorkeepers etc.," the Committee commented tartly:

"It will be seen by the Evidence, that a practice prevails among the Officers in the department of the Serjeant at Arms, of requesting or receiving Gratuities or Presents (see p. 139) as well from Members as from other persons. The Committee consider this practice to be in a high degree objectionable; and they therefore recommend that it should be hereafter strictly prohibited; and that the Fees properly payable in this department should be paid into the Fee Fund, from whence these Officers should be remunerated by fixed Salaries."

The income of the Deputy Housekeeper (see p. 141), Bellamy, they said, came from "so many sources, and are in some particulars so improper in principle, that the Committee propose to abolish the whole of them, and that in lieu of all Fees and Allowances made to the Deputy Housekeeper, and of all Perquisites of every description, or Gratuities or other Emoluments for use of rooms or otherwise, an annual Allowance be paid to him, out of which he is to find persons for keeping the House, Committee Rooms and Offices in proper order; such Deputy Housekeeper having apartments in the House (with coals and candles, but not furniture) for his own residence, the legal Fees being paid over to the Fee Fund."

The salary of the First Doorkeeper should be fixed at £300 a year (a decrease of £592), the Second Doorkeeper at £250 (a decrease of £558) and the four Messengers at £250 each (a loss per head of about £340 a year). The Ventilator Man, two Watchmen, two Day Porters and two Firelighters were left untouched—their salaries, anyway, were negligible, and they had no share in the gratuities.

However—"The Members' Waiting Room (i.e. the Cloakroom)," said the Committee, "is so essential to the Convenience of Members that it ought to be considered a part of the Establishment, and a responsible Person put in charge of it." They proposed :

One Superintendent at £200 per annum
One Assistant at £80 per annum
One Porter at £50 per annum

Thus, in the midst of all the economy and retrenchment a new office was created—an office which, only slightly modified, flourishes to this day.

THE VOTE OFFICE

Here the axe bit savagely indeed, and it was small wonder that the ailing Mr. Mitchell quitted the service of the House practically on the heels of the publication of the Committee's Report— though no doubt the receipts of his coal business would have perked up considerably as a result of receiving his full-time attention had he not unfortunately died towards the end of that year. The Committee had a great deal to say about the way this Office was conducted, though they were much less harsh in their attitude towards its Officers than they were towards the other members of the Serjeant's department:

"The manner in which the Officers in this Department are remunerated appears very objectionable, and extremely expensive to the Public, as a considerable proportion of the Emoluments of the principal Officer arises from the sale of Papers printed at the public expense, of which he receives a large quantity, either as perquisites of offices, as belonging to Members, or for Public Offices which have been abolished, or which do not require the Papers to which they are entitled, and which are then, by the custom of the Office, deemed to be a perquisite.

"This system has prevailed for many years, and no blame is therefore attributable to the Principal of this Office. Your Commitee, however, consider that no Public Officer should be allowed to dispose, for his own benefit, of any Papers printed at the public expense, and therefore recommend that the custom should be abolished, and that no Papers printed by the Order of the House should be allowed or delivered to any of the Clerks or Officers, except such as may be necessary for their official use.

"They also recommend that the Acts of Parliament, which have been hitherto delivered to the Messengers and Doorkeepers, with the intention of being distributed among the Members, should now be delivered from the Vote Office with the other Sessional Papers; and that the Proceedings of Public Committees, printed for the use of the Members, and Notes informing them of the days of meeting, which are now delivered each morning at a heavy expense to the Public, should be deposited in the Vote Office, and, together with any Letters placed in the Letter Office, be distributed by the Office Porters each morning with the Votes and Sessional Papers.

"To execute these duties, and to take charge of the printed Papers, an Establishment will be required of

One Principal at £600 per annum (but see p. 167)
One Assistant at £250 per annum
One Clerk at £100 per annum
One—do—at £50 per annum

"The contingent expenses of Office Porters for the delivery of the Votes and Papers should be defrayed under the control of the Serjeant at Arms (see p. 167), strict regard being paid to secure a regular and speedy delivery of the Papers, with a due regard to economy.

"It has been usual to charge each Member, for the delivery of his Sessional Papers and Votes in London, or for forwarding them by the Post when in the country, the sum of two guineas and a half each Session, it being considered that he is entitled to receive them at the House of Commons; this sum may still be received (see p. 168), and carried to the account of the Fee Fund."

The palmy days of the Vote Office, it seemed, were over, and its Principal became the poor relation of his colleagues. And the "Vote Office dinners", famous for several generations, were to grace no more the dining-rooms of the House.

THE LETTER OFFICE

It will be remembered that one of Bellamy's little extra jobs was the care of "the Twopenny Post"—a job that consisted of gathering up all the letters for posting, putting them into bags four times a day and sending them off to the General Post Office. The Committee disliked this system:

"The present arrangement made by the Post Office for the delivery of Letters, and the forwarding the same by the General and Twopenny Posts, is not only more expensive than necessary, but is also unsatisfactory.

"The Committee therefore recommend that a Person, to be appointed by the Post-Master-General, and under the usual Post-office regulations, with such deviations, however, as may be more convenient for the Members, should be in attendance during the Session, to take charge and to send and receive all Letters and Packets sent to or from the House of Commons by the General or Twopenny Post; also of all Letters which may be given to him for delivery by the Office Porters on Parliamentary business.

"An essential duty of this Officer will be to inform himself carefully of the Addresses of Members, and to give information to persons who may require it."

Thus this far-seeing Committee laid the foundations for today's system, under which a fully fledged branch Post Office staffed by officials of the Post Office itself, operates daily in the House—much to the convenience of both Members and staff.

THE SPEAKER

One might have thought that the Speaker, being an elected Member of the House—and flesh and blood of the Committee itself, so to speak—might have been spared the cut of the retrenching axe, but not a bit of it. The Committee was as impartial as it was thorough, and though the Speaker was not called to give evidence, violent hands were laid on his emoluments. The perquisites disappeared—the "£1,400 in lieu of 4,000 ounces of plate and £1,000 outfit allowance" (both payable each time he was elected) were abolished—and in their place a simple outfit allowance of £1,000, payable only upon first election, was substituted. Also, upon first election, a sum of £6,000 was to be spent on the purchase of "a Service of Plate for the use of the Speaker for the time being, which shall remain the property of the Public, and be attached to his Official Residence". And finally, though he should continue to enjoy the use of an official residence, his salary should be cut from £6,000 to £5,000 a year (at which level it was destined to remain until the mid-twentieth century).

THE SPEAKER'S SECRETARY

"The Salary and Emoluments of this Officer," said the Committee, "including the office of Secretary of the Commissioners for regulating the Offices of the House of Commons, fixed at £250, the duties of which appear to be unimportant, and including also £200 in lieu of an Official House, amounted in 1832 to £993 14s. 4d. The Committee recommend that all Fees payable to this Officer should be carried to the Fee Fund, and that the Speaker's Secretary should be allowed a salary of £500 a year for the performance of all the duties now belonging to his Offices of Secretary to the Speaker and of the Commissioners of the Fee Fund, without any official residence, or any allowance instead of it."

THE CHAPLAIN

The Committee found the practice of remunerating the Chaplain by giving him a Prebendal Stall after three years' service "highly objectionable", and recommended its discontinuance. "By this mode," they said, "appointments to high and dignified offices in the Church become dependent, not upon the possession of distinguished learning and piety, but upon the exercise, for probably a period of three years, of the moderate duties required by the Chaplain of the House of Commons." The Chaplain's services, they suggested, were worth no more than £200 a year, and so they recommended.

CONCLUSIONS

The domestic economy of the Commons staff had been found to be in a confused and sorry state indeed, and it is hardly surprising that the Committee should have directed its attention more to the pay structure than towards organisation. Organisational changes, in fact, were almost negligible in their recommendations.

In 1832, according to the Returns supplied by each Department, the whole of the services required to keep the Commons in operation were supplied by a mere handful of men—sixty-two in all. There were the Speaker with his Secretary and Chaplain; the Clerk with his two Assistants and a supporting staff of thirty-three; the Serjeant at Arms with his Deputy and a staff of twenty-one. From these, the Committee recommended the abolition of six posts—the four sinecure Principal Clerkships in the Committee Office, the Clerkship to the Committee of Privileges and the Clerkship of Ingrossment; and they proposed the creation of three new posts (all of them very minor) in the Serjeant's Department—a Principal and two Assistants, to look after the Members' Waiting Room at salaries of £200, £80 and £50 respectively together with the appointment of four new Juniors in the Committee Office at £100. These proposals would leave a total effective strength of sixty-three on the staff of the Commons.

But while the organisation itself was left reasonably intact, the incomes of its Officers were to be pruned cruelly—pruned, in fact, by a total of over £21,000. Savings in the Speaker's tiny department amounted to £1,493 14s. 1d. (allowing for the new item of £200 in respect of the Chaplain); in the Clerk's Department to over £12,000 and in the Serjeant's Department to more than £7,000 (allowing for the salaries of the new posts in each). Thus, a total expenditure (from all sources) on staff of about £51,000 per annum was to be cut by roughly 40 per cent to a mere £30,000 a year—all to be paid by the Treasury.

Surprisingly enough, the House itself did not wholeheartedly approve these proposals when the Committee at last reported in the usual way. It was felt by many Members that to cut a man's income so drastically after a lifetime of service in Parliament (many Officers, as has been seen, were to be offered less than half what they had been receiving hitherto) was hardly in accordance with that spirit of "liberal consideration" with which the Committee had identified itself in the preamble to their Report, and the resulting Act which they passed (4 and 5 Will. IV. c70) curtailed the recommendations to such an extent that they became almost nugatory in their effect.

The Act laid down that, although the House accepted all the recommendations *in principle*, no existing holder of office should suffer any reduction of salary or emolument or loss of residence —i.e. the existing state of affairs was to continue unchanged until the deaths of the present incumbents made the application of the new scales less hurtful to apply. This, of course, would have been really disastrous, adding new confusions to the old and the reformers refused to be checked. In the following year, 1834, a Committee which had been appointed originally to enquire into the payment of House Fees on Private Bills took time to have a sideways glance at the subject studied by their predecessors—and they found a state of affairs that was notably unchanged. The individual offices were still collecting their own Fees; copy-money was being paid just as it had been for generations; Committee Clerks were still being paid directly by the Treasury for work in Public Committees, and, above all, gratuities were changing hands as merrily as they had ever done.

It was in this year, 1834, that the Great Fire destroyed the Parliament buildings, but the reforming movement went forward in spite of that. 1835 and 1836 found two more Committees sitting on the same question, and between them they produced the "final solution"—final in the sense that, although their own recommendations contained little that was new, they did insist upon the proper implementation of the sound proposals of the 1833 Committee. All Officers appointed since 1833 went immediately on to the new scales of salary; older Officers were to be brought into line by 1840, and those engaged in Private Business were given the option of quitting the service of the House with compensation for loss of office (in which case they could carry on as Parliamentary Agents—a course which some adopted), or of giving up private business entirely and serving the House solely as full-time Officers, in which case suitable adjustments would be made to their salaries to make up, at least to some extent, what income they would lose from the private business field.

An interesting change was made in the status of the Vote Office, whose new Principal, Charles Paskin, earned a special word of praise from the Committee for the efficiency of his department. It will be remembered that hitherto the Vote Office had been run under the Serjeant at Arms (in his evidence before the 1835 Committee the Serjeant went on record that the Vote Office had always been "his best patronage" and that its loss would be a grievous blow to his income—a strangely incautious remark which underlined the fact that some subordinate officers not only paid cash down for their appointments but apparently continued to hand over a proportion of their incomes after appointment). The 1833 Committee had already drawn from the Serjeant the admission that "a great deal of responsibility" attached to the office of the Deliverer of the Vote and that "his labours were quite out of proportion" in comparison with the Serjeant's other officers (i.e. the Deputy Housekeeper, the Doorkeepers and the Messengers). "His duties are more confidential," the Serjeant had said. "They are of a quite different sort; they are entrusted with papers of value, and to take care of Ministers' boxes and confidential papers, which renders the situation superior to any of the other."

The new Committee, apparently, agreed completely with this appraisal, for they took the Vote Office out of the Serjeant's

Department altogether and placed it under the direct administration of the Speaker himself—a move which, in the long run, was to benefit both the Office and the quality of its service to the House. And not only did they confer this enhanced status on the fortunate Mr. Paskin; they also added a further £200 to the salary originally proposed by the 1833 Committee, making the Deliverer's income £800 a year instead of £600. The charges for actual *delivery* of the Vote, which the 1833 Committee had proposed should be paid into the Fee fund, were now completely abolished; since 1835 all Members have whatever Papers they are entitled to delivered to them—either in London or in the country—free of any charge whatever.

This time, the House endorsed its Committee's proposals, and the framework of today's organisation came into being. In 1836 another Committee dealt with claims for compensation made by Officers who felt themselves aggrieved by the 1835 proposals, and in their Report they reminded all concerned that participation in private business was to be henceforth prohibited under pain of dismissal. So private business disappeared for ever from the duties of the Commons' Clerks, and the powerful firms of Parliamentary Agents—many of them founded and carried on by Officers like Dorington, Jones, Walmisley, Dyson and Hall—moved outside the House to operate as ordinary business concerns, as most of them continue to do today. Several Committees have considered the question of Officers and their emoluments since 1836, but since none of their proposals have involved radical changes in structure it is unnecessary to study them in detail—what alterations and improvements have occurred in the interim will be seen in the account of today's structure of the Commons machinery.

Part Three

Modern Organisation

CHAPTER 10

Introduction

Though there are striking differences between the Commons' machinery of today and that of the 1833 era, there are also striking similarities, and the differences, where they exist, are more of degree than of kind. The whole organisation is, for one thing, on a vastly larger scale than a century ago, and though it is almost axiomatic to say that increasing size and complexity lead in general to greater vulnerability, greater likelihood of breakdown and decrease in efficiency, this is by no means the case in the Commons.

The reason for this can only be the greatly developed professionalism of the officers concerned in the administration of Parliament's domestic services—not only of the handful of very senior Officers of State who carry the ultimate responsibility for their Departments within the House, but of all grades and ranks down to the humblest servant. There is an *awareness*, today, that service to Parliament carries with it a satisfaction not to be found elsewhere, and although recent developments have brought most salaries up to a level where they can at last be compared with "outside" equivalents, the financial aspect is the least important. In fact, most of the Officers and officials now in service came into the House at a time when salaries were derisory, and it could never be said that they were attracted by the money.

The election of a Labour Government with a huge majority in 1945 had a variety of repercussions quite apart from the political ones. The *image* of Parliament changed dramatically overnight, and the older concept of the Commons as a rather remote and mysterious place where "they" drafted the laws to burden us disappeared. A whole young generation and a com-

pletely new section of the community felt suddenly and perhaps
for the first time, that Parliament was *their* Parliament and that
their voice had some real significance. The Commons, once
again, was seen in the "communes" sense by the people, and
public interest was aroused accordingly. The number of "tourist"
visitors, for example, increased enormously, and when the House
was sitting new Members found themselves heavily occupied in
taking round casual parties and organised groups from their
constituencies.

Parliament had "arrived" in the public's imagination, becoming patently accessible to the man in the street, and those who
worked inside its ancient walls were recognised at last as ordinary
human beings—kith and kin of those whose daily round took
them more openly beneath the public's gaze. The old mystique,
if so it could be called, evaporated, and "ordinary" people
realised that the Commons had not been run by an act of God,
but by men like themselves; men, certainly, with particular
qualifications and aptitudes, but with no more than could be
achieved by any intelligent citizen with enough sense of purpose
—and character—to benefit properly from his education.

Recruitment to the Commons staff had for a long time presented problems not unassociated with the poor rates of pay.
Salaries were not enough to live on, and perquisites had been
eliminated by the 1833 Committee and its successors. Before that
time, it will be remembered, senior Officers had been able to
make up their incomes either from the fees or by engaging in
private business, while the more junior members of the staff had
benefited hugely from the currently accepted system of fees and
"gratuities", but once the reformation had taken place to introduce merely fractional salaries where once had been richness, the
problem of recruitment became acute. Men had to live, after all,
and pay their rents and feed their wives and children, no matter
how dedicated to the service of an ideal, and what the Commons
offered in the way of pay was generally ludicrous.

In the second half of the nineteenth century, therefore, a
period ensued when nepotism became even more rife than it had
been before the reoganisation. Once again, there was nothing
dishonourable about this; it was simply the inevitable consequence of the dilemma in which the authorities of the House

found themselves. On the one hand, men were required who possessed an adequate standard of education and demonstrable integrity, with old enough heads on their shoulders to justify the assumption that they possessed also common sense and a certain amount of experience among their fellow-men. Such qualities, then as now, were essential in any Clerk in the House's service. But on the other hand, thanks to the economies of the 1833, 1834 and 1835 Committees, there was that meagre salary-scale which was—to say the least of it—far from tempting.

What ambitious young man of twenty-four or twenty-five, with a sound character and an engaging personality and a degree from a recognised University, would be likely to offer himself for a Commons' Clerkship, when by becoming, say, a Parliamentary Agent he could earn a salary several times greater than those in the House? Also, what young man with all these qualities was still unemployed at the age of twenty-four or five?

Once again, the problem was only solved by the subsidisation of the official salaries, though this time the subsidy came from the pockets of the appointees themselves—or from their families. For a time, then, recruits were to be found only among the ranks of those who could *afford* to accept a House appointment —"younger sons" of wealthy families, perhaps, or retired Service officers in enjoyment of a pension—and while this period certainly served to raise the social "tone" of the Commons Officers, it could not be said to be in the real best interests of the service as a profession. And until the service of the House *became* professional—as opposed to the pre-1833 practice of using a Commons appointment simply as a means of coming to close quarters with the "pickings" that were then generally available— it could never be a really good and efficient service.

Happily, that period is now past and the service is both professional and efficient. The Clerk, who still retains the ancient authority to appoint his own staff, now submits his proposed appointees for examination by the Civil Service Commission, and one can be quite sure that any young man who successfully surmounts the formidable obstacles of searching personal assessment and written examination to which he is subjected before acceptance as a Clerk in the Commons will be in every way suitable for his appointment.

The most striking difference between the present organisation and that reviewed by the 1833 Committee is the greatly increased size of the Speaker's Department. As will be seen, its earlier complement of Secretary and Chaplain has now swollen to a staff of no less than ninety-eight people, due in part to the transfer of the Vote Office from the Serjeant's Department but mainly to the vast expansion that has taken place in the Library. The Library performs a very different function today from that of a century ago and its services and responsibilities have been greatly widened.

The total staff of the House, which numbered a mere sixty-three in 1833, has now risen to 319 (sixty in the Clerk's Department, ninety-eight in the Speaker's and 161 in the Serjeant's) and as this total does not include a large number of people employed *in* the House but under outside authorities—e.g. the Post Office, the Ministry of Works, the Police, etc.—it is clear that an enormously greater amount of work is got through in the course of a day than was formerly the case. The machine has become very complex, and its co-ordination demands a high degree of skill and experience from the principal Officers in charge of the three Departments.

At the apex of the command pyramid are the Commissioners for Regulating the Offices of the House of Commons (appointed under the Act of 1812). These are the Speaker, the Chancellor of the Exchequer, the Attorney-General, the Solicitor-General and all Secretaries of State who are Members of the Commons : a former Commissioner, the Master of the Rolls, is now a Member of the Lords and is so ineligible. Any three Commissioners may form a quorum, but where executive action is called for, as when new posts are proposed or established posts come up for regrading, the Speaker, the Chancellor and at least one other Commissioner must approve the course chosen.

Since 1945 the Commissioners have been advised on staff matters by a Staff Board, consisting of the Clerk Assistant, the Speaker's Secretary, the Deputy Serjeant, the Deputy Accountant and the Senior Assistant Librarian, and since all ranks have access to this Board (through the Heads of their Departments) the claims or complaints of all the staff in all three Departments can be equably presented and dealt with. Salaries of all grades are now linked, by negotiated agreement, with those of equivalent grades in the Civil Service, and the Commissioners of today find themselves concerned less with organisation than with rates of pay.

Next to the Commissioners come the Speaker (in his capacity of Head of a Department), the Clerk and the Serjeant at Arms, all of whom appoint their own staff. In the Clerk's Department and in the Library—which is today practically a Department on its own—the higher officers are submitted to the Civil Service Commission before being appointed, while the Speaker personally appoints the Heads of Offices under his control. Lower grades of staff are appointed by the Heads of Offices, usually with the assistance of two or more members of the Staff Board.

It is interesting to notice, in passing, that all the principal posts in the Commons are still held by appointees of the Crown—the impact of Cromwell notwithstanding. The Speaker, though chosen by the House, is confirmed in his appointment by the Crown before he can take the Chair (it will be remembered that royal approval was withheld from Seymour in 1678 and that the House was forced to elect another in his place (see p. 99)); the Serjeant at Arms is a Royal Serjeant and is only attached to the Commons; the Clerk is appointed directly by the Crown by letters patent and the Clerk's Assistant similarly by sign manual. As long as this principle remains in practice the staff of the Commons can never become Civil Servants, and from that point of view the tradition is an important one.

CHAPTER 11

The Speaker's Department

When it is remembered that the Speaker is not only an elected
politician (with responsibilities to his constituents) and the
chairman of the debates in the House, but is also the administrative head of a large department, it is obvious that he can have
precious little time left for the pursuit of any affairs of his own.
His personal staff consists of his Secretary, Chaplain, Counsel,
Trainbearer and Assistant, shorthand-typist and one clerk (who
is permanently "on loan" to the Chairman of Ways and Means,
or Deputy Speaker), and his Department includes the Library,
the Fees Office (i.e. the Accountant's office, in modern parlance),
the Vote Office, the Sale Office and the shorthand writers of
Hansard. *All* their problems are his concern and he is responsible
to the House for their efficiency; and though the preparation of
the Vote and the Journal is done under the supervision of the
Clerk, their accuracy is entirely the Speaker's responsibility, as is
the accuracy of everything reported in Hansard.

The Heads of all offices in the Department are appointed
directly by the Speaker, though it is customary in modern times
for him to take advice, where the senior appointments are concerned, from two or three other senior officers—not necessarily
from his own Department. He has also, of course, absolute power
of dismissal over all his officers.

Bearing in mind the ultimate complete responsibility of the
Speaker for the correct and efficient working of all the offices
under him, his problem will perhaps be best understood by
looking briefly at those offices themselves and considering their
respective functions.

THE LIBRARY

Although one of the youngest of the House's major offices, the Library, because of the dramatic expansion of its function and services, has already become the largest single "command" in the Commons. Its beginnings were humble indeed—no more, in fact, than the holding of a small collection of books by the Clerk of the Journals at his premises in Abingdon Street in 1800—and even when the establishment became "official" in 1818 and was brought into the House itself it occupied a room a mere seventeen feet square. This accommodation was soon outgrown, and in 1827 new premises were built overlooking Cotton Garden and the river, but even these—2,530 square feet in area when completed—had become hopelessly inadequate by 1833. The Great Fire of 1834, though it destroyed so many precious and irreplaceable records and documents, came as a godsend from the point of view of accommodation, and in the Palace rebuilt by Barry the noble suite of rooms allocated to the Library set it up at last in the grand style it has maintained ever since. Its six great lofty rooms, which include the Speaker's own Library, lined from floor to ceiling with books and facing east over the Terrace on to the river occupy what is undoubtedly the finest position in the whole Palace of Westminster. Until 1945 the functions of the Library were fairly straightforward and simple to carry out since it was used mainly as a depository for papers, books and records, to which Members could refer when they needed information. Although the first Librarian, Benjamin Spiller, was reported to have "died from overwork" shortly before the sitting of the 1833 Committee, life in the Library nevertheless did continue to jog along at a fairly steady pace, and successive Librarians were able to preside with some show of leisured dignity at a desk actually in the Library itself. Here, they not only did their referencing and indexing (the preparation of the Index to the Journals was one of their most important and useful tasks), but also attended personally to the queries of Members. With a tiny staff of only three or four and a book stock of less than 4,000 volumes (in 1845) this sort of control was quite practical and effective, but it only remained possible so long as

Members' demands related simply to the whereabouts of the book or paper they wished to consult.

The new dynamism that entered the House in 1945 changed conditions in the Library overnight. The old leisurely service became at once too slow and too restricted to cope with the increasingly sophisticated demands made upon it by a new generation of M.P.s and it became clear within months of the new Parliament assembling that drastic reorganisation was going to be necessary. Although the Library had always been the responsibility of the Speaker (though it came under the Clerk for certain administrative functions for a short time during its early years) its development had been supervised until about 1862 by a series of Standing Committees. Between 1862 and 1922 the House seems to have been satisfied with the service it was getting and the Library was left to its own easy-going devices, but in 1922 Members decided that some form of direct control had again become necessary. Since 1922 there has always been an "Unofficial Committee", appointed by the House to advise the Speaker on Library affairs.

In 1945, however, even this Unofficial Committee was not considered adequate to deal on its own with the new problems of reorganisation required by the House, and a Select Committee (infinitely more powerful) was appointed to sort things out and to produce the ideal service. The key sentence in this Select Committee's Report set the standard of the Library as it is today. "The Library," they said, "should be far more than a repository of books and parliamentary papers. It should aim at providing Members rapidly with precise and detailed information on subjects connected with their duties."

The effects of this Committee's proposals soon began to be seen, and in the twenty years that have passed since it sat the Library has become a different place. In 1945 it had a total staff of seven, none of whom held professional Library qualifications, and its holdings consisted of a hotch-potch of odd purchases, donations of books unwanted by their owners, books written by Members (not all of them good ones!) and given as a compliment, as well as a mass of Parliamentary papers and records.

Today, the Library is run by a staff of thirty-nine, all of them highly qualified to carry out their particular function. Even the four part-time women cleaners have become expert, through long practice, at coping with the ever-present problem of dust among the books, a problem in London—and especially near the river—which is a perennial headache. And just as the number of personnel has multiplied, so has the size of the holdings. The main book stock consists of over *one hundred thousand* volumes and is supplemented by something like 130,000 Parliamentary papers as well as an enormous assortment of other national and international reports and publications. Practically all of these items may be taken out on loan by Members or Officers of Parliament, and where demands are made for books not held internally arrangements with some of the major London libraries allow for borrowing from outside. If required "in connection with his duty", a Member can obtain practically any book in the world, in any language (provided it is available) either from or through the Commons library—with the important exception of current fiction. *Some* fiction is held, but most of it is classical and only a few modern works are included.

But the book-borrowing service, vast though its organisation has become, is only a small part of the Library's service to Members. The Reference Room, for example, makes available something like 120 newspapers and 1,600 periodicals, as well as every reference work imaginable from the ABC Railway Guide, major encyclopaedias in four languages, travel information, general indexes and dictionaries, to handbooks on opera or photography and the leading works on medicine and surgery.

And even all this is only on the surface, the visible tenth of the iceberg. The modern emphasis in the Library is on research and a whole Division has been created to deal with it. Members' demands on this service are considerable, and it is easy to imagine how nerve-racking the work must be when it is remembered that the end-product of the clerks' researches are almost certainly going to be used in debate on the floor of the House. The variety of subjects into which research is required by Members is enormous and the amount of work involved is considerable. Four typical examples quoted in *The Library of the House of Commons* give some idea of the strange information the Reference Section may be required to dig out :

(1) A memorandum on which countries still employ women in the mines.
(2) Notes on the part played by Independent Members of Parliament.
(3) A memorandum on Public Ownership before and after 1945.
(4) The latest information on helicopter development.

The answers to queries like these are usually required urgently, and one can imagine that the Research Clerks have a fairly anxious time of it working with minute accuracy against the clock. In addition to carrying out research for individual Members, the Section also does work for the House itself, the Speaker and Committees, and prepares bibliographies, statistics and reference sheets in anticipation of forthcoming legislation.

The enormous holdings are catalogued under the headings of both author and subject, using the system of the London Library with modifications to embrace the special problems which exist in a Parliamentary Library of this size. A special Desk in the Reference Room keeps Members up to date on overseas publications (e.g. by international organisations and foreign governments), while the Parliamentary Division is responsible for all publications of the home Government. Among its more modern equipment, the Library has apparatus for "baking" and binding all new books in special transparent covers before placing them in the shelves, and has also the necessary machine for duplicating and photo-copying documents for Members. The present staff consist of :

    1 Librarian
    2 Assistant Librarians
    2 Deputy Assistant Librarians
    4 Senior Library Clerks
    5 Junior Library Clerks (plus 1 vacancy)
    1 Higher Executive Officer
    1 Cataloguer
    1 Information Clerk
    1 Chief Office Clerk
    5 Senior Office Clerks
    1 Office Clerk
    2 Senior Attendants

2 Attendants
1 Personal Assistant
5 Shorthand-typists
1 Temporary typist
4 Women cleaners (part-time)

THE FEES OFFICE (NEW STYLE)

In 1833 the Clerk of Public Bills had been appointed as "Paymaster of the House of Commons" to receive the fees from the Commissioners and to pay from them the salaries of all officers of the House except the Speaker, lodging what balance remained in a Special Commissioners' Account in the Bank of England (see p. 156). But this arrangement, as was eventually realised, was too cumbersome to work properly. In the same year an Accountant had been appointed to assist the Paymaster, but by 1918 he had taken over all the Paymaster's duties as far as the collection of fees and the payment of salaries was concerned and become an entity of his own. By the House of Commons Offices Act of 1849, it was decreed that all fees collected should be paid into the *"Consolidated Fund"* and that all charges and salaries (except that of the Speaker) should be paid on individual votes subject to the approval of the House. Audit was solely by the Speaker. This was the real beginning of the present professional service of officers paid directly out of public funds, by the Treasury but under the control of Parliament, and divorced completely from fees and private venture. In its quiet way, the nationalisation of the machinery of Parliament was something of a revolution and marked an historic moment in the service of the House.

The Accountant's office, known as the Office of the Collector of Fees, was small and quite specialised at its inception, concentrating as it did mainly on the assessment and collection of the fees on private business, but as new duties were added to its primary function it quickly grew in both size and importance. Although created originally in the Clerk's Department—to inherit the "fees" duties of the Clerk of Public Bills—the office was transferred to the Speaker's Department in 1918 thus making the Accountant responsible directly to the final auditor of his accounts—Mr. Speaker. The first major addition to the Accountant's responsibilities came when the payment of Members was introduced in 1911. Not all Members drew their Parliamentary salaries, and those who did were paid quarterly, so that the impact of this new duty was not heavy. Today, however, all Members draw their salaries (almost all of them monthly) and the amounts paid are complicated by all manner of variations in allowances and expenses, insurance stamps and tax, as well as by the fact that so many Members have income other than their Parliamentary salaries. The preparation of the monthly paycheque for 640 Members and 319 staff is a formidable task and involves a lot of money.

Another full-time and difficult job in the Fees Office is the administration of Members' free travel facilities. These, initiated in 1924 in respect of rail and sea, and extended to air travel in 1935, originally covered travel only between Westminster and the constituency, but in 1945 the privilege was extended to cover journeys between London and home and home and constituency. But in modern times Members have frequently to travel much more widely on the business of the House—i.e. as members of delegations to Colonies to present maces, etc., as members of Select Committees, and so on—and it is the Accountant's job to arrange both for their travel and for their necessary insurance.

Perhaps his biggest single task is the preparation of the annual Estimates of the House of Commons Vote, an enormous undertaking—it involved the expenditure of nearly three million pounds in 1965–1966—and one which demands his unremitting attention. The basic information for the Estimate comes to the Accountant from the Heads of the three Departments; the Accountant collates the items, checks their accuracy where checking is possible and prepares a draft estimate which he submits to both the Accounting Officer (i.e. the Clerk, who is *personally* responsible for all expenditure in the House) and the Speaker, whose approval must be signified before the Estimate goes forward. Under the 1846 House of Commons Offices Act this duty really belongs to the Speaker's Secretary, but under modern conditions the job is a highly specialised one and could only be done by a competent professional accountant. The law is satisfied, however, by the Secretary accepting responsibility for ensuring that the Estimate *is* prepared, and properly, at the right time every year.

In addition to the Estimate, the Accountant must also submit to the Treasury the Appropriation Account and the Forecast and Out-turn of the House of Commons Vote as well as preparing (and justifying) any Supplementary Estimate which, sadly, may be required.

These major items among the Accountant's duties, requiring minute and constant scrutiny, are themselves almost smothered by a host of ancillary tasks. As before, the assessment and collection of fees on Private Bills continues, together with the preparation of the necessary certificates on Taxation of Costs. He deals with the Treasury in all matters affecting staff, establishment and superannuation; supervises the day to day management of the House of Commons Vote, the House of Commons Members' Fund, the Members' Contributory Pension Fund, the funds of the History of Parliament Trust and the Speaker's Art Fund (under which comes the sale of books and postcards at the Bookstall in St. Stephen's Hall and the annual House of Commons Christmas Cards). His office also provides the secretariat of the Staff Board and keeps its records.

That all these duties can be performed—and performed with exemplary precision and accuracy—by a total staff of only eleven is a cause for wonder. The present personnel consist of :

1 Accountant
1 Deputy Accountant
2 Assistant Accountants
1 Superintending Clerk
1 Chief Office Clerk
5 Senior Office Clerks

THE SPEAKER'S OFFICE

Since this is such a small and compact department with all its officers responsible for direct service to the Speaker, it will be convenient to describe it under the one heading. Its functions are quite distinct from, say, the procedural functions of the Clerk's Department or the purely executive ones of the Serjeant, but its services, which include ceremonial, legal and financial responsibilities, and social arrangements, are just as essential to the overall working of Parliament.

The effective Head of this Office is the Speaker's Secretary. The post was first created in 1735, when a certain Mr. Fenton was appointed by Speaker Onslow, and though the duties of earlier Secretaries have already been described (see p. 147) it is fair to say that those of a century ago bear little resemblance to those performed today. Most of the old tasks are still there, but they have been so much added to that the post has become unrecognisable by former standards. Until the turn of the present century the main features of the duties centred around protocol and social arrangements (even when the Speaker's Secretary was made Secretary to the Commissioners under the 1812 Act it added little to his actual work), but as the general business of the House increased and the Speaker's Office became more and more involved in the day to day administration of the House's services, the Secretary began to find himself in some difficulty.

As a permanent member of the Staff Board, he is concerned with appointments, rates of pay, promotions, retirements, etc., of the staff of the whole House, while at the same time he is required to keep a special eye on the interests of his own Department. In practice, he is made to function as though he was indeed the executive Head of the Department (rather than Mr. Speaker) and is thus required to deal initially with every suggestion, complaint or difficulty that might come up from any of the six offices for which the Speaker is responsible. But unfortunately for the Secretary, from the point of view of getting things *done*, he possesses no actual power of his own and can neither make a ruling nor initiate an action without reference to Mr. Speaker. In the complex machinery of the modern House, this fact makes the Secretary's job difficult to a degree, and his lot is not an enviable one.

To say that he "deals with the Speaker's correspondence" seems a simple enough statement. But people write to the Speaker from all over the world, on subjects ranging from problems of Constitutional Law and precedent, history, protocol, requests for tickets to the Gallery and simple questions like, "Why don't you get rid of the Prime Minister?" Any Speaker's Secretary could write a book, and a good one, about his morning mailbag—and dealing with it can be a headache. Ministers and Departments, too, are in constant touch with the Speaker on matters affecting the Business of the House—all of it high-priority and confidential stuff—and once again it is the Secretary who takes the initial brunt.

Nor can he just sit down and get on with his work. The ceremonial side of the office requires his daily presence in the Speaker's Procession and in the Chamber, and his social duties cannot be neglected whenever the Speaker is "receiving".

The Secretary is the personal appointee of the Speaker and is appointed only during the Speaker's pleasure—though when a Speaker either retires or dies in office it is customary for the new Speaker to confirm the Secretary's status—and it has usually been the case that the man chosen for this important position is one who has already distinguished himself in some field or another outside the House.

His principal assistant is the *Trainbearer*, holder of an office created in 1730 when a Mr. Cox became a Trainbearer to Speaker Onslow (who also created the office of Secretary). As the title makes clear, the ceremonial duty of the Trainbearer requires him to carry the Speaker's train whenever he moves about on official occasions, and to escort him to meetings or functions when he attends them without his robe and wig. The Trainbearer is an essential figure in the Speaker's Procession which precedes the beginning of each day's sitting.

On the office side, the Trainbearer is responsible for the care of the Speaker's robes and wig, and must see that the arm of the Chair is furnished daily with whatever Bills, Order Papers and other documents may be necessary for the day's business. He looks after all filing in the Speaker's Office; runs the ballots for seats at such ceremonies as Trooping the Colour, Opening of Parliament, State Visits, and so on; issues tickets for the Distinguished Strangers Gallery and the Speaker's Gallery in the absence of the Secretary; he maintains all the necessary stationery and office equipment and types letters to Ministers, Government Departments and other official bodies when required to by the Secretary. His duties require him to remain on duty two nights a week, until the rising of the House; on the other two nights (or when the Trainbearer is absent) the duties are carried out by the

Trainbearer's assistant, who is a Senior Office Clerk. There is, in addition, a shorthand-typist who acts as Secretary to the Office.

The SPEAKER'S COUNSEL, who is listed in the Speaker's Office for the sake of convenience, does not come under the control of the Secretary, but has an office of his own. His function is a purely legal one, and his legal advice is taken by a great many people. He does *not* advise on procedural matters—the Clerk does that—but he is available to the Speaker and other Officers of the House whenever legal questions (other than procedural) require learned opinion. He also advises the Chairman of Ways and Means (the Deputy Speaker, *not* an Officer of the House) on the sometimes difficult aspects of private business, and is always at the call of the Model Clauses Committee and the Statutory Instruments Committee in respect of the knotty legal problems that often arise in conection with their duties to the House.

The office of Speaker's Counsel was instituted in 1838, but it was not until 1851 that he became the regular adviser to the Chairman of Ways and Means, in which capacity he is an *ex officio* member of the Court of Referees.

Also assisting the Chairman of Ways and Means, but held on the strength of the Speaker's Office for administrative reasons, is one PERSONAL ASSISTANT who runs the functional side of the Chairman's office.

The final member of the Speaker's own office is the Speaker's Chaplain (perhaps we should have *begun* with him, but no disrespect is intended). Prior to the appointment of a regular "preacher", in 1659, the daily business of Parliament had always been opened by special prayers—we learn from D'Ewes' Journal, for example, that in the Elizabethan Parliaments the Litany was read by the Clerk, kneeling at his desk, and that the whole House responded upon their knees. Then, when the Book of Common Prayer was prohibited in 1644, the customary formal (printed) prayers were discontinued and one was offered up by Mr. Speaker *extempore*. After the Restoration in 1661, however, a new set of official prayers were composed and printed and it is this set—with only a few amendments—that is still used today.

A delightful article in the *Pall Mall Gazette* of 28th February 1906 describes the hardships of the (then) Chaplain's Parliamentary existence :

"The actual official duties of the Chaplain of the House of Commons cannot be described as arduous, though they include the inexorable necessity of attendance at a precise spot at an exact moment every day that the House is in Session. It is the Chaplain's duty also to say grace at all official banquets. . . ."

Phew!

Today, however, although the Chaplain is still required to meet those ancient "inexorable necessities", he has other and perhaps more rewarding (certainly far happier) duties to perform. By pleasant tradition, it is possible for Members and Officers, their children—and in some cases their grandchildren—to be married or christened in the Crypt Chapel under St. Stephen's, and it is usually the Chaplain who comes over from his regular place in Westminster Abbey to officiate at these, rather rare, ceremonies. It is interesting to note, in passing, that ever since Cromwell "stabled his horses" in the Crypt (popular legend) it has ceased to be consecrated ground—and a Special Licence is required to make legal any nuptials performed here.

THE VOTE OFFICE

The Vote Office, much reformed and greatly more respectable, has been in the Speaker's Department since 1835, having been transferred thence from the control of the Serjeant who had enjoyed its proceeds since its creation (probably about 1682 (see p. 87). In common with all other Departments and Offices of the House, the Vote Office has had its duties and responsibilities so extended that the old "private enterprise" days described in earlier chapters seem now incredible.

The main function of this office is the quick supply of Parliamentary papers for use by Members "in connection with their duties", though it will be remembered that its original purpose had been the delivery of the Vote. It was for that reason that the Head of the Office was known as the "Deliverer of the Vote"— a fine-sounding title, with something of a ring about it, which unhappily disappeared during the early part of the present century when the then Head of the Office (for reasons to do with internal politics) began to call himself the "Principal of the Vote Office". In 1961, however, the Commissioners reversed the process and directed the then Principal—successor to the reformer—to revert to his ancient style and title, a change generally welcomed and in keeping with the best traditions of the House.

While in the realm of gossipy anecdote, an amusing story might be told of an incident affecting the Vote Office while the new House was being built after its war-time bombing. In the *old* building the Vote Office had enjoyed the possession of accommodation for its Store which ran the entire length of the Chamber, at ground level, while in the Architect's plans for the new, the Store had been placed underground in a former cellar, the floorspace of which was literally choked with supporting columns and arches. Not only this, but the Principal's own room —which by long tradition had been sited in the "Ministers' Corridor"—was now proposed to be placed in some similar sorry spot to the Store. The Principal protested; the Architect resisted; argument ensued. At last, it seemed, tradition triumphed, and the Principal was allocated the last room at the southern end of the new Ministers' Corridor; he awaited opening-day with a feeling of satisfaction. But was it sheer accident, one wonders, that when the day came and the Principal took possession of his new office, he found that the door was round the corner and that his room gave not on to the Ministers' Corridor but on to a stair-way and lift shaft? Perhaps, after all, the last laugh went to the Architect.

The amount of documentation provided for the use of Parliament has increased so much in recent years that the sheer physical handling of it has become a problem—one that is becoming acute as this book is written. Gone are the gracious days (which extended to within living memory) when the principal preoccupation of the office was the delivery of the Vote and the occasional Acts of Parliament, and when other Parliamentary papers—not normally *delivered*—were so infrequently issued that Members came personally to the Deliverer to request a copy. Gone too, alas! with those same leisurely days, is the happy custom many Members had during the Summer Recess of sending to the Deliverer and his staff the surplus products of their hunting-shooting-fishing expeditions among the moors and highlands of this sceptred isle!

Today, the Vote Office is kept working at full stretch by the flood of reports, bills, white papers, statutory orders and Hansards which flow like a daily tide into the House from the Stationery Office. After a General Election every Member is sent a Sessional Demand Form on which he is invited to indicate (*a*) if he wishes papers to be delivered to him; and (*b*) if so, which ones, and where to? Four types of publication qualify for this "full delivery" treatment:

The Vote
All Bills, as issued
The Financial Statement (produced for the Budget)
Supplementary Estimates.

In addition, a Minister may direct from time to time that some paper to which he attaches particular importance should go out on full delivery, in which case it, too, is sent to all Members who have applied for papers. The deliveries are taken out by hand by a staff of seventeen part-time Porters, who report for duty each day at 7 a.m. and carry the day's papers to the addresses of Members who live within a three-mile radius of the House and to the Ministries. Papers are sent by post to Members who live outside the radius.

But the full-delivery papers, comprising as they do a regular and known quantity, represent the least of the problems facing the Vote Office in modern times. Under the orders of the Speaker (advised by the Publications and Debates Committee of the House) the office is required to maintain in stock, and issue *on demand* (no waiting) every paper issued in the current and preceding Session—and when it is considered that the total number of papers handled per Session tops the million and a quarter mark, it will be appreciated that this is no simple task. It is complicated, too, by the lack of shelf-space in the Store. Because of the cramped quarters, it is only possible to keep thirty copies of each paper once its initial issue is over, and as there are 640 Members —who might all decide to ask for a particular paper on a particular day—maintaining the "on demand" condition of the service can become tricky. It becomes downright hair-raising at times, because if the Vote Office should fail to produce a paper which a Member should rightly have in connection with the day's business the Member can appeal to the Speaker to stop the debate.

To avoid such a catastrophe, at least as far as *current* papers are concerned, the Vote Office staff make a point of studying the list of "next week's business" which is announced in the Chamber each Thursday, and then topping up the stock of whatever papers they estimate will be in demand for the various debates. This system is only workable because of the long experience possessed by the officers concerned and their knowledge of Members' interests; together with an ingenious programme of referencing and filing that has been developed in the office itself.

Since 1961 it has been the responsibility of the Ministers to put into the Vote Office sufficient quantities of papers *older* than the two Sessions, when they are considered relevant to a current debate; and this has added a whole new dimension to the work of the office. In response to the increasing demand from Members for more and more background information, Ministries tend to supply a veritable flood of older papers for every piece of legislation coming before the House and the handling of all these extra documents (sometimes as many as six or seven thousand for a single small measure) adds greatly to the already complicated duties of the office.

To maintain this comprehensive service the Deliverer must keep a continuous and close liaison with the Speaker, Members, Ministries, the Departments of the House and the Stationery Office and keep himself informed of the feeling of the House by going frequently into the Chamber to see what is going on. The office is open from seven in the morning until the rising of the House and the staff virtually work two shifts, each clerk doing two nights a week as well as the early mornings. Either the Deliverer or his Deputy must be on duty during all the hours the office is open, available to attend the Speaker instantly should he require it, either in the Chamber or in his office.

The staff consist of the following:

Deliverer
Deputy Deliverer
Chief Office Clerk
6 Senior Office Clerks/Office Clerks

THE SALE OFFICE

The Sale Office, which at first sight appears to be a parallel organisation to the Vote Office, in fact performs a very different function. Under the regulations of the House, Members are entitled to only one copy of every paper issued, up to six copies of the daily Hansard and six copies of every Bill (they may have twenty-five copies of a Bill by special application to the Speaker) and if they require more copies than the free issue allows they can buy them from the Sale Office. Generally, however, the free issue is adequate for the needs of most Members, and the main clientele of the Sale Office is composed of the staffs of the Parliamentary Agents, to whom a source for obtaining Government publications inside the House itself is a great convenience. In addition to stocking and selling papers the two-man staff (one chief and one Senior Office Clerk) are responsible for the supervision and maintenance of two photo-copying machines which are available for use by Members and/or their secretaries, and for collecting the relevant charges.

THE OFFICE OF THE OFFICIAL REPORT

The Office of the Official Report (i.e. Hansard) is the final component of the Speaker's Department, and its staff are the only staff in the Commons to belong to and be represented by a trades union. This follows a ballot which took place in 1960, when the entire staff of the House were invited to state their preference, by secret vote, for or against trades union representation in respect of their pay and conditions of work. Only the Official Reporters opted *for*, and they have been represented ever since by the Institution of Professional Civil Servants; the Hansard typists belong to the Civil Service Clerical Association. (The remainder of the House's staff, of course, deal directly with the Staff Board through the Heads of their Offices.) Both systems seem to work quite satisfactorily side by side under the same roof.

Just as the House has always reserved the right to exclude strangers from its debates (the cry, "I spy strangers!" is still enough to have the galleries cleared, even today), so it has reserved the right to protect the privacy of its proceedings by prohibiting any reporting of individual speeches. Thus, the activities of the Office of the Official Report constitute a daily breach of privilege, flying right in the face of Orders which, though not now enforced, are still lawfully in existence. There were many instances of these Orders being invoked to procure "Secret Session" debates during the last war—though the ban on publication of those proceedings was lifted, by Order, in 1945.

There were two good reasons for the original—and long-lasting—prohibition of "reporting". First, to make possible absolute frankness and freedom of speech in debates in the House; and second, to avoid misrepresentation—either accidental or wilful—in the country outside. In 1628, it will be remembered, (and again in 1640), the Clerk was forbidden to "make notes of particular men's speeches" (see p. 32) or to "suffer copies to go forth of any arguments or speech whatsoever", and in 1641 it was ruled by the House that "no Member shall either give a copy, or publish in print any thing that he shall speak here, without leave of the House". Also, "that all the Members of the House are enjoined to deliver out no copy or notes of anything that is brought into the House, or that is propounded or agitated in the House". And these orders, which have the force of law, still stand in the Journal.

It is true that during the Cromwellian period the House from time to time released reports of its proceedings, and that in 1681 they began to print *and publish* the "Votes and Proceedings", but after the Restoration the old clamp-down was re-imposed and applied even more rigorously. In 1738 the House re-affirmed, under Walpole, that outside publication of its proceedings would constitute "a high indignity and a notorious breach of privilege", but newspapers and magazines all over the country were becoming extremely restive over the restraints this attitude placed on them, and many of them got round the ban by reporting the actual debates while using fictitious names for the House and its Members. One imagines that this could have been hilarious at times.

The Gentleman's Magazine, for example, classified all its (illegal) Parliamentary reports under the title of "Debates in the Senate of Great Lilliput" and gave only the first and last letters of a Member's name with a dash between. Samuel Johnson was at one time Parliamentary reporter for this magazine. Note-taking being absolutely prohibited inside the House, he used to sit in the Gallery and memorise the salient arguments in the debate, writing up his "fictitious" account in his own words afterwards, and the result of this was sometimes astonishing. "The eloquence of Greece and Rome," cried Voltaire in admiration, "is revived in the British Senate!" Little did he know, never actually having visited Westminster.

Johnson, on being asked how it was *possible* to carry a long debate in his head and then to write it up accurately later, declared that he *did* it and that his reports were absolutely true and impartial, though he confessed privately to Boswell that he "took care that the Whig dogs should not have the best of it" (!) which explained a mystery which Walpole told the House he found insoluble. "I have read," he said, "professed debates of the House, wherein all the wit, learning and argument appeared on the one side, and on the other nothing was shown but what was low, mean and ridiculous; and yet, strange to say, the division had gone against the side which, according to the report, had reason and justice to support it!"

Gradually, however, public feeling had its way and Parliament ceased to act against reporters of its proceedings—so long as their accounts were manifestly fair and accurate. In 1803, an unofficial but tacitly "recognised" series of Parliamentary reports was produced by William Cobbett, printed for him by the firm of T. C. Hansard (long associated with the House's printing) and later published by them under the title of "Parliamentary Debates". When the "*Official* Report" was established in 1909 inside the House itself it was produced under the title of "Parliamentary Debates, Official Report", thus perpetuating on its title-page both its traditional name and the new attitude towards its existence; but people had by then become so accustomed to the idea of "reading it in Hansard" that the name stuck. The "Official Report" continued to be known as "Hansard". But it was not until 1943 that the name "Hansard" was, by order, incorporated into the title page of the "Official Report".

Today's Office of the Official Report is a large, busy and very efficient organisation, responsible for recording all proceedings of the House itself (including Committees taken in the Chamber) and of its Standing Committees. (It should be noted that Select Committees' proceedings are reported by the shorthand-writer to the House—whose appointment is in the Department of the Clerk.) The Editor of Debates, or Editor of Hansard as he is still more generally known, is directly responsible to the Speaker for the production of the Official Report, and the Speaker is answerable to the House for its accuracy. There is a widespread misconception that Hansard is an exact, full and "unexpurgated edition" of every statement made in the House, but this is not so. The Select Committee on Parliamentary Debates which sat in 1907 to define the status, duties and responsibilities of the proposed "Official Report" organisation defined "a full report" as being one "which, though not strictly verbatim, is substantially the verbatim report, with repetitions and redundancies omitted and with obvious mistakes corrected, but which on the other hand leaves out nothing that adds to the meaning of the speech or illustrates the argument". The tradition set by Samuel Johnson, it seems, was to be perpetuated—as it still is, of course, today.

The Hansard Reporters have their own Gallery, adjoining those occupied by the Press, above and behind the Speaker's Chair, and each reporter does only a ten-minute spell in the Gallery before being relieved, to minimise the possibility of errors caused by tiredness or flagging concentration. Out of the Gallery, he has then to arrange for the transcription of his shorthand and for the typing of his notes. Hansard is produced daily while the House is sitting, but the proofs are sent to the Stationery Office for printing at 10.30 each night so that when the House goes late the proceedings *after* 10.30 p.m. are not published until the Hansard of the next day but one. The daily parts are collected into the Weekly Hansard (which reports from Friday to Thursday) and into the Bound Volume, which is produced in its distinctive pale blue cover about every three weeks. Members are entitled to draw up to six copies of the daily part and one copy of the Weekly from the Vote Office, while one copy of the Bound Volume is sent to them direct from the Stationery Office. They can also have up to six copies of the "Loose-leaf Hansard", which is in separate, single-sided pages, like galley-proofs, and which was produced originally for Members to mark off any corrections they wished to be made in the Bound Volume when it came out. (The Loose-leafs, however, are very handy for sending copies of one's speech, question, etc., to one's local newspaper, and they are widely used for this purpose—thus saving a copy of the complete daily part.)

The present staff of Hansard consists of :

 1 Editor
 1 Deputy Editor
 2 Assistant Editors
20 Reporters
 7 Hansard typists
 2 Senior Office Clerks

These thirty-three, however, are reinforced by temporary reporters when more than five Committees are sitting simultaneously, but as this book is being prepared some interesting experiments with mechanical recording equipment are taking place, and it may be that in the fairly near future science will move into the field of Parliamentary reporting as it has done in so many places elsewhere.

CHAPTER 12

The Clerk's Department

Although the Clerk's prime function has been almost smothered in modern times by a host of administrative duties in connection with his Department, as well as by the tremendous variety of advisory services he is called upon to provide for the House and for the Speaker, the original element remains unchanged and is always quoted when the Clerk's duties are defined. It is "to keep the records".

Today's Clerks, like their unbroken line of predecessors, are appointed by letters patent of the Crown, and will, in every case, have served a long apprenticeship at the Table before the Prime Minister's recommendation results in their ultimate promotion to be Clerk of the House. From the fact that the Clerk "moves up" along the Table, so to speak, it may appear that his eventual appointment to the top is no more than a formality, but this is not so. At every successive stage of his progress from junior Clerk upward, the aspirant is subject to the closest scrutiny by the Clerk, the Speaker and the House itself, and when the time arrives for the final accolade to be conferred upon him there is no shadow of possible doubt but that he is completely equipped for his great and distinguished office.

Enormous care, for example, is lavished on the selection of the Second Clerk Assistant (who may eventually become Clerk). The candidates for the appointment—themselves already highly qualified men in the Clerk's Department—are screened from every possible angle, not only in respect of their intelligence, efficiency, experience and probity, but also very much in respect of their personality; for while the hand of the Clerk must be of the hardest iron, its glove must be of gossamer. Upon the recommendation of the Speaker (advised by the Clerk) the successful candidate is then appointed by sign manual of the Crown. The appointee may serve for years at the Table as Second Assistant before death or retirement at the top creates a vacancy for Clerk Assistant, but his onward promotion is not automatic. If the earlier assessment of his abilities has proved too optimistic, for example, or if his health has proved unequal to the long hours of duty, he will not find himself recommended for the Clerk Assistant post—a recommendation which, once again, is made by the Speaker and endorsed by the Crown by sign manual. Having become Clerk Assistant, however, he will now spend more years adding greatly to his experience and qualifying for the ultimate promotion.

When the House is in Committee, it is the Clerk Assistant who sits at the Table to assist the Chairman in the same way that the Clerk assists the Speaker when the House sits as a House—proving himself, in this way, under operational conditions. The House can observe him at leisure, work with him, assess his capabilities and savour his personality, and when the day arrives for a new Clerk to be appointed the Prime Minister knows exactly what manner of man is next in line for the job. It would be a strange thing indeed, in modern times, if *any* outsider could be found of comparable stature; the waiting candidate would be, by now, the world's leading authority on Constitutional Law and Parliamentary procedure, as well as a man already known intimately —and trusted—by Members of the House.

In addition to his long and detailed experience of the procedural affairs of Parliament, however, this candidate for the Clerkship would also be highly expert in the domestic machinery of the Commons, since by virtue of his office as Clerk Assistant he is also Chairman of the Staff Board and his duties in this connection have concerned him closely with the activities of every Department and Office in the House.

Having been recommended by the Prime Minister and approved by the Crown, the new Clerk—still officially styled the "Under Clerk of the Parliaments, to attend upon the Commons"—is required to appear before the Lord Chancellor and to swear a declaration that he will, among other things, "make true entries, remembrances, and journals of the things done and passed in the House of Commons." His letter patent from the Crown, strangely modern in appearance among the dusty trappings of traditions in which they are created, consist of a type-written document which is signed, not by the Monarch, but by the Clerk of the Crown in Chancery. Or rather, it is not signed; the Clerk of the Crown's surname is simply *typed*, in capitals, at the foot of the document—a procedure which would seem to make it an easy thing to forge a "letters patent" for one's self. Such a forgery would, in fact, be quite simple to do; though it should be pointed out to anyone who might contemplate doing such a thing that it is an offence— and that the penalty for committing it is still death by the axe!

In office, the Clerk finds himself responsible for a vast complex of administrative machinery as well as for his duties in the Chamber. As has been mentioned earlier, it is the Clerk who signs all Addresses, votes of thanks, and Orders of the House, as well as certifying all Bills sent from the Commons to the Lords. At the Table, he reads aloud the titles of Bills about to be considered (fragmentary tradition of the days when he read the whole Bill for the information of Members). He has an interesting duty to perform, too, when the House is electing a new Speaker. The Speaker's Chair being empty, it is the Clerk who calls upon the Proposer and Seconder of the new occupant, but since the Clerk has no voice in the Chamber (except by order of the Speaker) he "calls" them in silence, merely rising in his place and pointing his finger. When new *Members* are sworn it is the Clerk who administers the oath and introduces the Member to the Speaker and the House.

As he sits at the Table, one ear always on the debate so that he can advise the Speaker on any points of order which may arise, he maintains that famous "book of minutes" started by Seymour in 1547 from which will spring both the Journal and the Vote, while at the same time dealing with a continuous flood of procedural queries which come from every part of the House. Each morning he must find time to assess the business for the day's sitting, consider any difficulties which may arise, and brief the Speaker in depth on every aspect of it; this is done at a daily conference just before the House meets. As the acknowledged authority on Constitutional Law and procedure, his advice on all procedural matters is constantly sought by both the Government and Opposition Front Benches, back-bench Members, the Committee of Privileges when it sits, and by outside authorities and other Departments of the House. He is personally responsible, as Accounting Officer, for all the money voted by Parliament for the running of the House, and should a shortage occur he would be obliged to make it good out of his own pocket. It is perhaps unnecessary to say that he has an official residence within the Palace of Westminster—with a job that occupies him almost twenty-four hours a day while the House is sitting, he most certainly needs it.

THE CLERK ASSISTANT, as has been mentioned, acts as Deputy of the Clerk when required, but has a whole range of responsibilities of his own—similar to those of the Clerk except that his liaison is with the Chairman of Ways and Means instead of the Speaker. When Committees are taken on the Floor of the House under the control of the Chairman of Ways and Means, it is the Clerk Assistant who officiates at the Table. He has special advisory duties in respect of Committees of Supply and of Ways and Means and advises the Chairman both before and during the Committee debates. Being also Chairman of the Staff Board he spends a great deal of time on the staffing and pay problems of all the Departments of the House.

THE SECOND CLERK ASSISTANT, who also officiates at the Table, is responsible for the Table Office, a fairly recent creation whose duties will be described later.

THE FOURTH CLERK AT THE TABLE occupies the newest post in the Commons, one which was created for a special purpose as lately as 1953. As the title implies, he relieves at the Table when relief is required, but his main responsibility is to represent the Clerk in his relations with Commonwealth Parliaments. In this connection he travels widely, advising new Parliaments on procedure and helping them to produce workable Standing Orders for their particular conditions of work. He is responsible, also, for the instruction here of Commonwealth clerks who come to Westminster on attachment to learn for themselves the tried and tested procedures of the Mother of Parliaments.

THE CLERK OF PUBLIC BILLS is intimately involved with all the Government legislation that comes before the House. As we have seen earlier, a Bill is prepared by the Parliamentary draughtsmen to be as concise and accurate a statement as possible of the Government's legislative intentions, but that by itself is not enough; the Bill must be correct, too, in the *Parliamentary sense*—that is, it must comply with the complicated Standing Orders that have been evolved over the centuries to safeguard the interests of those to be affected by the proposed legislation (even if it is only the taxpayer!). So long as the Standing Orders are observed, especially in Bills dealing with money matters, the Government cannot become a dictatorship, and it is the Clerk of Public Bills' responsibility to ensure that the Orders are rigidly adhered to. The proposed Bill comes to him first in draft form and is submitted to a very close scrutiny before it is sent back to the Ministry for printing, and until the Clerk is satisfied that it is completely in order, it will not be proceeded with. He maintains a continuous liaison with the office of the Parliamentary Counsel, all the Ministries and the Stationery Office, and he is the chief fountain of advice for all Members seeking to introduce a Private Member's Bill. (These are not *"Private Bills"*, since once the House has given a Member permission to introduce his measure the Bill is printed at Government expense and goes through the House—if proceeded with—under Public Bill procedure.)

The Clerk of Public Bills supplies, through his CLERK OF STANDING COMMITTEES, the Clerks for all the Standing Committees of the House. Some Bills—the Finance Bill is a good example—go through all their stages, including the Committee stage, on the Floor of the House itself, but if this treatment were applied to all Bills the House would become choked in no time. At the beginning of each Session, therefore, Standing Committees are set up, each with its own Chairman, and to them are referred the Committee stages of whatever Bills do not require full House treatment. The Committees are a microcosm of the House itself, representing in their composition the balance of the political parties, and—like the Speaker—the Chairman becomes an impartial authority. And to the Chairman, though naturally on a smaller scale, the Clerk gives a similar service to that supplied by the Clerk of the House to the Speaker.

THE CLERK OF THE JOURNALS carries a much wider responsibility than his title may suggest, though his ancient function (see p. 49) still continues unchanged. It has often been suggested, in the cause of labour-saving, economy and speed, that the Journal might be telescoped into a simpler, more direct form rather like the Votes and Proceedings (see p. 53). Indeed, it has even been proposed that the two should be identical so that the one preparation and the one printing should suffice for both—but this has always been strongly resisted, and it would be a pity if the reformers had their way. Both are prepared from the Clerk's "book of notes"; which is sent out from the Table at frequent intervals during the day's sitting; but whereas the Vote consists of merely a series of minutes—though complete and detailed ones—of occurrences in the Chamber, the Journal (which is written up the next day) is maintained in the fuller narrative form initiated by Seymour in 1547 and continued (with only a small break) ever since. Any departure from this tradition would be a sad loss in more ways than one. From the point of view of the historian the Journal more than earns its keep; but also, since its entries can be accepted as evidence before the Courts (under Section 3 of the Evidence Act 1845) belated intereference with its *form* might represent a real complication.

The Journal Office is responsible for all research that may be required by the Clerk of the House—as when, for example, he may be called on to provide chapter and verse on the precedents. Since most of these are in the Journal itself, the Index maintained by the Journal Office is invaluable. The Office is responsible, too, for the form and presentation of Statutory Instruments, i.e. Orders made by a Minister under powers vested in him by a parent Act of Parliament. This is a very complicated aspect of Parliamentary procedure and one that demands constant vigilance on the part of the officer concerned. The final responsibility of this Office is the handling of Public Petitions presented to the House, in respect of which the Clerk of the Journals advises the Select Committee—a Committee, which, it might be said, has for long possessed almost the authority of an Ombudsman and could well be used in that capacity.

THE CLERK OF COMMITTEES provides Clerks for all the *Select* Committees set up by the House. Unlike the Standing Committees already referred to, Select Committees (generally—there have been odd special exceptions) have nothing to do with the Committee stages of Bills. They are set up to enquire into specific matters and have power to summon witnesses, to take evidence and to inspect documents—and very powerful bodies they are, as can be imagined. In addition to the usual services expected of a Committee Clerk, the Clerks to the Select Committees must be able to offer advice as to *what* witness should be summoned, and what papers called for, and how and where they should be obtained; and when the Committee eventually forms its opinion (or opinions) on the matters defined in its terms of reference, it generally looks to its Clerk to draft its Report to the House. Two Deputy Principal Clerks in this Office have special responsibilities towards the powerful Public Accounts Committee and the Estimate Committee—undoubtedly the widest-ranging, deepest-probing and most complicated Committees in the House.

The duties of the CLERK OF PRIVATE BILLS are apparent, though this is not to suggest they are simple. He works closely with the Chairman of Ways and Means, who has a special responsibility to the House for the conduct of all Private Business, and provides a Senior Clerk to serve as Secretary to the Chairman. As with Government legislation, Private Bills must conform exactly with the requirements of the Standing Orders governing their passage through the House, and the Clerk of Private Bills is responsible for their correctness. The Office supplies Clerks for the Private Bill Committees, and the duties here are very different from those which obtain in both the Select and Standing Committees of the House. The principal difference lies in the fact that when Private legislation is being considered both the Proposer and the Opposer come from outside the House— they may be either private citizens or corporate bodies—and that they are not infrequently represented by Counsel to argue the merits of the respective points of view. The Committee (of Members, not necessarily lawyers) listen at length, and then form their own conclusion to report to the House. The Clerk's function, under these circumstances is vital—but unenviable.

As of old, the Office still maintains the Register of Parliamentary Agents, the Register of Private Bills (with notes on their current position in the House) and a list of deposited Petitions, and acts as a clearing house between the Commons authorities, Agents and interested parties outside.

The last of the Clerk's offices is the TABLE OFFICE, created only at the end of the last war, but already a vital element in this busy Department. Under the administrative control of the Second Clerk Assistant, the Table Office has three main responsibilities, all of which are of paramount importance to the daily sittings of the House, comprising as they do the preparation of the Order Paper, Parliamentary Questions and Notices of Motions. Each of these three items is so hedged about by rules of order that they must be handled with meticulous care and unremitting attention, since any mistake that *might* escape the scrutiny of the Office can only be discovered on the Floor of the House itself—and much too late for correction. It is not necessary to say much about the preparation of the Order Paper, although a moment's thought will show that if the Order Paper itself should not be completely accurate and rigidly within the rules of order of the House it would be quite impossible to proceed with Business.

Parliamentary Questions present a problem since they, too, must be "in order" from several points of view (as typical examples; a Minister cannot be questioned about something over which he has no Departmental control; a question must not anticipate a forthcoming debate; personal accusations must not be hidden in an alleged "question"). It may seem a statement of the obvious to say that questions are supposed to be put to elicit information, but in fact many are not—Parliamentary reputations have been built on a skilful use of Question Time! But questions must not only avoid "anticipation", they must not be repetitive. If a Member puts down a question which has already been answered in the current Session the question is rejected by the Table; if it were not, there would be trouble. Since the Table Office *passes* something over 16,000 questions per session, it will be seen that this scrutinising is a formidable task, and it is in fact only possible at all because of the highly ingenious system of cross-indexed filing specially developed by the Office for the purpose. To claim that the system *cannot* err might be an exaggeration, but it has certainly been foolproof throughout the twenty years of its existence. It is applied, too, to the checking of Motions, which must satisfy roughly the same conditions as questions, and by the end of a Session the files and indexes are swollen and complicated in the extreme.

THE SHORTHAND WRITER. This appointment has some curious and interesting aspects, some of which make it unique among the offices of the House. Following Speaker Abbot's introduction of the freelance W. B. Gurney as "shorthand writer to the House" in 1813, with the recognition of Gurney himself as an Officer of the Commons, the work of reporting Select Committees and Private Bill Committees remained in the hands of the family for the next fifty or sixty years, still on a freelance or contractual basis.

When the Gurneys died out, however, the firm continued its business (which was not confined to the Commons, but covered the Law Courts and other "outside" employments) under the original name, and it is still the company of W. B. Gurney and Sons that serves the Commons today. As of old, they continue to have considerable outside interests, and it may seem strange that the head of an independent commercial firm should enjoy the status of a full Officer of the House. This status, in fact, seems to have been in doubt—and not invoked—for nearly a century, and it has only recently been re-established (in 1965).

Today's Shorthand Writer serves both Houses and is appointed jointly by the Clerk on behalf of the Commons and by the Clerk of the Parliaments on behalf of the Lords, his tenure of office dependent upon "good behaviour". He and his Deputy, with a staff of ten or eleven stenographers—reinforced from their headquarters in Victoria Street when necessary—are the only staff in the Commons still paid by "fees" (which are agreed through the Treasury), but the Shorthand Writer himself is paid a House Retaining Fee, personal to himself. Still in harness on the staff is one reporter who is, as far as I know, the only person in the world today still using the old "Gurney" form of shorthand writing—more modern systems are generally used now, most of the female reporters preferring the Palantype machine system.

This thumbnail survey of an extremely important and busy Department can do no more than indicate the mere outline of its duties; any *detailed* account would require a book for each Office—and if done properly, would probably be incomprehensible to anyone outside the House. In describing the framework within which the work is done, it is impossible to convey the feeling of constant, though quiet, *busyness* that is always present when the House is sitting; the comings and goings between offices as consultation takes place—at all levels—to ensure that the machine is producing an overall efficiency; the telephone calls, the memos and the personal contacts between Officers and Ministers and Members that serve so often to iron out on the spot some difficulty that would occupy "normal channels" for weeks. Every Clerk is aware that his sole function is to facilitate the work of the House and that he is only important to the extent that his labours help towards that end. And every Clerk is content that this should be so and is happy to be judged—as judged he is, every day of life—by this high standard. The framework of the Clerk's Department is substantially the same as it was when the 1833 Committee had done with it, but the men are of a different sort. With "private enterprise" perquisites shorn from their incomes, today's Clerks, with their high qualifications and personal qualities, could certainly earn much better salaries outside the House; the fact that they do not marks them as that special kind of man who is an Officer of the Commons and who is prepared to develop to a point of high professionalism a service which can only be described as a vocation.

CHAPTER 13

The Serjeant at Arms's Department

Like the Clerk, the Serjeant at Arms is appointed by letters patent under the Great Seal, but with this difference—that whereas the Clerk is appointed *for life*, the Serjeant holds his post only "during his good behaviour". The Serjeant, in fact, can be sacked if the House so desires, as happened in the case of Sir James Northfolke in 1675 (see p. 82).

Traditionally, the appointment of a Royal Serjeant is the sole prerogative of the Sovereign, and that it was so regarded into the latter half of the nineteenth century is illustrated by the pronouncement of Disraeli in 1875 ". . . the appointment of the Serjeant at Arms is in the gift and *entirely in the gift* of Her Majesty the Queen. There is no person, whatever his position in this House, who has any influence whatever in that appointment." But changes were on the way. First, it became customary for the Crown to accept advice from the Lord Chamberlain in respect of candidates for the post, a procedure for which the Commons had no great liking but which they were to accept for over half a century. It was not until 11th December 1962, in fact, that the Lower House intervened, and though the Royal prerogative was in no way challenged, the Commons made it clear that *they* would be the ones to advise the Crown regarding any future appointments into their own House. On that date the Prime Minister stated that "the Queen in making future appointments would welcome and bear in mind any soundings which Mr. Speaker might take to inform her of any feelings there might be in the House".

Although the Serjeant's Patent states that he shall "attend upon her Majesty in person when there is no Parliament and at the time of every Parliament to attend upon the Speaker of the House of Commons", the first part of this instruction is now only a formality. The Serjeant's multifarious duties keep him in the House whether Parliament is sitting or not. These duties fall under two headings: Order and Ceremonial, and Housekeeping (this latter under the Act of 1812): and the two functions are surprisingly distinct and different.

The maintenance of order and security in a building as big and as rambling as the Palace of Westminster is a formidable task, and one that demands considerable organisation and control. Not only must any form of demonstration be prevented within the precincts (in spite of the fact that mass lobbying is permitted), and strangers be confined strictly to non-private areas of the building, but the Serjeant is responsible for order actually inside the Chamber itself—including the Galleries and Lobbies. Symbolic of this particular responsibility, the Serjeant on duty in the Chamber is required to carry his sword at all times and is the only armed person allowed to enter—except for the Speaker's Trainbearer, who is armed only during the Procession that precedes each day's sitting.

An interesting incident occurred in this connection in the 1960's, when objection was taken to the presence of a Scottish Member wearing the kilt and skean dhu—surely he had come "armed" into the Chamber and contravened the rules of order? The complaint was taken seriously enough for the Chair to give a subsequent ruling on the matter; the skean dhu, said the Speaker, was not to be considered "a weapon" in the sense intended by the rules, but rather as a decoration or ornament and a necessary part of a recognised costume; and the honour of the Scots was preserved. Fifteen or so years earlier, however, a member of the staff who had appeared in the corridors similarly adorned had been quietly but very firmly discouraged.

More serious breaches of order occur, however, when, for example, a Member may refuse to obey the Chair. As often as not, this would occur when the Speaker found it necessary to direct the Member to withdraw an "unparliamentary expression"; on the Member's continued refusal to retract, the Speaker would be obliged to "name" him, after which the offender, suspended for the rest of the day with loss of pay, should leave the

Chamber. Should he insist on remaining in his seat, however, it
becomes the duty of the Serjeant to remove him—not only from
his seat, but from the entire premises—and for this exercise the
Serjeant calls in as many of his Doorkeepers as may be necessary to do the job quickly and with a minimum of fuss.

It should be said that these expulsions, which are extremely
rare and have not been seen in the Commons for nearly fifteen
years, have usually been conducted in a spirit of goodwill between the culprit and the Serjeant. The offending Member,
having made his point and established his principle, has generally permitted himself quite gracefully to be lifted from his seat,
borne gently along the corridors and staircases and deposited
upon the pavement in Parliament Square without so much as a
murmur against the Serjeant and his men. During the "Irish
days", however, I believe it went rather differently.

Disorder in the Galleries, too, meets with summary justice from
the Serjeant. Earnest citizens who jump to their feet during the
debate to cry "What about the workers!" or "Down with the
Government", are seized instantly by the Doorkeepers, acting
under the Standing Orders of the House, and taken to the Prison
Room, where they remain in custody until the rising of the
House. This has happened fairly often when the House has gone
on to sit all through the night, and though the offenders are
always well-treated by the police and given tea and buns and so
on from time to time, one wonders just what excuse they really
offer at home next morning after their all-night absence. To an
irate spouse, no doubt, the *truth* must appear unlikely in the
extreme.

The Serjeant is directly responsible for the admission of
strangers to all Galleries, except the Speaker's Gallery; he controls the issue of passes and tickets to both the national and
world Press; and he must take care that no unauthorised person
is permitted to stray into the Members' Lobby (Lobby journalists
are granted access, but not other members of the Press Gallery).
He is also in complete control of photography and car parking
in the precincts and is required to co-operate with the Kitchen
Committee in regard to the regulations governing the use of
rooms for dining, having tea, entertaining guests and so on.

The Serjeant's principal duties in connection with ceremonial are those involved in his attendance upon the Speaker. Although, in modern times, real executive power lies with the Commons rather than with the Crown, the ancient tradition of extending royal protection to Parliament (symbolised by the Royal Mace) persists. Thus, whenever the Speaker moves about from place to place *as Speaker*, whether in the House or outside it, he is preceded or accompanied by the Serjeant with his Mace, presenting between them a combination of popular and royal authority that is irresistible. This display of symbolic power is seen at its best in the daily procession of the Speaker from his residence into the Chamber—a procession which, incidentally, does not follow the obvious and shortest route but makes its way down the Library Corridor and through the Central Lobby before approaching the Chamber from the "wrong" end (i.e. the end *opposite* to the Chair). This being so, the public are able to observe the impressive dignity with which the little ceremony is conducted.

The procession is headed by a large and military-looking Doorkeeper in Court dress, who not only leads the way but sets the pace, adjusting his stride according to the size of the Speaker (small Speaker, short steps, etc.). The procession's approach is heralded by the stentorian voices of the police stationed along the route, who, as soon as they catch sight of the Doorkeeper in the distance, remove their helmets and cry "Make way for Mr. Speaker!" They enjoy this little exercise, which breaks the monotony of their day, very much. Behind the Doorkeeper paces the Serjeant at Arms, Mace over his right shoulder; and behind him, the Speaker, suitably wigged and gowned to take the Chair, represents the power of the People. The Trainbearer, also in Court dress, and wearing that curious black rosette at the back of his collar (which in earlier days served to keep his wig-powder off his uniform) comes next, the Speaker's train in one hand while the other balances the hilt of his fine ceremonial sword sheathed in handsome white leather. Behind the Trainbearer, the Speaker's Secretary and the Chaplain bring up the rear side by side, and as the procession enters the Central Lobby the Inspector of Police calls out, "Hats off, strangers!" Members and officers and others who know the ropes bow as the Mace goes by, and the crowd of sightseers are kept stationary until the procession has cleared the Lobby and disappeared into the Chamber.

While the House is sitting the Serjeant remains responsible for the Mace and positions it either "on" or "below" the Table according to the movement of the Speaker. When the Commons sit as a House, with the Speaker in the Chair, the Mace lies in its cradle-rests on top of the table and plays its constitutional part in the proceedings; but should the House "go into Committee" the Speaker's act of leaving the Chair signals to the Serjeant to remove the Mace. Whereupon the Serjeant steps smartly up to the Table, bows before the mace, then lifts it from the rests and places it in others *below* the Table top, after which it is deemed not to be present. The Speaker then quits the Chair and the Chamber becomes just a Committee-room.

The Housekeeping, or domestic, duties of the Serjeant are legion and complicated. He is responsible for the allocation of all accommodation in the Commons' end of the building, and since *everyone* is continually crying out for more space, this job is a headache. He arranges all rooms for the sitting of Committees and supplies them with attendants and necessary stationery, etc.: in co-operation with the Ministry of Public Buildings and Works he is responsible for the entire fabric of the building —its cleaning, maintenance, decoration, heating, lighting, furnishing, ventilating and so on. (Some of the cleaning work is done by Ministry cleaners, but since in most parts of the House security aspects have to be considered *most* of the cleaning is done by cleaners of the Serjeant's staff.)

The Serjeant must maintain close liaison with the G.P.O. on Post Office services supplied in the House—i.e. the Post Offices in the Central Lobby and the Members' Lobby, the telephone and telegraph facilities and the division bell system. He is responsible for the allocation of desks and filing cabinets to Members and their secretaries and must equip and maintain the various writing, typing and interview rooms both in the building itself and in premises outside. He has also to maintain the Members' Cloakroom, the Changing Room, Barber's Shop and Bathrooms, and the Wireless and Television Rooms, as well as supplying all stationery, laundry and a host of other stores throughout the House. But these are only routine matters which the Serjeant and his staff can take in their stride. The Serjeant himself, forming as he does an important contact between the users of the building and those responsible for its administration, finds himself the constant recipient of everyone's complaints and suggestions—and the trouble is, from his point of view, that he generally has to *do* something about them.

He is assisted by three Officers. The DEPUTY SERJEANT, as the title implies, can deputise for the Serjeant in all matters, and is often called upon to do so. In addition, he has special responsibility for pay, stores, the Staff Board and Press Gallery matters. The ASSISTANT SERJEANT, as the executive officer of the Department, is in charge of all the office organisation and security arrangements, seating accommodation in the Galleries and all forms of communication—i.e. postal, telephone and messenger. He also specialises in the "ceremonial and order" aspects of the Serjeantcy functions. The DEPUTY ASSISTANT SERJEANT has overall responsibility for the detailed supervision of the Housekeeping duties of the office. The three subordinate appointments are completely within the gift of the Serjeant, and though he is at liberty to appoint anyone he pleases to the posts, in practice he always seeks the Speaker's approval of his proposed candidate. Modern Serjeants are always chosen from distinguished military or naval circles.

The Serjeant and his officers occupy a suite of rooms which act as administrative centres for the particular functions for which each is specially responsible, but there is, in addition, a general office which supples the secretarial and other services for the Department. The Clerk-in-charge of this office, with an Assistant Clerk, is responsible for the payment of the Serjeant's staff, together with the maintenance of all the necessary records. He orders and accounts for all stores, stationery, etc., and prepares the Department's Annual Estimates and Appropriation Account. He is responsible for all the newspapers and periodicals with which the reading rooms and tea rooms are furnished, and for all uniforms and protective clothing used by personnel in all Departments. Writs for by-elections, Orders of the House, Addresses to the Sovereign and Warrants of the House all pass to this office for action when the Serjeant receives them from the Speaker, and to it come all enquiries regarding lost property.

It is surprising, sometimes, what things visitors seem to leave lying about behind them. The Reporters' Gallery List and the Lobby List are compiled and kept up to date here and the necessary tickets issued by the Serjeant's Personal Assistant and one shorthand-typist, and of course the office looks after all routine and confidential correspondence and keeps detailed records and files.

As with every other office of the House, however, a mere recital of the official duties can give no real idea of the surge and swirl of events that make up the day to day occupation of those concerned. A regiment of telephones, constantly ringing, pump in an endless stream of enquiries from the world outside—queries from radio and television authorities concerning protocol; from police and other organised bodies seeking information covering mass lobbying; foreign embassies requesting tickets for the Galleries; authors, journalists and broadcasters checking facts and backgrounds. Outside queries alone, in fact, could well occupy one man's time each day. But in addition to those there are the enquiries, instructions and complaints continually arising within the House itself, and these are, after all, the Serjeant's main concern. He, or his staff, are available at all times to all Members of Parliament, Ministers, Government Departments and officers of the House, and are required to arrange rooms for conferences and interviews, to confer with the Architect and Ministry of Public Buildings and Works in connection with minor alterations and repairs, to squeeze a few extra seats into the Press Gallery, inspect the accommodation in the tea-rooms, smoke-rooms and dining-rooms—in fact, the Serjeant's responsibilities are so widespread and touch the daily life of the House at so many points that for him simply to walk the length of the Lobby is the equivalent of running the gauntlet. *Somebody* will find *something* for him to do at almost every step he takes.

THE DOORKEEPERS

The English language being what it is, it would be a mistake to assume that Doorkeepers "keep doors". In fact, of the thirty-four Doorkeepers on the Serjeant's staff, only two do so. These two, the Principal and Second Principal Doorkeeper, are stationed at the approach to the Chamber while the House is in session, and it is their responsibility to ensure that only authorised people pass through the Churchill Arch, which is the entrance proper. Only Members and Officers of the House are permitted inside during a sitting, and Officers are only allowed in as far as the Bar of the House—a white line on the floor which is deemed to be the limit of the Chamber itself. When Divisions are called, it is the Head Doorkeeper who activates the mechanism for ringing the division bells which are strategically placed all round the building (and in homes and clubs outside, too, by private arrangement).

The Principal Doorkeeper is the guardian of an old and pleasant tradition which is quite outside his official duties. Since smoking of any kind has always been prohibited in the Chamber, it has long been the custom for a box of snuff to be kept in the Principal Doorkeeper's Box for the use of Members, and those who avail themselves of it are served by the Doorkeeper with a good deal of formality. The present snuff-box, with a continuing supply of the finest snuff, was presented by Winston Churchill, to whom this tradition—like all other traditions of the Commons—was part of the stuff of life itself.

Of the remaining thirty-two Doorkeepers and Assistants, sixteen serve inside the Chamber, one attending the Serjeant (whose chair is just outside the Bar, facing the Speaker) two more attending behind the Speaker's Chair and thirteen supervising the public and Press Galleries. Four more stand by to relieve these sixteen posts as required. One Doorkeeper and one Assistant look after the Letter Board in the Members' Lobby and see to it that any messages, letters or packages left there for Members are delivered promptly to the addressee.

The remaining ten Doorkeepers serve as "card messengers", working from the Central Lobby. The Central Lobby marks the limit to which the public are admitted to the Palace of Westminster; beyond that point a stranger can only move about the building by invitation—either from a Member or an Officer, who must accompany his guest; or from the authorities of the House, in the form of a ticket to one of the Galleries.

A member of the public who wishes to speak personally to his Member of Parliament can enter the Central Lobby and ask to see his M.P. He will be directed to a desk which is guarded by a police officer and will be given a Green Card on which to write his name, the name of the Member he wishes to see, and the nature of his business, and this card will be taken by one of the ten "card mesengers" (Doorkeepers) into every part of the building in search of the Member named in it. Collections are made from the desk by the Doorkeepers every twenty minutes throughout the day while the House is sitting. The Doorkeepers are selected from men who have attained the rank of Warrant or Chief Petty Officer and have completed twenty-one years' regular service in H.M. Forces.

THE HEAD OFFICE KEEPER. This official, who lives in the building, has executive responsibilities for the Serjeant's housekeeping function. He, or one of his Office Keepers, must be on call twenty-four hours a day and between them they supervise the work of thirty-one Attendants, eight Night Watchmen, forty-five Women Cleaners and the Members' Hairdresser.

THE CHIEF STORE-KEEPER, with an Assistant and three Attendants, maintains and orders all stores and stationery, supplies and maintains all lavatories with soap, towels, etc., supervises the laundry services and makes up and dispatches official stationery ordered by the Members on repayment.

THE SUPERINTENDENT OF THE MEMBERS' WAITING ROOM is responsible for the Members' Cloakroom and for the collection and distribution of the newspapers and periodicals that are suplied to the Reading, Tea, Smoking and Lady Members' Rooms.

THE HALLKEEPER, who has an Assistant and six attendants, is responsible for booking in staff, acceptance and delivery of letters both inside and outside the building, the actual *delivery* of Members' stationery within the London area, and the escorting of visitors to Ministers' offices. He also deals with all lost property matters in the precincts.

THE SUPERINTENDENT OF THE REPORTERS' GALLERY is responsible for the whole of the accommodation occupied and used by both the domestic and foreign Press. He has one Assistant and two attendants.

The final component of the Serjeant's Department is THE ADMISSION ORDER OFFICE, a little organisation that has quite a chequered history behind it. As we have seen from the Serjeant's evidence before the 1833 Committee, the admission of strangers into the Galleries was largely in the hands of the Doorkeepers who made considerable revenue from the process. When important debates were to be introduced in the Chamber it was always possible, under the old system, for a Member to reserve a seat, or seats, for his friends so long as he paid the Doorkeeper handsomely enough. And the Doorkeeper, for his part, was usually obliging enough to place one or two of his own men at the head of the queue to wait in the visitor's stead and to occupy his seat for him until he was ready to occupy it himself. Not unnaturally, there was a good deal of dissatisfaction among the less influential visitors who were denied entrance to the Galleries because of this exercise of privilege, dissatisfaction which amounted at times to outright fury, and disturbances outside the Chamber and at the entrances to the Galleries became so frequent that the House was compelled to take action.

In 1885 it was decided to appoint "two gentlemen of the status of clerks" to superintend the issue of admission orders for strangers—this, on the assumption that "gentlemen" would be above accepting tips in respect of their duties—but for some reason the experiment only continued for three years; in 1888 the control of admission went back to the Doorkeepers. This reversion, however, was displeasing both to the House and the public, and in 1893 a select Committee on Admission to the Strangers' Gallery recommended that two Junior Clerks should be appointed to issue Admission Orders under the supervision of the Speaker's Secretary—a system that worked quite successfully until 1908. In that year, though, the whole question was opened up again as the result of a series of serious disturbances in the Ladies' and Strangers' Galleries, and a new Committee proposed the setting up of an Admission Order Office in the Central Lobby under the direct control of the Serjeant at Arms. This is the organisation in use today.

The Admission Order Office is staffed by one Chief Clerk and one Second Clerk, both of whom are either ex-officers commissioned from the ranks or ex-Doorkeepers, a female Senior Office Clerk and one Attendant, and between them they are responsible for all aspects of admission to the Galleries (except for those tickets which the Serjeant himself issues personally to Members inside the Chamber). They also arrange the special late-night transport that takes the staff home when the House sits after midnight.

CONCLUSION

The inner workings of the Commons machinery present a strange and subtle pattern to anyone not acquainted with the operations of the House—as opposed to the operations of either the Government of the day or the Opposition—and the number of people actually employed to keep the machine in motion will come as a surprise, I think, to *everyone*. To adapt a military analogy, the operational force of 630 Members of Parliament is attended in action by 319 support troops, who are officers and officials of the House, with a 570-strong "tail" of supply services (see Appendix A) a formidable total, and one which represents only a conservative count since so many of the supply services are heavily reinforced in times of special need.

Small wonder it is, that with a total work-force of 1,519 persons packed into the narrow confines of the Palace of Westminster—which cannot, itself, expand—the problems of accommodation and integration of services have become acute. The position is complicated, too, by further large numbers of people not included above. Members' secretaries and the staffs of the typing services, all necessary to the day to day functioning of the House, add to the congestion; and the "public"—either as individuals, or delegations, or lobbying groups, or witnesses for Committees—forming as they do a sizeable daily procession into and through the building, add their quota to the problem of control and accommodation. The Select Committee on the Palace of Westminster, set up in 1965 to take a fresh and modern look at the whole administration of the Commons' services, have this problem of accommodation in mind, and while it is certain that they will introduce significant changes into the *machinery* of the House, it can also be confidently expected that they will work out a solution to the problem of space. What that solution will be is impossible to see at the moment, but when it is found—and it will be found—the resulting Commons' service, and its officers, will provide a rich study for some future historian.

Appendices

Attached Services

As has been mentioned, there are many people working inside the Palace of Westminster who are not on the staff of either House, and as far as those employed in the Commons' end are concerned their liaison is (in varying degrees of closeness) with the Serjeant. Since none of them are officers of the House it will only be necessary to mention them briefly.

CATERING STAFF

Since the thousand-odd members and staff of the Commons necessarily spend long periods of time in the building, it is obvious that eating and drinking facilities must be available—often for practically twenty-four hours a day—and this situation poses special problems in catering. The extended "opening hours", for example, make double staffing or split-shift work obligatory at several points, and the fact that the personnel of the Refreshment Department are not servants of the House brings an added complication. It will be remembered that in the days of the 1833 Committee all catering was the prerogative of the redoubtable Bellamy, who found his own staff, provided his own supplies and charged his own prices. Today, however, a much higher standard of service and a much greater variety of accommodation are demanded by the House, and the arrangements have been placed in the hands of a Select Committee which is appointed every Session to supervise the catering facilities. The catering staff, as the servants of this Committee, do not enjoy the status of House officials, nor do they have the same pension rights or security of employment—an anachronism that may well be dealt with by the Committee currently considering the running of the Palace of Westminster.

In practice, the Committee appoints professional managerial staff to organise and run the Department. In overall charge is the Catering Manager, who is assisted by his Chief Cashier (an accountant), his Personnel Officer and an office staff of eight; and between them they are responsible for engaging, supervising and paying an operational staff of waiters, waitresses, bar-men and bar-maids, chefs, supervisors, cleaners and kitchen-hands of between 180 and 190 regularly employed people. Extra help is employed when required.

Although the Kitchen Committee, as the employing body, report direct to the House on catering matters, the Serjeant at Arms is responsible for all accommodation used by the Refreshment Department and for the application of rules and regulations laid down by the Speaker for their use.

POLICE

An important part of the Serjeant's function is his responsibility for the security of the Commons' precincts, and in this duty he is assisted from two outside sources. When the House is *not* sitting, officers of the Palace of Westminster Corps of Custodians are sent into the Commons to carry out the necessary supervisory and guard duties; but while the House is in session its security is in the hands of regular police officers under control of the Serjeant.

These officers are a remarkable body of men—all volunteers—and they have a remarkable job to do. Recruited from the Metropolitan "A" Division, with headquarters at Cannon Row, they are not generally accepted for this special service until they have had up to eight or ten years' experience of routine police work outside the House, and once they are accepted on to the strength of the Commons' force they normally stay with it until the completion of their service. For the one inspector, two sergeants and forty-nine constables, the duty is not an easy one, hedged about as it is by restrictions and considerations of Parliamentary privilege quite outside the experience of an ordinary police officer. Neither Members nor House staff, for example, carry passes or identity-cards, but because the police officers possess almost unbelievable memories for names and faces one seldom hears of an authorised person being challenged on entering the building. Unauthorised people, however, are pounced on at once.

No police officer has any power to arrest within the precincts, except by the authority vested in the Serjeant at Arms by the House, and the Commons force is no exception. They are responsible solely to the Serjeant. They are not permitted to enter any of the Galleries of the House in police uniform, and if they *should* be required to enter them to assist the Doorkeepers in cases of grave disorder, they could only do so in civilian jackets. (There are always one or two plain clothes men in the Galleries, anyway, to lend initial assistance to the Doorkeepers when required.) However, should the Speaker be forced to *suspend the sitting* in the face of uncontrollable disturbances, uniformed officers may enter the Galleries to deal with it.

The Commons police spend long hours at their posts, strategically placed throughout the House, and since they must remain within a very small radius—fully dressed, including helmets, and standing all the while—their daily tour of duty is tiring to a degree. On those occasions when the House sits past midnight, however, some compensating relief appears, for by long custom, they are allowed to remove their heavy helmets and to sit down—if there happens to be a seat close to their post. And when the day is finally over, and the Mace is removed from the Table, it is the police who pass the glad cry "Who goes home?" from post to post through the corridors of the House until it is called, at last, by the Constable on the pavement of Parliament Square—often to the great surprise of passing citizens!

THE POST OFFICE

Prior to 1833 the Post Office facilities were in the hands of Bellamy, the Deputy Housekeeper, who was paid a small sum annually to make up and dispatch "bags of Twopenny Post four times a day"; but the Committee concluded that the work would be better done if performed by Post Officials actually inside the House, and they so directed (see p. 163).

That the present organisation could have sprung from such a modest directive is surprising, for the House today is equipped with complete and extensive Post Office facilities. There are two fully fledged Post Offices, one in the Members' Lobby and one in the Central Lobby, a Sorting Office for letters and parcels, a dispatch room, a telegraph service and a messenger service. The facilities are available from 6 a.m. until half an hour after the rising of the House on sitting days, and from 8 a.m. to 6 p.m. during the recess and there are frequent collections and deliveries of mail throughout the day. The Postmaster is assisted by one Deputy, sixteen Postal and Telegraph Officers, seven postmen and six telegraph messengers—or "young postmen" as they are called nowadays.

The large Telephone Exchange, which does not come under the House of Commons Postmaster, but directly under the Central Area Telephone Manager, has a day staff of two Assistant Supervisors and eighteen telephonists, and a night staff of one Telephonist-in-Charge with five switchboard operators (male). During an average sitting day, from 8 a.m. to 8 p.m., rather more than 5,000 calls are handled—"unvalued" calls, in Post Office parlance, which means that if they were valued in such a way as to equate them with the accepted average time taken by calls throughout the system, the House of Commons exchange would be credited with something like 10,000 "average-time" calls a day. Parliament, however, is not noted for short-windedness and calls from and to the Commons are often (necessarily, let's face it!) of lengthy duration. It is interesting to note that even during the night hours the exchange averages 100 (unvalued) calls.

In addition to the telephone exchange itself, there is a rank of nineteen kiosks known collectively as the "Members' Telephone Room", where casual in-coming calls for Members are received and the messages passed on. (These kiosks are in addition to the very numerous kiosks and open instruments dotted around the building for the use of Members individually.) The Telephone Room is open from 9 a.m. till the rising of the House on sitting days and from 9 a.m. to 5 p.m. during recess; it is staffed by two Supervisors and fifteen telephonists (male).

MINISTRY OF PUBLIC BUILDINGS AND WORKS

The number of Ministry personnel in the building at any one time is impossible to define with accuracy since it varies with the amount of construction work and decorating being done, but an approximate figure can be given of those who work permanently in the Commons. There are three main divisions of function; Works, which covers day to day maintenance (including such cleaning as does not come under the Serjeant at Arms), repairs to the fabric of the building, and all decorating; engineers, who are responsible for heating, ventilation and lighting; and Supplies, who look after all furniture, requirements, carpets, curtains, etc.

The non-industrial personnel comprise one Resident Engineer, one Resident Depot Superintendent (formerly Clerk of Works), one Surveyor, one Superintendent of Works, eight Control Room Officers, six boiler house foremen, two works foremen and six office staff. The non-industrial staff are: Works forty-five; Engineers ninety; Supplies eighty-five; a total of 246 persons in all, who are, as has been said, considerably reinforced from time to time from outside when the work requires it.

THE TRANSPORT OFFICE

This final element in the Serjeant's domain is a branch office of Thomas Cook's travel agency which operates inside the building to make all travel enquiries and bookings required by Members. Originally established in 1941, this office was used at first purely to arrange *official* journeys undertaken by Members on behalf of the House, but in recent years its services have become more general until today it operates a travel agency, similar to those outside, which sells travel to Members as individuals or to Officers of the House. The staff of seven travel clerks is controlled by a Transport Officer who is, incidentally, the only branch manager in the Cooks' organisation to enjoy this particular title. The office is open from 9 a.m. to 5.30 p.m. on sitting days and until 5 p.m. during recess.

APPENDIX B

Speakers of the House of Commons

1377 Hungerford, T.	1429 Alington, W.
1377 De la Mare	1431 Tyrrel
1378 Pickering	1432 Russell
1380 Goldsbrough	1433 Hunt
1382 Waldegrave	1436 Bowes
1383 Pickering	1436 Tyrrel
1394 Bussy	1436 Burley
1399 Cheney	1439 Tresham, W.
1399 Dorewood	1445 Burley
1401 Savage	1447 Tresham, W.
1403 Redford	1449 Say, J.
1404 Savage	1450 Popham, J.
1405 Esturmy	1451 Oldhall
1405 Cheney	1453 Thorpe
1406 Tiptoft	1453 Chalton, T.
1407 Chaucer	1455 Wenlock
1413 Stourton	1459 Tresham, T.
1414 Hungerford, W.	1461 Green
1415 Chaucer	1461 Strangewaies
1415 Redmayne	1463 Say, J.
1415 Beauchamp	1472 Alington, W.
1416 Flower	1482 Wode
1420 Hunt	1483 Catesby
1421 Baynard	1486 Lovell
1422 Flower	1487 Mordaunt
1423 Russell	1489 Fitzwilliams
1425 Wauton	1492 Empson
1426 Vernon	1496 Drury
1428 Tyrrel	1496 Bray

1505	Dudley	1659	Say, W.
1509	Englefield	1660	Grimstone
1510	Sheffield	1661	Turnour
1514	Neville	1672	Charlton, J.
1523	More	1672	Seymour
1529	Audley	1678	Sawyer
1533	Wingfield	1678	(Seymour)
1537	Rich	1678	Gregory
1540	Hare	1681	Williams, W.
1542	Moyle	1685	Trevor
1547	Baker	1689	Powle
1553	Dyer	1690	Trevor
1553	Pollard	1695	Foley
1554	Brooke	1698	Littleton
1554	Heigham	1701	Harley
1555	Pollard	1705	Smith
1558	Cordell	1708	Onslow, R.
1558	Gargrave	1710	Bromley
1562	Williams, T.	1713	Hanmer
1565	Onslow, R.	1714	Compton
1571	Wray	1727	Onslow, A.
1572	Bell	1761	Cust
1577	Popham, J.	1769	Norton
1585	Puckering	1780	Cornwall
1589	Snagg	1789	Grenville
1592	Coke	1789	Addington
1597	Yelverton	1801	Mitford
1601	Coke	1802	Abbot
1603	Phelips	1817	Manners-Sutton
1614	Crewe, R.	1835	Abercromby
1620	Richardson	1839	Lefevre
1623	Crewe, T.	1857	Denison
1625	Finch, H.	1872	Brand
1627	Finch, J.	1884	Peel
1640	Glanville	1895	Gully
1640	Lenthall	1905	Lowther
1653	Rous	1921	Whitley
1654	Lenthall	1928	FitzRoy
1656	Widdrington	1943	Clifton Brown
1658	Chute	1951	Morrison
1658	Long	1959	Hylton-Foster
1659	Bamfylde	1965	King

APPENDIX C

Clerks Since 1363

1363 Robert de Melton
1385 John de Scardeburgh
1414 Thomas Haseley
1440 John Dale
1461 Thomas Bayen
?1503 Thomas Hylton
1510 William Underhill
1515 Robert Ormeston
1548 John Seymour
1567 Fulke Onslow
1603 Ralph Ewens
1613 John Wright
1640 Henry Elsynge
    the younger
1649 Henry Scobell
1658 John Smythe
1659 John Pheleps
1659 Thomas St. Nicholas
1660 William Jessop
1661 William Goldsborough

1678 William Goldsborough
    the younger
1683 Paul Jodrell
1727 Edward Stables
1732 Nicholas Hardinge
1748 Jeremiah Dyson
1762 Thomas Tyrwhitt
1768 John Hatsell
1820 John Ley
1850 Denis Le Marchant
1871 Erskine May
1886 Reginald Palgrave
1900 Archibald Milman
1902 Courtenay Ilbert
1921 Lonsdale Webster
1930 Horace Dawkins
1937 Gilbert Campion
1948 Frederic Metcalfe
1954 Edward Fellowes
1962 Barnett Cocks

APPENDIX D

Serjeants at Arms Since 1414

	FROM	TO
Nicholas Maudit	1414	1417?
John Bury	1461?	1471
Maurice Cethyn	July 1471	Oct. 1471
Robert Siddale	Oct. 1471	1472
Nicholas Brytte	Oct. 1472	1485
John Harper	Sept. 1485	1488
	Mar. 1488	1517
John Smythe	1517	
John Sent John	Sept. 1533	1555
Thomas Hale	Jan. 1555	1575?
Ralph Bowyer	July 1576	1590
Roger Wood	Aug. 1590	Mar. 1610
Edward Grimstone	May 1610	Dec. 1640
John Hunt	Nov. 1640	Jan. 1646
Edward Birkhead	Jan. 1646	Apl. 1660
Sir James Northfolk	Apl. 1660	Oct. 1675
Sir William Bishop	Oct. 1675	July 1693
Samuel Powell	July 1693	1709
Thomas Wybergh (Confirmed S at A in 1716)	Feb. 1709	Aug. 1717
Thomas Spence	Oct. 1717	June 1737
Wentworth Odiarne	Dec. 1737	Sept. 1762
Nicholas Bonfoy	Oct. 1762	Oct. 1775
Edward Colman	Nov. 1775	May 1805
Francis John Colman	May 1805	Dec. 1811
(John Clementson)(?Acting)	Jan. 1812	Mch. 1812
Henry Seymour	Mar. 1812	1835
Sir William Gosset	1835	Mar. 1848
Lord Charles Russell	Mar. 1848	Apl. 1875
Sir Ralph Gosset	Apl. 1875	Sept. 1885

	From	To
Sir H. David Erskine	Oct. 1885	June 1915
Admiral Sir Colin Keppel	June 1915	Oct. 1935
Brigadier Sir Charles Alfred Howard	Oct. 1935	Dec. 1956
Major-General I. T. P. Hughes	Jan. 1957	Aug. 16, 1962
Lieut.-Colonel Peter F. Thorne	Aug. 17, 1962	Oct. 25, 1962
Rear-Admiral Alexander H. C. Gordon Lennox	Oct. 26, 1962	

Appendix e

Principal Officers of the Commons, 1965

THE SPEAKER—Dr. Rt. Hon. Horace King, MP
CHAIRMAN OF WAYS AND MEANS—Sir Samuel Storey, Bt, MP
DEPUTY CHAIRMAN OF WAYS AND MEANS—
Roderic Bowen, Esq., QC, MP
CLERK OF THE HOUSE OF COMMONS—
Sir Barnett Cocks, KCB, OBE
CLERK-ASSISTANT—D. W. S. Lidderdale, CB
SECOND CLERK-ASSISTANT—R. D. Barlas, OBE
PRINCIPAL CLERKS
CLERK OF PUBLIC BILLS—K. R. Mackenzie, CB
CLERK OF THE JOURNALS—S. C. Hawtrey.
CLERK OF THE COMMITTEES—H. R. M. Farmer.
FOURTH CLERK AT THE TABLE—C. A. S. S. Gordon.
CLERK OF STANDING COMMITTEES—A. C. Marples, CBE
CLERK OF PRIVATE BILLS—T. G. Odling.
DEPUTY PRINCIPAL CLERKS—D. Scott, E. E. Taylor, PhD, M. H. Lawrence, F. G. Allen, A. A. Birley.
SENIOR CLERKS—
R. S. Lankester, K. A. Bradshaw, D. A. M. Pring, MC, J. H. Willcox, J. P. S. Taylor, C. A. James, H. M. Barclay, M.'T. Ryle, D. McW. Millar, C. J. Boulton, J. F. Sweetman, TD, A. A. Barrett, D. W. Limon, J. R. Rose, R. K. Middlemas, G. S. Ecclestone, C. B. Winnifrith.
ASSISTANT CLERKS—A. J. Hastings, W. R. McKay, R. J. Willoughby, S. A. L. Panton, R. B. Sands.
SUPERINTENDENT OF PRINTING THE VOTES AND PROCEEDINGS—
F. G. R. Turmaine; DEPUTY—G. H. Bright.
EXAMINERS OF PETITIONS FOR PRIVATE BILLS—T. G. Odling, E. D. Graham.

TAXING OFFICER—T. G. Odling.
CHIEF OFFICE CLERKS—D. A. Brown, J. B. Brown, E. Broomfield.

DEPARTMENT OF THE SPEAKER

SPEAKER'S SECRETARY—Brigadier Sir Francis Reid, CBE
COUNSEL TO THE SPEAKER—Sir Robert Speed, CB, QC
CHAPLAIN TO THE SPEAKER—Rev. Canon M. S. Stancliffe, MA
TRAINBEARER TO THE SPEAKER—J. Green
LIBRARIAN—Strathearn Gordon, OBE
ASSISTANT LIBRARIANS—D. C. L. Holland, D. Menhennet, DPhil.
DEPUTY ASSISTANT LIBRARIANS—R. F. C. Butcher, VRD,
    D. J. T. Englefield.
    SENIOR LIBRARY CLERKS—E. C. Thompson, H. J. Palmer,
        G.F. Lock, M. A. Griffith-Jones.
    JUNIOR LIBRARY CLERKS—Miss J. M. Hodlin, Miss M. C.
        Gichard, Miss J. B. Tanfield, Miss V. Willis, Miss H. R.
        Rimington.
    EXECUTIVE LIBRARY ASSISTANT—R. G. Brown.
    INFORMATION CLERK—Miss M. R. O'Reilly.
    CATALOGUER—Miss F. M. Walsh.
    CHIEF OFFICE CLERK—S. E. Dickason.
ACCOUNTANT—F. J. Wilkin, DFM
    DEPUTY ACCOUNTANT—H. McE. Allen.
    ASSISTANT ACCOUNTANTS—G. Powter, F. A. Byford.
    SUPERINTENDING CLERK, FEES OFFICE—N. E. E. Hatt.
    CHIEF OFFICE CLERK—A. C. Langford.
OFFICIAL REPORT OF DEBATES (HANSARD)
    EDITOR—L. W. Bear.
    DEPUTY EDITOR—W. M. Bussey.
    ASSISTANT EDITORS—R. P. Dring, L. A. Giles.
    SENIOR REPORTERS—C. A. H. Allen, H. Jochimsen,
        H. W. S. Scott, R. E. G. Slade, E. D. Holmes.
    REPORTERS—W. P. Brooks, R. H. Dagworthy, G. B. Parry,
        G. E. Rudd, P. D. Adam, K. S. Morgan, H. C. Bacon,
        R. V. Hadlow, L. R. Johns, F. G. Brotherston, C. Watson,
        J. Robinson, J. Gourley, P. Walker, J. Withers.
VOTE OFFICE—DELIVERER OF THE VOTE—P. K. Marsden;
    DEPUTY DELIVERER OF THE VOTE—G. R. Russell; CHIEF
    OFFICE CLERK—H. McNally.
SALE OFFICE—CHIEF OFFICE CLERK—C. C. Clarke.

Department of the Serjeant at Arms

SERJEANT AT ARMS—Rear Admiral A. H. C. Gordon Lennox, CB, DSO

DEPUTY SERJEANT AT ARMS—Lieutenant Colonel P. F. Thorne.

ASSISTANT SERJEANT AT ARMS—Commander D. Swanson, DSO, DSC, RN(Retd.)

DEPUTY ASSISTANT SERJEANT AT ARMS—Major G. V. S. Le Fanu.

CLERK IN CHARGE (SERJEANT AT ARMS DEPARTMENT)—C. T. Plymen.

ASSISTANT CLERK IN CHARGE (SERJEANT AT ARMS DEPARTMENT)— D. J. Mouat.

ADMISSION ORDER OFFICE—G. P. Smith, E. J. Blake.

PRINCIPAL DOORKEEPER—W. R. Lishman, SECOND PRINCIPAL DOORKEEPER—W. Perkins.

SHORTHAND WRITER TO THE HOUSE—A. R. Kennedy.

DEPUTY SHORTHAND WRITER—A. P. M. Brewin.

SURVEYOR—L. W. Brimley.

RESIDENT ENGINEER—T. A. Hoyland.

SUPERINTENDENT OF WORKS—J. Mathews (Surveyors' Department). W. Watson, MBE (Engineers' Department).

POSTMASTER—W. G. Birch.

INSPECTOR OF POLICE—G. Blackmore, DCM

REFRESHMENT DEPARTMENT MANAGER—E. G. Roberts.

Bibliography

Appropriate House of Commons Journals.

Select Committee on Establishment of the House of Commons 1833 (H.C. 648, 1833)

Select Committee on Private Bill Fees (H.C. 540, 1834)

Select Committee on Printed Papers relative to the House of Commons 1835 (H.C. 606, 1835)

Select Committee on House of Commons Officers' Compensation 1836 (H.C. 249, 1836)

Select Committee on Parliamentary Debates 1907 (H.C. 239, 1907)

Select Committee on House of Commons Accommodation etc. 1953 (H.C. 309, 1953)

Select Committee on Palace of Wesminster 1965 (H.C. 285, 1965)

Parliament Past and Present, Wright and Smith (Hutchinson)

The Clerical Organisation of the House of Commons 1661–1850, O. C. Williams (Oxford University Press)

The Book of Parliament, M. MacDonald (Ibster)

The Reporters Gallery, M. MacDonald (Ibster)

"Erskine May", 17th Edition. Edited by Sir Barnett Cocks, KCB, OBE

The English Parliament, Kenneth Mackenzie (Pelican)

Our Parliament, Strathearn Gordon (Cassell)

A Compleat Journal of the Votes, speeches and debates, both of the House of Lords and the House of Commons throughout the whole reign of Queen Elizabeth (etc.)—D'Ewes (Sir Symonds)

Index